# THE DREAM OF
# ENLIGHTENMENT

Also by Anthony Gottlieb

*The Dream of Reason: A History of Philosophy from the Greeks to the Renaissance*

# THE DREAM OF ENLIGHTENMENT

*The Rise of Modern Philosophy*

## ANTHONY GOTTLIEB

LIVERIGHT PUBLISHING CORPORATION

A Division of W. W. Norton & Company

*Independent Publishers Since 1923*

New York   London

For information about permission to reproduce selections from this book,
write to Permissions, W. W. Norton & Company, Inc.,
500 Fifth Avenue, New York, NY 10110

For information about special discounts for bulk purchases, please contact
W. W. Norton Special Sales at specialsales@wwnorton.com or 800-233-4830

Manufacturing by Berryville Graphics
Book design by Helene Berinsky
Production manager: Julia Druskin

Library of Congress Cataloging-in-Publication Data

Names: Gottlieb, Anthony, author.
Title: The dream of enlightenment : the rise of modern philosophy /
Anthony Gottlieb.
Description: First edition. | New York : Liveright Publishing Corporation, a
division of W. W. Norton & Company, [2016] | Includes bibliographical
references and index.
Identifiers: LCCN 2016015063 | ISBN 9780871404435 (hardcover)
Subjects: LCSH: Philosophy, Modern—History.
Classification: LCC B791 .G68 2016 | DDC 190—dc23 LC record available
at https://lccn.loc.gov/2016015063

W. W. Norton & Company, Inc.
500 Fifth Avenue, New York, N.Y. 10110
www.wwnorton.com

W. W. Norton & Company Ltd.
Castle House, 75/76 Wells Street, London W1T 3QT

1 2 3 4 5 6 7 8 9 0

*For my father and in memory of my mother*

# CONTENTS

# INTRODUCTION
## *The Kingdome of Darknesse*

WESTERN PHILOSOPHY IS NOW TWO AND A HALF MILLENNIA OLD, BUT a great deal of it came in just two staccato bursts lasting some 150 years each. The first was in the Athens of Socrates, Plato and Aristotle, from the middle of the fifth century to the late fourth century BC. The second was in northern Europe, in the wake of Europe's wars of religion and the rise of Galilean science. It stretches from the 1630s to the eve of the French Revolution in the late eighteenth century. In those relatively few years, Descartes, Hobbes, Spinoza, Locke, Leibniz, Hume, Rousseau and Voltaire—most, that is, of the best-known modern philosophers—made their mark. All these people were amateurs: none had much to do with any university. They explored the implications of the new science and of religious upheaval, which led them to reject many traditional teachings and attitudes. What does the advance of science entail for our understanding of ourselves and for our ideas of God? How is a government to deal with religious diversity? What, actually, is a government for? Such questions remain our questions, which is why Descartes, Hobbes and the others are still invoked and argued with today.

It is because they still have something to say to us that we can easily get these philosophers wrong. It is tempting to think that they speak our language and live in our world. But to understand them properly, we must step back into their shoes. That is what this book tries to do.

The seeds of the eighteenth-century Enlightenment were sown in the seventeenth century, when some people came to think that history was the wrong way round. It was not Plato and Aristotle who were the ancients to be revered: the admirable ancients are us. Francis Bacon (1561–1626) was apparently the first to crystallise this thought. But among the many who echoed Bacon, Blaise Pascal (1623–1662) perhaps put it best, in his writings about vacuum—which was not abhorred by nature at all, according to recent experiments, despite what the ancients had said:

> Those whom we call ancient were really new in all things, and properly constituted the infancy of mankind; and as we have joined to their knowledge the experience of the centuries which have followed them, it is in ourselves that we should find this antiquity that we revere in others.

Pascal also pointed out that if the ancient Greeks had shown the same overawed reverence for their predecessors that later ages showed to the Greeks, they would never have achieved the things for which they are admired.

Bacon was an effective propagandist for the new idea that all old ideas are suspect. We must, he insisted, go out and find the facts instead of wasting our days in dusty books. This will let us unlock the secrets of nature, which we can then exploit to make the world a better place for mankind. Bacon's advocacy of careful and systematic observation won him adoption as the mascot of the Royal Society of London, one of Europe's first clubs of scientific investigators, which was formed in 1660. A hundred years later, he was proclaimed a hero of mankind's new dawn by the French Enlightenment's *Encyclopédie*, though these French admirers conceded that his own scientific ideas had come to seem misguided. Bacon overlooked, misunderstood or failed to see the point of what we now regard as the most notable scientific developments of his time. He had little time for Galileo or Kepler, because they were tiresomely mathematical, and he did not think much of Copernicus, whose astronomy "I am convinced is most false." Nevertheless, what Bacon had set out to achieve was, in his words, "to ring a bell to call other wits together," and in this he succeeded. His condemnation of the "degenerate learning" of recent centuries rang true to some of the keener minds of what was becoming a new age:

> the schoolmen . . . having sharp and strong wits, and abundance of leisure, and small variety of reading, but their wits being shut up in the cells of a few authors (chiefly Aristotle their dictator) as their persons were shut up in the cells of monasteries and colleges, and knowing little history, either of nature or time, did out of no great quantity of matter and infinite agitation of wit spin out unto us those laborious webs of learning which are extant in their books—cobwebs of learning, admirable for the fineness of thread and work, but of no substance or profit.

To Thomas Hobbes (1588–1679), who was briefly Bacon's assistant, the medieval style of philosophy, which still had all too much influence in universities, was part of "the Kingdome of Darknesse." Superstition and intolerance were also at work in this metaphorical kingdom. The challenge was to find ways of escaping it.

∞

How it came about that some people in the seventeenth century were ready to look askance at the ancients, and at the authority of the Church and at medieval science and philosophy, is discussed in *The Dream of Reason: A History of Philosophy from the Greeks to the Renaissance*, to which this book is a sequel. (A revised edition of *The Dream of Reason* is being published simultaneously with this book.) A future volume will take up the story of philosophy again, starting with Immanuel Kant, whose most influential work was published in 1781, three years after the deaths of Voltaire and Rousseau. A new phase of the subject started with him.

All histories of philosophy are selective: some suggestions for further reading about the seventeenth and eighteenth centuries may be found at the end of this book.

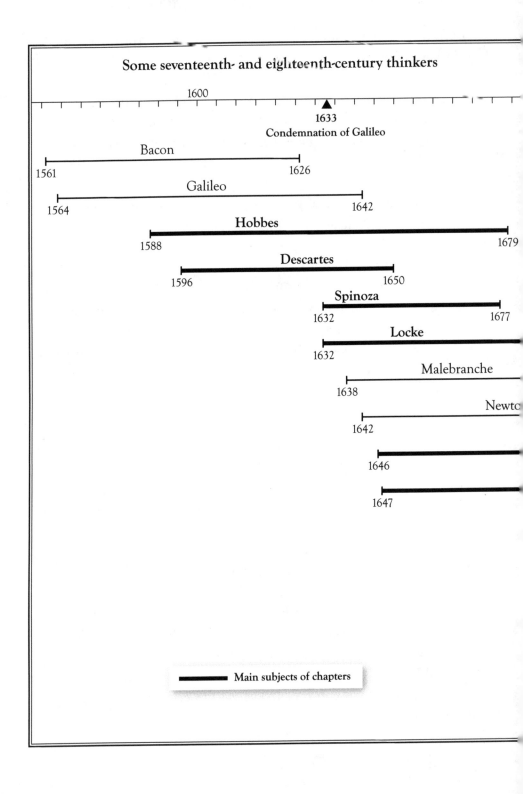

Some seventeenth- and eighteenth-century thinkers

1600

▲
1633
Condemnation of Galileo

Bacon
1561                    1626

Galileo
1564                         1642

Hobbes
1588                                              1679

Descartes
1596                    1650

Spinoza
1632              1677

Locke
1632

Malebranche
1638

Newto
1642

1646

1647

━━━ Main subjects of chapters

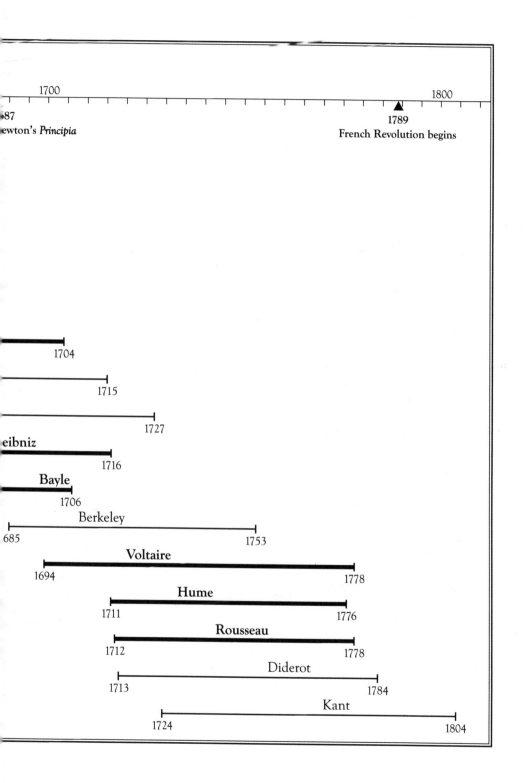

1700                                                      1800

87                                                        1789
ewton's *Principia*                              French Revolution begins

                    1704

                         1715

                              1727

eibniz
                    1716

**Bayle**
        1706

        Berkeley
685                                    1753

        **Voltaire**
1694                                              1778

            **Hume**
    1711                                      1776

            **Rousseau**
    1712                                      1778

                Diderot
        1713                              1784

                    Kant
            1724                                  1804

# The Dream of Enlightenment

# 1

## STARTING AFRESH
## *Descartes*

DESCARTES (1596–1650) WAS A PARTICULARLY KNOWLEDGEABLE MAN, but he is more famous for what he pretended to doubt than for what he actually knew. How can I be sure that I am not dreaming?, he asked. How can I be certain that some deceitful demon is not filling my head with falsehoods? In the spirit of Francis Bacon's proverb, "if a man will begin with certainties, he shall end in doubts; but if he will be content to begin with doubts, he shall end in certainties," Descartes invited his readers to join him in a cold bath of scepticism—which he himself had found to be wonderfully invigorating:

> since I now wished to devote myself solely to the search for truth, I thought it necessary to . . . reject as if absolutely false everything in which I could imagine the least doubt. . . . Thus, because our senses sometimes deceive us, I decided to suppose that nothing was such as they led us to imagine. And since there are men who make mistakes in reasoning . . . and because I judged that I was as prone to error as any-one else, I rejected as unsound all the arguments I had previously taken as demonstrative proofs. Lastly, considering that the very thoughts we have while awake may also occur while we sleep without any of them being at that time true, I resolved to pretend that all the things that had ever entered my mind were no more than the illusions of my dreams.

Descartes soon found something which could not be an illusion, however—something he could know to be true even if he were dreaming. He had found his first certainty:

> I noticed that while I was trying thus to think everything false, it was necessary that I, who was thinking, was something. And observing that this truth, "*I am thinking, therefore I exist,*" was so firm and sure that all the most extravagant suppositions of the sceptics were incapable of shaking it, I decided that I could accept it without scruple as the first principle of the philosophy I was seeking.

"I think, therefore I am"—*ego cogito, ergo sum,* as he put it in Latin—became the most famous slogan in philosophy, and is an odd sort of first principle. It seems indubitable enough, yet also too simple to serve as the foundation for anything. How much useful information can possibly follow from it? As we shall see, Descartes's route from his own mere existence to a whole new system of knowledge was somewhat indirect, and has been widely misunderstood. But he was convinced that with "I think, therefore I am," he had found the right place to start.

He was also convinced that he could virtually finish the job, for one thing that the great doubter never really questioned was his own importance. Not only were the principles he eventually arrived at "so certain and evident that whoever rightly understands them will have no occasion to dispute them," they were also, he believed, sufficiently wide-ranging to provide definitive answers to all scientific questions. Descartes's grandiose ambitions even extended to "a system of medicine founded on infallible demonstrations." He once said that the preservation of health had always been "the principal end of my studies," and he believed he was on the verge of discovering how to prolong human life. He apparently thought that, given enough time on this earth, plus some artisans to make equipment for him, he could complete the task of science himself:

> I venture to say that I have found a way to satisfy myself within a short time about all the principal difficulties usually discussed in philosophy [which for Descartes included what we call science]. What is more,

I have noticed certain laws which God has so established in nature, and of which he has implanted such notions in our minds, that after adequate reflection we cannot doubt that they are exactly observed in everything which exists or occurs in the world.

Aristotle had never expressed himself with such confidence. Perhaps the intervening centuries of faith in Christianity helped to make such self-assurance possible. After all, if the truth about religious matters can be stated definitively, how much of a problem could the truth about nature be? Descartes's familiarity with the new science of Galileo (1564–1642) fuelled his optimism. The "mechanical philosophy" seemed an enormous leap forward after centuries of stagnation; surely the truth was now just around the corner. The same sense of excitement has been felt in our own time by some physicists, who expect recent advances to culminate in a "final theory" that will explain literally everything. In 1980, an eminent cosmologist, Stephen Hawking, wrote that this might well happen within the next twenty years. This turned out to be somewhat premature, as similar pronouncements regularly have been since the end of the nineteenth century. In 1894, Albert Michelson, the first American to win a Nobel prize in science, said that all the main laws and facts of physics had already been discovered. In 1928, Max Born, another Nobel prize-winner, said that physics would be completed in about six months' time. We can now see that Descartes had less justification for his hopes than our modern optimists have for theirs. But he can hardly be blamed for not realising this. Besides, he had a special reason for confidence in his ideas. They had walked unscathed through the valley of deepest doubt, and were also the first to be put to this gruelling test. How, then, could they fail to be correct?

DESCARTES was in a position to speak with authority about the new science, for he was one of its principal authors. Modern applied mathematics is largely based on an invention of his, namely analytic geometry, which uses algebra to solve practical problems about space and motion. He did more than anyone else of his day to illustrate how mathematics could be put to work throughout the sciences. Galileo and Kepler were the pioneers in this project, but their efforts were fragmentary ones. Descartes's work was more comprehensive. He laboured to construct a unified account of nature that would be as all-encompassing as Aristotle's, but based on the un-Aristotelian "mechanical" principle that physical phenomena are to be explained in terms of contact between moving bodies and the motions and shapes of their parts. In physics and cosmology, Descartes propounded theories which were for a time serious rivals to those of Isaac Newton (1642–1727) and which stimulated some of Newton's ideas. A few years after Newton's death, Voltaire (1694–1778) wrote, "I don't think we really dare compare in any way [Descartes's] philosophy with that of Newton: the first is a sketch, the second is a masterpiece." Nevertheless, Voltaire continued, "the man who set us on the road to truth is perhaps as noteworthy as the one who since then has been to the end of the road."

Most of Descartes's scientific work except for his mathematics has been superseded, which is partly why he is now remembered as an abstract thinker rather than as a man of science. This tends to obscure the fact that much of his life was spent not in ruminating about the topics of what he called "first philosophy" or "metaphysics"—the nature of the soul, the limits of knowledge and the existence of God, for example—but rather in experiments, dissections, observations and calculations. Despite Descartes's current reputation, the man himself seems to have been less interested in metaphysics than in applying algebra to geometry, and delving into the innards of cows. While living in Amsterdam in around 1630, he visited butchers' shops every day to fetch carcasses for dissection. His explanation of the rainbow was a landmark in experimental science, and it was almost right. He independently discovered, and was the first to publish, the law of refraction, known in English-speaking countries as Snell's Law, which explains why a straight stick can appear bent when partly immersed in water. He also conducted research in physiology, medicine, meteorology, geology and all the other mysteries that the "mechanical philosophy" promised to illuminate. It was Descartes who first demonstrated in detail that the workings of human bodies could be studied as if they were machines. He seized on William Harvey's discovery of the circulation of the blood, and generalised such ideas to develop a comprehensively mechanistic physiology. He also, however, made several incorrect criticisms of Harvey, and misdescribed the function of the heart.

Descartes was so fascinated by machines and all kinds of mechanical contraptions that, according to a piece of widespread gossip, he was often accompanied by a life-sized working doll that was practically indistinguishable from his illegitimate daughter, Francine. This tale, with its suggestions of infernal cleverness and of madness bordering on impropriety, became current in the latter half of the eighteenth century, when extreme versions of materialism and even atheism were defended by some radicals in France. Descartes's mechanistic science and his rationalist world-view were by this time widely seen as having sown the seeds of these ghastly outgrowths, much though Descartes himself would have abhorred them. He did not maintain that people were machines, as some others later did, only that people's bodies were machines. And he was apparently untouched by any doubts about the main dogmas of the Catholic Church.

∞

RENÉ DESCARTES was born into the upper bourgeoisie on March 31, 1596, in a village then called La Haye, in the Loire valley. Always a secretive man—his motto was *Bene vixit, bene qui latuit* ("He lives well who is well hidden")—he would not allow his date of birth to be published in his lifetime, for fear that someone might cast his horoscope. His father had hoped that he would follow him into legal practice and provincial officialdom, and marry well. In the event, René disappointed his father's dynastic ambitions, though his older brother, Pierre, delivered the goods, and the family acquired the lowest degree of nobility in 1668. René inherited some farms from his mother's family, and then sold them to help pay for his life as a gentleman scholar. His father said that he was the only son to have disappointed him, because he was "ridiculous enough to have himself bound in calfskin."

Descartes's mother died when he was fourteen months old, and his father entrusted his upbringing to relatives. At the age of ten, René was sent to the recently established Jesuit college of La Flèche. In 1614, he left the Jesuits to study law at Poitiers, graduating and rejoining his family two years later. How he then occupied himself is a mystery, but in 1618 he began his travels, aiming, as he later said, to "roam about in the world, trying to be a spectator rather than an actor in all the comedies that are played out there." He decided to enroll as a gentleman (i.e., unpaid) soldier in the army of Prince Maurice of Nassau, outside Breda, on the truce lines between the north and the south of the Netherlands. Descartes was rather bored, contenting himself with some painting, military architecture, and learning Flemish. It was thanks to an apparently chance meeting in the street in Breda that his intellectual career began to take shape.

On 10 November 1618, Descartes was trying to read a mathematical puzzle posted in Flemish on a billboard, and asked a passerby, Isaac Beeckman, to translate it into Latin. Seven years older than Descartes, Beeckman had just completed his medical degree while earning his living as an engineer and candlemaker. He was interested in applying mathematics to mechanics, explaining regularities in physical phenomena in terms of the behavior of their minute constituents—an approach to science that began to flourish in the Netherlands in the late sixteenth century. The two men struck up a close friendship, and Descartes became, in effect, Beeckman's apprentice, using his mathematical skills (which were apparently superior to Beeckman's) to solve problems set by his master. It is unclear whether or not Beeckman was one of the catalysts for the revelation that Descartes claims to have had at the age of twenty-three, a year to the day after his first meeting with him. That was when he went to bed after a day's excited contemplation in which he discovered the "foundations of a marvellous science," and had a series of vivid dreams which he said changed his life. Possibly, this was a nervous breakdown rather than the intellectual breakthrough that Descartes later made it out to be. Either way, within a few years he seems to have been set on a life of learning, focussing on the natural sciences and mathematics.

Descartes realised the dangers he faced as an innovator. He was rightly worried that some of his scientific work might prove unacceptable to the Church and to the educational establishment, especially after hearing of Galileo's recent treatment at the hands of the Inquisition. Galileo had been censured for, among other things, repeating the cardinal "error" of Copernicus, namely his heliocentrism. The Church still maintained that the sun moved around the earth, not vice versa. After all, the Psalms say that the earth cannot be moved; Genesis says that the earth was created before the sun; and Joshua told the sun and the moon to stand still while the children of Israel attacked the Amorites, which (it was argued) he would not have done if the sun had already been still. Descartes knew that the earth did move. He wrote to his old friend, Marin Mersenne, that if this view is false, then "so too are the entire foundations of my philosophy." In 1633, when the news about Galileo's condemnation reached him, Descartes cancelled the planned publication of his first major scientific treatise, *The World*. Although little harm could have come to him in the Protestant part of the Netherlands, where he then lived—or, probably, in France, where there was no Inquisition, and considerable sympathy for Galileo—Descartes was keen to avoid rows with the Church. At this point, his scientific researches pretty much came to an end.

One lesson of Galileo's trial was that religion and science could not ignore one another. If Descartes's work was to be accepted as that of a new Aristotle, which he desperately wanted it to be, then he would have to find a way to pacify the pious. There is nothing Descartes would have liked better than to have had his scientific works used as texts in schools such as the Jesuit college at La Flèche. This is one main reason why he then decided to present these works in the context of a wider philosophical project. If he could demonstrate not only that his science was based on irrefutable principles but also that he could use it to establish the truths of religion in a new and better way, then he need have little to fear. This is what he sought to do in 1637, when he published four short books in one: three scientific essays, prefaced by a *Discourse on Method*. The essays would show what his approach to science could achieve—"Compare the deductions I have made . . . about vision, salt, winds, clouds, snow, thunder, the rainbow . . . with what the others have derived," he wrote proudly to a friend. The prefatory *Discourse* would show, among other things, how religion and science could proceed best if they walked hand in hand.

The scientific essays which he chose to publish in this collection steered clear of the most controversial topics. They consisted of his innovative *Geometry*, a treatise on *Meteorology*, and one on *Optics* that was largely concerned to establish which shape of lens would most improve the performance of the recently invented telescope. The *Discourse* also contained a selective summary of his general physics, carefully omitting anything liable to cause offence or misunderstanding, such as the Copernican theory of the solar system and the idea that people's bodies are machines. But the main business of the *Discourse* is conducted in the form of an intellectual autobiography, which starts with an attempt to doubt as much as possible, and goes on to report Descartes's discovery of the following alleged truths.

Since I—that is, Descartes—can doubt that my body exists, but cannot doubt that I myself exist, it follows that I am not the same thing as my body. What I am is a thinking soul, not a piece of matter, and I know about this soul and its thoughts better than I know about any physical thing. Because I am aware that my knowledge of some things is inferior to my knowledge of others, I am aware that I fall short of perfection. Now, this idea of "perfection" with which I contrast my own imperfect state is a remarkable one, says Descartes. How did I get it? I could not have come up with it on my own, and in fact it can only have been planted in me by a being who is Himself perfect, i.e., by God. Therefore God exists (or so Descartes says; he also produces a second and equally unconvincing argument for the existence of God).

One fact which I know about God, Descartes continued, is that He is not a deceiver, since deceitfulness is an imperfection and God is perfect. It follows that He will not deceive me, nor allow me to be deceived by anyone else, when I am doing my best to get at the truth. So I may rest assured that I will not go far wrong in my attempts to understand the world, provided I am careful in these efforts. Armed with this guarantee of God's goodwill, I can now justifiably dismiss the radical doubts that I entertained at the beginning of my search for truth. That is, I can discount the possibility that I do not know anything at all about the physical world because I might be dreaming or deceived by a powerful demon.

The *Discourse* thus demonstrates Descartes's credentials. It shows that he has tried to be supremely cautious and responsible, doubting everything which it is possible for him to doubt before going so far as to claim any knowledge. It shows that, for all his apparently materialistic interest in the "mechanical" philosophy, he considers his soul as separate from his body and therefore as something which may be expected to survive his body's death. It shows that God exists—indeed, it shows this twice. And, above all, it proves that in order to know about nature you must first know about God. It was theology which assured him that scientific knowledge was obtainable, for if Descartes had not found reason to think that there is a benign God, he would not have been able to rule out the possibility that he is massively deluded about the world. And if he cannot rule this out, then there is little that he or anyone else can rule in. Thus even somebody whose main ambitions lie in the field of science must admit that theology is the senior discipline.

There is no reason to question the sincerity of this. True, the *Discourse* was written partly as an exercise in propaganda, to recommend Descartes and his work to the Church, but it seems to have been propaganda that Descartes himself on the whole believed. One might well wonder, though, how much this philosophising has really revealed about the basis of his controversial scientific ideas. In the *Discourse*, Descartes often referred to a "method" that had enabled him to obtain new and useful knowledge in the sciences. Unfortunately, it is not clear what method he is talking about. In one place, he lists four cardinal rules that he says he has followed in his enquiries; but, as the German philosopher Leibniz (1646–1716) later pointed out, these rules are so vague as to be almost vacuous. The first is "never to accept anything as true if I did not have evident knowledge of its truth . . . and to include nothing more in my judgements than what presented itself to my mind so clearly and so distinctly that I had no occasion to doubt it." The second is "to divide each of the difficulties I examined into as many parts as possible." The third is "to direct my thoughts in an orderly manner, by beginning with the simplest and most easily known objects in order to ascend little by little . . . to knowledge of the most complex." And the fourth is to "make enumerations so complete, and reviews so comprehensive, that I could be sure of leaving nothing out." Leibniz was surely right to be unimpressed by these maxims. If we were to adapt them to the task of cooking a perfect meal, for example, we might end up with something like the following advice:

Consult only what you are absolutely certain is the best recipe.
Do not try to perform too many steps at once.
Make sure you do them in the right order.
Do not forget any of the ingredients.

If there was anything more specific to Descartes's method, he had difficulty in saying exactly what it was. The four rules were excerpted from
a book he never managed to finish and which even in its uncompleted
state contained no fewer than twenty-one "rules for the direction of the
mind." A few of these rules shed some light on the techniques he used in
mathematics, but none captures what was distinctive about his work as
a whole. They do not seem to reveal much of a link between his style of
science and his general philosophy. Elsewhere in the *Discourse*, however,
there are some clues to the connection between Descartes's belief in the
"mechanical philosophy" and his musings on God, the soul and the limits
of certainty. There is, he says, a fundamental error that infects people's
thinking: "they never raise their minds above things which can be perceived by the senses." Here is the mark of Descartes's real method, if it
can be called a method. What guided all of his reasoning, including his
thoughts about physics, was his determination to escape what he saw as
the limitations of the senses. How exactly it did so emerges more clearly
in his masterpiece, which was published in 1641.

I would not urge anyone to read this book except those who are able
and willing to meditate seriously with me, and to withdraw their minds
from the senses and from all preconceived opinions.

THUS WROTE DESCARTES in his *Meditations*, which is presented as a diary
of six days of contemplation. In case those who were willing to meditate
with him should nevertheless find themselves unable to agree with him, he
issued the work together with a large number of comments and objections
which he and his friend Mersenne had solicited to a draft of it, followed

hy his replies. The comments were by a French Jesuit; a Dutch Catholic theologian; Thomas Hobbes; Mersenne himself; Pierre Gassendi, a philosopher-mathematician who was influenced by ancient scepticism and the atomism of Epicurus; Antoine Arnauld, who became one of the most eminent philosopher-theologians in France; and various others, some of them unknown. This appendix of energetic debate is seven times longer than the *Meditations* itself. Debates about the debate are many times more extensive: the *Meditations* turned out to be the most-discussed philosophical work of the early modern period.

Yet its themes and preoccupations are strikingly ancient. In particular, they are Platonic. Descartes urged his readers to focus above all on things that are "objects of the intellect alone and are totally separate from matter," which is an unmistakable echo of Plato's main piece of advice to his aspiring philosopher-kings. Like a true follower of Plato, Descartes repeatedly insisted that we must turn aside from the world of the senses and look in our own minds to find the truth. Indeed, the extreme doubts which he entertained at the beginning of his meditations were useful not only because they could strip us of erroneous preconceptions, but also because they provided "the easiest route by which the mind may be led away from the senses." Many ancient Platonists had looked for such a route, and one Platonist, namely St Augustine, trod virtually the same path as Descartes.

In his *Confessions*, which were published at the end of the fourth century, Augustine had examined the contents of his own mind to see if there was anything about which he could be absolutely certain. He noted that he might, for all he knew, be dreaming, but that he could not be mistaken about his own existence: "If I am deceived, I exist!" Introspection revealed other certainties as well, none of which had anything to do with the senses, and Augustine maintained that these seeds of knowledge point to the existence of a God who has planted them in our minds. Augustine cited the now-famous proof that one cannot be mistaken about one's own existence in at least six of his books.

Descartes was not pleased to be informed that his best-known idea was therefore far from original. He was a proud man who groundlessly accused former collaborators of stealing his ideas, and who was exceptionally abusive to those of his contemporaries whom he saw as rivals: he dismissed the work of the great mathematician Pierre Fermat, for example, as "shit." Descartes acknowledged that Augustine had come first in inferring his own existence from the fact that he was thinking, but Descartes quickly added that this inference was in fact so simple and natural that it "could have occurred to any writer." (Indeed, it seems to have occurred to some thinkers at least two centuries before Augustine.) The genuine novelty, Descartes insisted, lay in what he—and only he—had gone on to prove about the nature of the soul: "I . . . show that this *I* which is thinking is an immaterial substance with no bodily element."

As we have seen from his *Discourse*, Descartes's reasons for believing that his soul or self must be something non-material were as follows. I cannot doubt that I exist. But I can doubt that I have a body. Therefore I am something separable from my body. Unfortunately for Descartes's claims of novelty, Augustine had once again come first and argued in the same way: "the mind . . . is certain about itself, as is clearly shown from what we have already said. But it is by no means certain whether it is air, or fire, or a body, or anything of a body. It is, therefore, none of these things."

Still, the spirit of Descartes's project was different from Augustine's, even if its letter was sometimes the same. Augustine's meditations were passive appreciations of God's truth: he reflected on how the mind is divinely illuminated and how it is therefore well-stocked with the knowledge that man really needs. Descartes, on the other hand, aimed actively to exploit the natural power of human reason, not only in order to prove old truths but also to discover new ones. Although Descartes maintained that all knowledge depends ultimately on God—because it is the existence of a benign God which guarantees that our basic beliefs are correct—he saw that this does not mean we can leave everything up to Him. For one thing, we need to work out precisely which of our beliefs are covered by the divine insurance plan. Thus, while Augustine mused on how much God had done for us, Descartes aimed to show how much intellectual work we can and need to do for ourselves. As a result, Descartes's investigations are usually more searching and sophisticated than Augustine's.

Descartes's diary of *Meditations* rambles back and forth as he tells the story of his discoveries, raising questions but then deferring them and picking up the threads later when a pertinent thought strikes him. This carefully contrived informality helps to make the work engaging; but it can also make it hard to spot exactly how Descartes manages to get from his own mere existence to such large matters as the reality of things outside him and the truth of the "mechanical philosophy."

At the start of the nineteenth century, Hegel made heavy weather of "I think, therefore I am." Ripped from its context, the slogan was taken to illustrate how Descartes had propounded a subjective view of the world, in which the "I" is the foundation of everything. This reading of Descartes continues to have wide currency, especially in Catholic circles. In 1994, for example, Pope John Paul II wrote that, for Descartes, "only that which corresponds to human thought makes sense. The objective truth of this thought is not as important as the fact that something exists in human consciousness." And in a later book, John Paul II argued further that the philosophical revolution brought about by Descartes downgraded God and put the mind of man in His place: "according to the logic of *cogito, ergo sum*, God was reduced to an element within human consciousness." In other words, Descartes inaugurated a shift to a view of the world in which the "I" is the foundation of everything, and a selfish monstrosity rules.

Descartes often lost his temper when dealing with his critics. One can barely imagine what he would have said privately about this pope, for he had repeatedly explained that his own existence (and that of the world) depends on God, not the other way around. Those who suspect Descartes of rampant subjectivism have confused the style of his reasoning with its substance. He cast his philosophical enquiries in an autobiographical style, and looked within himself. But there was nothing subjective about what he found:

> When I consider the fact that I have doubts, or that I am a thing that is incomplete and dependent, then there arises in me a clear and distinct idea of a being who is independent and complete, that is, an idea of God. And from the mere fact that there is such an idea within me, or that I who possess this idea exist, I clearly infer that God also exists, and that every single moment of my entire existence depends on him. . . . And now, from this contemplation of the true God, in

whom all the treasures of wisdom and the sciences lie hidden, I think
I can see a way forward to the knowledge of other things.

Although Descartes wrote that the certainty of his own existence is the
"first principle" of his philosophy, this just turns out to mean that it is
the first certainty that he decided to accept, not that anything else is
based upon it. Actually, Descartes infers nothing from his own existence.
Instead, he asks how he comes to possess this one certainty, so that he can
then find others in the same way. The secret of that certainty is just that
it involved "a clear and distinct perception of what I am asserting." Crucially, Descartes then introduces God. Having satisfied himself, by various
philosophical arguments, that there must be a God, he reasons that this
God, being good, would not allow His creatures to be seriously deceived,
provided that they exercise some restraint and confine their beliefs to what
they clearly and distinctly perceive to be true. Thus Descartes's system of
knowledge depends not on his own existence but on God's.

With the existence of God safely established, all Descartes had to do
was find and stay within the limits of "what the intellect clearly and distinctly reveals." So how much did the intellect reveal about matter? The
goodness of God was enough to guarantee the existence of some sort of
physical reality. Descartes said that he had such a strong propensity to
believe that his sensory perceptions were caused by objects outside him
that God would have to be reckoned a deceiver on a grand scale if this
were not generally so. However, Descartes warned that these objects "may
not all exist in a way that exactly corresponds with my sensory grasp of
them, for in many cases the grasp of the senses is very obscure and confused." Still, "at least [external objects] possess all the properties which I
clearly and distinctly understand."

These properties, it emerged, are the ones which "are comprised within
the subject-matter of mathematics." Descartes found that he had a clear
understanding of measurable dimensions in space, of geometric shape, of
duration and of motion, but that "as for all the rest, including light and
colours, sounds, smells, tastes, heat and cold and other tactile qualities, I
think of these only in a very confused and obscure way." He saw—or so
he believed—that "heaviness and hardness and the power to attract, or to

purge, and all the other qualities which we experience in bodies, consist solely in the motion of bodies, or its absence, and the configuration and situation of their parts."

Thus it turns out that the sort of physical facts covered by the divine insurance plan just happen to be those that feature in the "mechanical philosophy." God's guarantee that we shall not be deceived applies only to those of our ideas which we can form in a clear and distinct way, and in the case of material objects this means, according to Descartes, only the ideas of the so-called "primary qualities," such as shape, size, position and state of motion which Galileo and the Greek atomists took to be the sole objective qualities in nature. Descartes therefore dismissed from his physics all the dubious and subjective "secondary" qualities, such as colour, which are merely creations of the senses and which cannot, he believed, be treated mathematically. The fact that, like mechanics, his physics as a whole focussed on "shapes and sizes and motions" was "its most praiseworthy feature," he claimed, for it meant that it used "no reasoning which is not mathematical and evident."

Another advantage of the mechanical approach to nature, Descartes claimed, was its practicality: "Whatever I concluded to be possible from the principles of my philosophy actually happens whenever the appropriate agents are applied to the appropriate matter. . . . This part of philosophy . . . has useful and practical consequences, and so any mistakes in it result in financial loss." In Descartes's hands, the project of leading the mind away from the senses has thus taken a distinctly un-Platonic turn. Plotinus and other Platonists had used arguments against the trustworthiness of the senses in an effort to encourage a spiritual withdrawal from the material world. But now Descartes was using the same arguments to show people how to make money. He cast doubt on the "confused and obscure" evidence of the senses in order to advocate a mathematically oriented physics that would, among other things, supposedly aid technology, and thereby produce bankable results.

Descartes's investigation of what could be made clear and distinct in his ideas of matter led him to conclude that its essential nature is to be "extended," that is, to occupy the three dimensions of space. Indeed, he came to think that matter and space amounted to the same thing, and that various important truths followed directly from this fact. It followed, for instance, that there could be no such thing as completely empty space, for if matter is the same thing as space, then there can be no space without matter. Descartes accordingly reasoned that all of the universe was a brimming sea of tiny particles. He thought that swirling whirlpools or "vortices" of invisible particles accounted for the phenomena of gravitational and magnetic attraction. There was no limit to how small these particles of matter could be. Descartes regarded it as obvious that space was infinitely divisible—any length, breadth or width could in theory be halved again and again *ad infinitum*—so he inferred that matter was infinitely divisible, too. All this meant that he was forced to disagree with two ancient atomists, Democritus and Epicurus. They believed that everything was ultimately composed of individual particles, and that the universe had plenty of empty space or "void" between clusters of these "atoms." Although Descartes shared their mechanical view of the universe (indeed, their physics was an ancestor of his own), he took the opportunity of this disagreement to describe their ideas as "empty theories which have nothing to do with me."

Descartes was only too pleased to be able to put a safe distance between himself and the Greek atomists. Since these people regarded the soul as just another form of matter—and were generally supposed to have been godless—it was prudent to avoid their company. For Descartes the difference between soul and matter was the most fundamental difference in creation. While the essence of matter was "extension," or existence in space, the essence of the soul was something else altogether. Descartes reckoned that a malicious demon could in theory deprive him of all his attributes except one: "At last I have discovered it—thought; this alone is inseparable from me." He could clearly and distinctly conceive of himself as existing without a body, but not as existing without thought. And he could clearly and distinctly conceive of matter as existing without thought, but he could not conceive of it as unextended (i.e., as not occupying space, as a body does). I am, Descartes concluded, essentially "a thinking thing," whereas matter (or body) is essentially an extended thing. "It is true," he added,

> that I . . . have . . . a body that is very closely joined to me. But nevertheless, on the one hand I have a clear and distinct idea of myself,

insofar as I am simply a thinking, non-extended thing; and on the other hand I have a distinct idea of body, insofar as this is simply an extended, non-thinking thing. And accordingly, it is certain that I am really distinct from my body, and can exist without it.

By the end of his *Meditations*, there were thus plenty of things of which Descartes was certain. By closing his eyes to the material world and concentrating instead on the ideas that played in his inner theatre, he found the indubitable truth about God, the soul and matter unfolding before him. The senses loitered uselessly outside during this show. Although it was the senses that gave him information about particular physical objects, it was his reflections on his own "clear and distinct" ideas which revealed how far this information could be trusted, and which gave him "firm and certain" knowledge about the essential nature of soul and matter. Or so he says. In fact the whole exercise is a shadow play. If Descartes had stuck to his principles and questioned every assumption as rigorously as he said he was going to, he would never have been able to claim so much.

Everything depends on Descartes's proofs of the existence and nature of God. Without them, he admits, he would have no firm and certain knowledge. Yet his theological arguments are flimsy. Each one relies on principles that he had no right to accept. For instance, in one place Descartes asserts that "the same power and action are needed to preserve anything at each individual moment of its duration as would be required to create that thing anew if it were not yet in existence." This maxim is a crucial step in one of his arguments for the existence of God, and it is, Descartes claims, "manifest" by the natural light of reason. But not even all the philosophers of his own day found much truth in it, let alone those philosophers who came afterwards.

We do not need to go far into the details of Descartes's dubious proofs to demonstrate that his edifice is built on sand. We need only consider what he says about the impossibility of being misled by God. He writes that God "cannot be a deceiver, since it is manifest by the natural light that all fraud and deception depend on some defect." But according to the Bible, as Descartes's friend Mersenne pointed out, God had deceived people in the past—Pharaoh, for example—so the matter cannot be so simple. One philosopher of the early twentieth century, J. E. McTaggart, neatly put his finger on the flaw in Descartes's reasoning about divine deception:

> A God . . . will doubtless regard deceit as an evil. But there is, beyond doubt, much evil in the universe, and, if we are satisfied that there is a God, we must regard this evil as in some way compatible with his goodness. And then why not that further evil of a misleading divine revelation?

How can we be sure, McTaggart continued, that deceiving us about something might not sometimes be the best thing God can do for us? It might be "bad in itself, but good as the means of avoiding some greater evil." Perhaps God sometimes deceives us in order to test our faith, or to remind us how weak and fallible we are. He is, after all, infamous for working in mysterious ways. If Descartes was prepared to take seriously the outlandish possibility that he had merely dreamed most of what he thought he knew, why did he never even consider the possibility that God might want to mislead him?

There are other problems, too. Even if we overlook the fact that God's guarantee is not worth the paper Descartes wrote it on, how can Descartes be sure that any particular idea is sufficiently clear and distinct to be underwritten by it? He plainly did not have any reliable way of telling, since several of his allegedly clear ideas were not clear at all. Besides, the fact that many of his fundamental tenets have been rejected by other thinkers suggests that one man's "clear and distinct" ideas are another man's muddy misconceptions.

Thus Descartes's project backfired. He not only failed to win over the theologians of his day, but forever weakened his philosophy in trying to do so: the flimsiest parts of his *Discourse* and *Meditations* are his proofs of the existence of God and his argument that God would not deceive us. If we are as critical and sceptical as Descartes aimed to be, we can see that he did not after all succeed in proving the existence of God, the existence of physical objects or the correctness of the "mechanical philosophy." What he did succeed in doing was raise some doubts that he was then unable to assuage.

When he conjured up his radical doubts, Descartes had in effect put each person in a prison of his own ideas, confident that the proof of an undeceptive God would be able to release him. But the rescue mission failed and man was left in a state of ignorance about the world around him. That, at any rate, is how many of the philosophers after Descartes have seen the situation, and plenty of effort has been devoted to remedying it. While few have accepted his theological answer to the problem of knowledge, many have been captivated by his way of formulating the problem. They have followed Descartes into the prison, but then understandably do not trust his way out.

What Descartes had to say about dreaming illustrates his skill at enticingly reframing the old sceptical questions of Greek philosophy. According to Plato, Socrates had asked how one can tell whether one is asleep or awake. Descartes asked this question too, but he also asked another one, which is closer in spirit to a puzzle posed by some ancient Sceptics who regarded themselves as followers of Pyrrho (c. 360–c. 270 BC). Why, these Pyrrhonists wondered, should we regard our waking visions as more accurate than our sleeping ones? Even if I am awake, my sensations might not correspond to anything real. The ancient Sceptics did not press this point with any great urgency; it was just one among many disconcerting possibilities that they had up their mischievous sleeves. But Descartes homed in on it:

> every sensory experience I have ever thought I was having while awake I can also think of myself as sometimes having while asleep; and since I do not believe that what I seem to perceive in sleep comes from things located outside me, I did not see why I should be any more inclined to believe this of what I think I perceive while awake.

His point is that, whether I am awake or not, there is a gap between subjective experience and the external world—between the ideas inside me and the reality outside. The fact that when I am asleep it can seem to me that I am perceiving, say, a tree shows that perceiving and merely seeming to perceive are two different things. So maybe even when I am awake, I only seem to perceive trees.

Thus Descartes drew a line between the ideas or images in my mind and the "things located outside me." On one side of this line lay the intimate world of my own consciousness, which included images, thoughts, sensations, emotions and "everything that is within us in such a way that we are immediately aware of it." On the other side lay the distant world of matter. This notion that my ideas are the walls of a private garden is one of Descartes's main legacies to philosophy. It was largely because of him that later thinkers, particularly in the seventeenth and eighteenth centuries, wrote so much about internal "ideas" and their relation to external objects.

It was also largely because of Descartes that the relation between mind and body came to seem an acute problem. His distinction between the inner and outer worlds raised the question of how man could live in both of these worlds at once. Although Descartes believed that he would exist without his body after he was dead, he did not deny that he existed very much with it while he was alive. He acknowledged, "I am not merely present in my body as a sailor is present in a ship, but . . . am very closely joined and, as it were, intermingled with it." The evidence for this intermingling was as clear as day. His mental states affected his body (for example, when he consciously moved a part of it), and his body affected his mental state (for example, when something injured him and he felt pain). The question was how this interaction between internal mind and external body managed to take place.

For Descartes, the mind or soul inhabited the body rather like a "ghost in the machine," as one twentieth-century philosopher memorably put it. Critics of this idea, which is often known as "dualism," tend nowadays to be sceptical of the ghost, but in Descartes's time they were more puzzled by the machine. How, they wondered, could an automaton that was essentially like a clock or a mechanical doll possibly be conscious, even if it was haunted? Descartes's answer was that people, but not dolls, or animals either, have souls which communicate with the mechanisms of their bodies through a particular junction in the brain. The ghost talks to the machine and the machine talks to the ghost at the point where they meet, which is in the pineal gland.

According to Descartes's theory of physiology, the nervous system is a network of tubing which conveys the "animal spirits," a gaseous stream of tiny and fast-moving particles derived from the blood and purified in the brain. These animal spirits (which, despite their name, are entirely physical) carry information to and from the pineal gland. For example, when I see something or feel pain, the animal spirits in my eyes or in the relevant part of my body are affected and pass a message to the pineal gland. When I wish to move my hand or to speak, the pineal gland carries a message back to the relevant muscles. Descartes likened the way in which the animal spirits make the muscles do the biddings of this gland to a series of water-driven contraptions:

> you may have observed in the grottoes and fountains in the royal gardens that the mere force with which the water is driven as it emerges from its source is sufficient to move various machines, and even to make them play certain instruments or utter certain words depending on the various arrangements of the pipes through which the water is conducted.

One reason why Descartes believed that it was the pineal gland which acted as the junction between body and soul is that he believed it to be the only structure in the brain which is not duplicated in the brain's two hemispheres. There had to be a place, he reasoned, where the twin images from the two eyes are resolved into a single image, and the pineal gland seemed to be it.

Many mysteries remain today about the functioning of this gland, which exists in all vertebrates with a cranium. It secretes a hormone, melatonin, in response to darkness, and it acts as some sort of biological clock and also regulates the sex hormones. But nobody knows quite how it works. Even in Descartes's time, few people accepted his account of it, not because they knew more physiology than he did, but because they were rightly baffled by the idea that there can be physical communication between the realm of soul and the realm of matter, either in the pineal gland or indeed anywhere else. One of his readers who pressed him on this point was Princess Elizabeth of Bohemia. She was the daughter of Elector Frederick, against whom Descartes had campaigned during a youthful career as a gentleman-soldier. In a long correspondence with the princess, Descartes tried to explain the mysterious union of body and soul which existed in the grottoes of the brain. But he never quite satisfied her on the subject.

One recent scholar has argued that Descartes's account of the mind as an immaterial substance was at best a provisional theory, aimed at providing support for the Catholic doctrine of the immortality of the soul, and that he may not have been altogether happy with his dualism. The suggestion is not that Descartes doubted the immortality of the soul, but that he may not have been wholly convinced that the activity of thinking required an immaterial substance rather than a physical one. Descartes's dualism is certainly not quite what it is often taken to be. In a 1994 best-seller, *Descartes' Error: Emotion, Reason, and the Human Brain*, a neurologist, Antonio Damasio, reported that Descartes believed in an "abyssal separation between body and mind." This is actually the opposite of what Descartes thought. He held that we "experience within ourselves certain . . . things which must not be referred either to the mind alone or to the body alone," and that these arise "from the close and intimate union of our mind with the body." In his best-known writings, Descartes did indeed stress the differences between matter (which occupies space) and thought (which does not). But he also maintained that, in human beings, mind and body are mysteriously and inextricably combined, as he tried to spell out in letters to Princess Elizabeth. He could not explain how it is that mind and body are united, but he was sure that they were.

The pervasive myth that Descartes stressed a "profound separation" between "our intellect and the physical world" has been fancifully employed by environmental campaigners—including a former American vice-president, Al Gore, and the heir to the British throne, Prince Charles—to blame Descartes for the doctrine that "we are separated from the earth, entitled to view it as nothing more than an inanimate collection of resources that we can exploit how we like." This rather oversimplifies the long history of man's relationship with the rest of nature.

Fortunately for the survival and development of mankind, the desire to make use of inanimate materials has not been confined to those who have been convinced by the dualist strain in Descartes's writings.

His last book, *The Passions of the Soul*, began life as a treatise which he wrote for Princess Elizabeth on the intermingling of mind and body, and related subjects. The final version ranged over questions from the physiology of perception to the nature of shame, impudence and disgust, and ended with a defence of the ancient Stoic doctrine that "the chief use of wisdom lies in its teaching us to be masters of our passions and to control them with such skill that the evils which they cause are quite bearable, and even become a source of joy." In the judgement of later thinkers, however, this book did not succeed in explaining how a ghost can live and work in a machine, either joyfully or otherwise.

The moral ideas of the Stoics had long appealed to Descartes. In his first major publication, the *Discourse on Method*, he wrote that one of his maxims was "to try always to master myself rather than fortune, and change my desires rather than the order of the world." "Nothing," he said, echoing Epictetus, "lies entirely within our power except our thoughts." It must be said, though, that Descartes seems to have made a poor job of mastering his passions in the way that a good Stoic is supposed to do. His letters are ripe with intemperate ire: the writings of one French mathematician, for instance, he found "so impertinent, so ridiculous and so despicable"; the rector of the University of Utrecht was "stupid," "malicious" and "incompetent."

Descartes's rather pedestrian Stoic preaching caught the attention of another royal reader, Queen Christina of Sweden, to whom he dedicated his completed book on the passions. It is said that she used to read it while out hunting. Christina invited him to Stockholm to give her lessons in philosophy, and he went in 1649. But the rigours of life at the Swedish court did not suit Descartes at all. In fact, it seems they killed him.

Descartes had always been a late riser. Even at school, perhaps because of frail health, he was excused from early-morning exercises and allowed to stay in bed musing to himself instead. He developed a lifelong habit of meditating during his lie-ins. On several such occasions he apparently experienced a dreamlike state in which he was, at first, unsure whether he was dreaming or awake. In Stockholm, however, he could not indulge his languorous habits. In the coldest Swedish winter in sixty years, he found himself obliged to give his lessons standing bare-headed in Christina's library at five in the morning, so that his teachings could be fitted into her busy schedule. It was a cruel change for a man who was not exactly a morning person. He caught pneumonia and died in Stockholm on 11 February 1650, at the age of fifty-three. Four years later, the queen abdicated and converted to Catholicism, prompted, she wrote, by Descartes's philosophy, though this did not make the Church any less suspicious of his writings.

He was buried in Sweden under a simple wooden monument that was allowed to rot. Seventeen years later, his remains were exhumed and taken on a six-month journey to France, except for his right forefinger, which the French ambassador to Sweden was allowed to keep, and his head, which was removed by a captain in the Swedish guards. In France, his body was exhumed and reburied three more times before coming to rest in a former Benedictine monastery in Saint-Germain-des-Prés. The Musée de l'Homme, in the Palais de Chaillot, near the Eiffel Tower, claims to have Descartes's skull, but the claim is weak. It seems that the great dualist's head is still missing.

∞

WITHIN A FEW YEARS of his death, wrote Descartes's first biographer, it was no more possible to count the number of his disciples than it was to count the stars in the sky. This may well have been so, but the numerousness of Descartes's opponents was impressive, too. It is hardly surprising that a man who aimed to call everything into question and start out afresh should suffer a mixed reception. His work was condemned by the Catholic Church and by French universities throughout the rest of the seventeenth century. Traditional-minded academics did not appreciate Descartes's trampling of Aristotle and of Aristotelian concepts. The Inquisition objected, as it had done to Galileo, that the "mechanical" philosophy was inconsistent with the dogma of transubstantiation; and it worried that Descartes did not make the mind sufficiently independent of the body. This second worry suggests that the seventeenth-century Inquisition had a better grasp of his ideas than some recent popularisers. In 1663, several of Descartes's works were placed on the Index of Prohibited Books, where they were in distinguished company. Earlier works on the Index included books by Abelard, Erasmus, Luther, Calvin, Bacon, Pascal and Montaigne, which were later joined by the novels of Stendahl, Balzac and Flaubert, among many others.

In 1720, seventy years after his death, Descartes achieved part of his ambition when some of his books were put on the curriculum at the University of Paris. They did not, however, supplant Aristotle's texts, as Descartes had always dearly wanted, but were instead set for study alongside Aristotle's.

Descartes had intended to appeal to the good sense of educated laymen and women, not just to win over priests and academics. That is why he wrote his *Discourse* in French rather than in Latin—a French version of the *Meditations* was issued, too. This strategy worked. His ideas were discussed with great interest in the salons of Paris long before they were fully appreciated at the Sorbonne. Literary and court circles heard readings from Descartes's works and listened to talks about people like Nicolas Malebranche (1638–1715), an acute thinker who turned from church history and biblical criticism to science and philosophy after becoming enthralled by one of Descartes's books in 1664. The salons of noble ladies, such as Mme de Sévigné, succumbed to a vogue for discussing scientific and general topics from the "new philosophy." These Cartesian women provided the subject for a comedy by Molière, *The Learned Ladies*, which was produced in Paris in 1672. The play features plenty of banter about the rival attractions of reason and the senses, and has an obscure joke based on Cartesian philosophical terminology. The ladies seem acquainted with the theories of Descartes's physics, and do not find much to quarrel with in them:

> ARMANDA: I love his vortexes.
> PHILAMINTA: And I his falling worlds.

Despite the obstacles which Descartes's books encountered from the Church and educational authorities in the seventeenth century, the scien-

tists who mattered loved his vortexes too. Descartes's theories in physics
held the stage until they were superseded by those of Newton at the start
of the next century. Newton himself was a more or less orthodox Cartesian
in the 1660s, and it is sometimes said that his later work would have been
unthinkable without the start that Descartes had made in overthrowing
the Aristotelian system to put a "mechanical" one in its place. The Cartesian revolution continued to make headway in many fields of science, from
astronomy to physiology, while conservative university professors looked
on nervously from the wings.

In the meanwhile, Descartes's more purely philosophical ideas were
making their mark, sometimes in ways that would have surprised him.
Political reformers claimed to apply his method of systematic doubt and his
emphasis on "clear and distinct ideas" to dislodge unexamined prejudices
and defeat arguments against the causes they believed in. The rights of
women was one such cause in the 1670s—though, like all political topics,
apparently, it did not interest Descartes himself. He had focussed more
on the general nature of knowledge than on any social consequences of
enlightenment. He would have been more gratified by a widely read treatise called *Logic, or the Art of Thinking*, which was published in 1662 and
which was deeply influenced by his views on the mind. This book began
with a declaration that captured the essence of Descartes's project in the
*Discourse* and *Meditations*: "As we can have no knowledge of what is outside us except by means of the ideas in us, the reflections we can make on
our ideas are perhaps the most important part of logic, since they are the
foundation of everything else."

The *Logic*, written by Arnauld and another philosopher-theologian,
Pierre Nicole, was the most important treatise on its subject since Aristotle, and remained influential until the late nineteenth century. In the
course of offering what was intended to be a complete guide to the art of
reasoning, it endorsed Descartes's most distinctive views about knowledge.
It agreed that all certainty depends on intellectual introspection. It agreed
that such introspection reveals various self-evident truths, of which it cites
"I think, therefore I am" as one example. And it agreed that the basic facts
about both mental and physical reality may be found in such truths. The
book also joined Descartes in disparaging sensory experience and prais-

ing reason; it relied on his touchstone of "clear and distinct" ideas; and it echoed his sentiment that the mind is better known than the body and the rest of the physical world.

Malebranche shared these Cartesian views, but he added a larger theological dimension. In his *The Search After Truth*, which was published in 1674–1675, he stressed that the union of soul and body was an unhappy marriage between the divine spark of reason and the defiled realm of matter. "We must constantly resist the body's influence on the mind," he wrote, because

> a man who judges all things by his senses, who follows the impulses of his passions in all things, who perceives only what he senses and loves only what flatters him, is in the most wretched state of mind possible. In this state he is infinitely removed from the truth and from his good. But when a man judges things only according to the mind's pure ideas, when he carefully avoids the noisy confusion of creatures, and, when entering into himself, he listens to his sovereign Master with his senses and passions silent, it is impossible for him to fall into error.

Malebranche subtly infused Descartes's philosophy with a stronger dose of religiosity than Descartes himself had found it necessary to stomach. In his account of the wretchedness of bodily life, Malebranche harked back to the Orphic element in Platonism (see *The Dream of Reason*, pp. 25–28), which Descartes had largely outgrown. And he closely identified reason with God, the "sovereign Master," which Descartes never explicitly did. Echoing St Augustine, Malebranche wrote of rational introspection as if it consisted of listening to God whispering in our ears: "the mind's attention is in fact only its conversion and return to God, who is our sole Master, who alone teaches us all truth."

In Malebranche's universe, God also did rather more than that. Malebranche believed that God has a more intimate involvement in the physical world than Descartes ever got round to acknowledging. Every event, Malebranche argued, is really brought about by Him: "there is only one true cause because there is only one true God." Descartes had said that matter is in itself inert and derives its power of motion from God, but Malebranche and others went further and inferred from this that when, for instance, one billiard ball hits another, it is God rather than the first ball which makes the second ball move. According to this theory, the impact of the first ball is not the cause of the second one's movement, but merely the "occasion" for God to nudge it into motion somehow.

One main attraction of this bizarre hypothesis was that it seemed to answer the question of how the mind and the body can interact. It answered it by saying that they do not literally interact at all, but only appear to do so. Nothing interacts with anything, except with God. It is God who makes things happen in the soul and in the body, and He does it in such a way that the two seem to affect one another. When a pin pricks my finger, for instance, it is God who causes the sensation of pain in my mind. Mind and body thus function independently yet remain in step— they are, as another dissident Cartesian put it, like two synchronised but unconnected clocks. This idea was supposed to make more sense than the orthodox Cartesian view that the body acts on the mind and the mind acts on the body.

"Occasionalism," as this theory came to be called—because a pin-prick was said to be the "occasion" of my pain rather than its "cause"—was the most widespread heresy in the young church of Cartesianism, but it soon died out. Another deviation from Descartes's own ways of thinking was more consequential and is still with us. This modification of Cartesianism was more a matter of emphasis than of doctrine. Descartes himself had regarded his discussions of the topics of "first philosophy," or metaphysics, as no more than a prologue to the business of finding out about the world. Problems about knowledge, certainty, mind and body were supposed to be only a small part of philosophy as a whole, for this included everything that we now count as science. But in the hands of Malebranche and many others, these metaphysical problems came to seem the most important part of the subject.

This would have surprised and disappointed Descartes, who thought there was little left to be said about such subjects after what he had written about them. He explained that the reason why he had dealt at length with the challenge of scepticism, for example, was so that "everyone does not have to tackle the job for himself, or need to spend time and trouble meditating on these things." One should not, Descartes warned Frans Berman, a student who interviewed him in 1648,

> devote so much effort to the *Meditations* and to metaphysical questions, or give them elaborate treatment in commentaries and the like. Still less should one do what some try to do, and dig more deeply into these questions than the author did: he has dealt with them quite deeply enough. It is sufficient to have grasped them once in a general way, and then to remember the conclusion. Otherwise, they draw the mind too far away from physical and observable things, and make it unfit to study them. Yet it is just these physical studies that it is most desirable for men to pursue, since they would yield abundant benefits for life.

In other words, he was delivering the same message as some of today's anti-philosophical scientists, who scoff that philosophers should focus on up-to-date physics or biology and get on with some real work. Descartes gave the same advice to Princess Elizabeth, but it was not generally heeded. By the end of the seventeenth century, the topics of his *Meditations* and similar writings attracted much wider interest than his scientific work. This is partly because Descartes's *Meditations* did not in fact resolve quite as much as he thought they did. If he had really been able to answer all the excellent questions he had raised, there would have been no need for later philosophers to tackle the job themselves. It was also partly because his scientific ideas were rapidly eclipsed by those of Newton and others. Descartes the philosopher waxed just as Descartes the scientist was waning.

This is not to say that all or even many thinkers endorsed his philosophical opinions down to the last detail. When Voltaire pronounced judgement on Descartes in 1728, he declared not only his physics but also his views on knowledge and the soul to be old hat. According to Voltaire, John Locke (1632–1704) had exposed the errors in Descartes's old philosophy and established a new one himself, just as Newton had established a new physics. Whereas Descartes had written a fanciful novel of the soul, said Voltaire, Locke had "modestly written its history." Voltaire's estimation of Locke's achievement was somewhat exaggerated; it reflected his preference for English ways of thinking over French ones—a preference he seems

to have developed after fleeing to England in 1726, following an altercation
with a bullying and thuggish Parisian aristocrat. But Descartes still loomed
larger than Voltaire was prepared to acknowledge. All the major philosophers were followers in his footsteps even if they did not embrace all his
ideas. By the eighteenth century, Descartes, and especially the topics of his
*Meditations*, was a popular starting-point for any philosophy that regarded
itself as modern. Even Voltaire's hero, Locke, who was often as far removed
from Descartes's opinions as anyone of the times, said that he got his first
"relish of philosophical studies" from reading Descartes.

In a snapshot of the rival views of Descartes and Locke, Voltaire high-
lighted an issue that historians subsequently decided was a central one for
modern philosophy. Voltaire's picture was partly distorted, but something
like it found its way into many albums:

> Our Descartes, born to uncover the errors of antiquity but to substitute
> his own, and spurred on by that systematizing mind which blinds the
> greatest of men, imagined that he had demonstrated that the soul was
> the same thing as thought, just as matter, for him, is the same thing as
> space. He affirms that we think all the time, and that the soul comes
> into the body already endowed with all the metaphysical notions,
> knowing God, space, the infinite, having all the abstract ideas, full, in
> fact, of learning which unfortunately it forgets on leaving its mother's
> womb.

Locke, on the other hand, "having destroyed innate ideas . . . establishes
that all our ideas come to us via the senses."

Descartes did indeed hold the strange view that we never stop thinking. He could not see how to avoid this consequence of his thesis that
"thought . . . alone is inseparable from me." But his supposed theory that
we are born with a great deal of knowledge, which we promptly forget and
then have to rediscover, is a mischievous exaggeration on the part of Voltaire. According to Voltaire, Descartes maintained that

> a few weeks after my conception I was a most sapient soul, already
> knowing a thousand things that I forgot at birth, having quite point-

lessly possessed in the uterus knowledge that escaped me as soon as I was in a position to need it and which I have never been able to regain properly since.

This charge was brought against Descartes in his own lifetime and he angrily rejected it, ridiculing the suggestion that he believed children know things in the womb. He did maintain that we have certain "innate ideas"—that is, some concepts and some truths which are somehow implanted in us—but what he mostly meant by this is just that we have "a natural power that enables us to know" various things. "I have never written or even thought that such ideas are actual," he justly objected. It was only the potential for knowledge that was inborn.

Still, Voltaire was on to something when he pointedly contrasted Descartes's talk of innate ideas with Locke's theory that the raw materials of our knowledge are provided by experience. Descartes's most revealing definition of innate ideas is that they are what "we come to know . . . by the power of our own native intelligence, without any sensory experience." For example, when I reflect that the angles of a triangle must always add up to 180 degrees, or that God cannot have any imperfections, these thoughts count as "innate" ideas in Descartes's sense of the term. I am not born with them, because this native intelligence is as yet undeveloped; but they do come "solely from the power of thinking within me." One key problem in Descartes's philosophy, as Locke realised, was that too much of what Descartes asserted had no other warrant except that it allegedly came from this internal faculty.

Descartes frequently spoke of the "natural light" of reason and of various truths that were "self-evident." His proofs of the existence of God, and of the fact that God would not deceive us, rest on allegedly self-evident premises that were seen by this natural light. Several key principles of his physics were also supposedly revealed by natural reason (for instance, that matter is infinitely divisible and that empty space is an impossibility). Of course, Descartes did not believe that reason reveals the whole story about the physical world. As we have seen, he was a keen experimentalist and observer who liked to dissect livestock. Having arrived at his fundamental principles, he acknowledged that it was necessary to put points of detail to the test of experience. But he believed that the fundamental principles themselves came from "certain seeds of truth which are naturally in our souls," and did not require any further confirmation.

Thus Descartes tried to work out too much in his head. In the case of his basic principles, both in physics and in general philosophy, he was too quick to assume that whatever seemed to him to be necessarily true was in fact so. This failing is, of course, far from unique to Descartes. The history of science as well as of philosophy is full of work that is later judged to have depended on assumptions that ought to have been questioned. This is inevitable, because it is often hard to see which parts of a theory ought to have been scrutinised more closely until somebody suggests a workable alternative to them. Even some of Euclid's geometry has now been not only questioned but rejected—though nobody blames him for trying to work out too much in his head. Nobody blames Euclid for failing to see that he could have abandoned some of his assumptions and adopted alternative geometries, because these substitute geometries were not developed until the nineteenth century.

But Descartes did not have Euclid's excuse. Virtually all of his theories were criticised by someone or other in his own lifetime. Alternative accounts of the mind, of the soul, of God and of matter and space were at least being sketched, for example in the extensive *Objections* which he commissioned to his *Meditations*. Thus, except for his pride and for his faith in his own unusually bright light of reason, there was little to prevent Descartes from realising that perhaps he did not have all the answers.

Descartes's quest for "infallible demonstrations" in all branches of science, even including medicine, and his confident deduction of proofs about God, the soul and matter, showed the excessive influence of mathematics on his mind. Perhaps this is understandable in a mathematician of genius. Locke, by contrast, advocated a more cautious and experimental approach to philosophical questions, and this difference between Locke and Descartes came to seem crucially important. Voltaire believed that it accounted for their many differences of opinion about the soul and other matters. Later historians went even further. It was said that all the main battles of modern philosophy stemmed from this dispute between indubitable reason versus fallible experience.

In his *Critique of Pure Reason*, which was published in 1781, Kant contrasted two rival schools of philosophers, the "empiricists" and the "noologists" (from the Greek word for intellect, *nous*). Two prize pupils from the first school were said to be Aristotle and Locke, who stressed the role of experience in the formation of knowledge. Two from the second were Plato and Leibniz, who emphasised reason instead. This way of dividing philosophers into opposing teams derives from two rival sects of Greek medicine in the third century BC. One sect developed ambitious theories about the inner workings of the body; the other aimed to do without any theories, and based its treatments on whatever seemed to have worked in the past. As the great medical writer Galen (c. 129–c. 200) put it: "[doctors] who rely on experience alone are . . . called empiricists . . . those who rely on reason are called rationalists." These are the names that stuck when Kant's contrast caught on as the best way to encapsulate recent philosophical history. Philosophy from Descartes to at least Kant was a struggle between empiricists and rationalists—or so it was claimed, and often still is.

This myth was established in its present form by an enormous history of philosophy that was written in the mid-nineteenth century by one of Kant's admirers. The book spread two influential ideas. First, it said that Descartes had made the problem of knowledge the most basic question of philosophy. Secondly, it said that two three-man teams had devoted themselves to tackling this problem: the empiricists, consisting of John Locke, George Berkeley (1685–1753) and David Hume (1711–1756); and the rationalists, consisting of Gottfried Leibniz (1646–1716), Benedict de Spinoza (1632–1677) and Descartes himself. The six men are still mainly thought of as members of these teams, though it is sometimes admitted that this neat grouping would have baffled the players themselves. Berkeley, for example, saw himself as above all an opponent of Locke's, not as a teammate. As for the idea that the theory of knowledge became the focal point of philosophy in Descartes's day and remained so for some time, this thesis became especially popular in the twentieth century, when many philosophers liked to think of themselves as pioneers who had finally found something better to focus on, namely language.

Thus one influential work of philosophy in the second half of the twentieth century stated that "Descartes made the question, 'What do we know, and what justifies our claim to this knowledge?' the starting-point of all philosophy; and, despite the conflicting views of the various schools, it was accepted as the starting-point for more than two centuries." This author goes on to say that everything has, of course, now changed, because Ludwig Wittgenstein (1889–1951) and Gottlob Frege (1848–1925) instituted a new revolution. They established the philosophy of language, or theory of meaning, as the foundation of the subject instead. Questions about what we know were thereby set aside and relegated once more to the inferior status from which Descartes had temporarily raised them.

Was the problem of knowledge really the heart of philosophy for more than two centuries? Most of the philosophers of the time did not think so, and they ought to know. The work of Hobbes, who is now remembered mainly for his political thought, and to whom we turn next, certainly does not bear out the myth. Nor do the writings of Spinoza or Leibniz. Locke and Hume fit the traditional picture somewhat better. But, as we shall see, plenty of their best work was not especially concerned with knowledge. As for Descartes himself, he would have been puzzled by the question of whether or not the theory of knowledge was central to philosophy. Of course he himself had seen fit to devote plenty of effort to questioning and then justifying what we think we know; but in so doing he had resolved all such issues, or so he thought, and thus philosophers were free to move on to more consequential matters, such as how to extend human life.

By addressing the old challenge of scepticism, Descartes did accidentally help to give philosophy a new direction, or rather to remind it of an old one, since the question of whether our beliefs can be justified, and, if so, how, was a very lively one in Hellenistic times too. But philosophers always travel in several directions at once, and the story of scepticism in seventeenth- and eighteenth-century philosophy is not the whole story of that time. Besides, the impact of scepticism was not felt only via the writings of Descartes. Nor did it affect only those topics which Descartes chose to discuss. Spinoza's revolutionary view of God and nature may be said to have reflected his sceptical attitude towards traditional religion. This was a momentous development in philosophy, but it had little to do with Descartes. It certainly had nothing to do with the sort of general questions

about knowledge that Descartes had allegedly made the focus of the subject. Such sceptical puzzles bored Spinoza.

The distinction between empiricists and rationalists is a vague and
confusing one, anyway. Several of the so-called rationalists of the seventeenth century took a greater interest in the empirical sciences than
their "empiricist" counterparts; Leibniz and Descartes knew far more
about these sciences than Locke or Hume ever did. And Hobbes, who
is conventionally classified as an empiricist, in effect sided with Leibniz
and against Hume by playing down the role of experience in scientific
knowledge.*

Bacon, like Hobbes, is placed by historians in the empiricist camp, yet
he himself ridiculed "the *empirical* brand of philosophy" for producing "more
deformed and freakish dogmas than the . . . rational[ist] kind, because it
is . . . founded on . . . the narrow and unilluminating basis of a handful
of experiments." Bacon maintained that there are really three kinds of
philosophers: ants, spiders and bees. Empiricists are like ants. They "simply
accumulate and use; Rationalists, like spiders, spin webs from themselves;
the way of the bee is in between; it takes material from the flowers of the
garden and the field; but it has the ability to convert and digest them. . . ."
Bacon advocated the way of the bee: one should combine the best parts
of the experimental and rational faculties. Descartes, Hobbes, Locke, Spinoza, Leibniz and Hume all aspired to be bees, though none of them quite
put it that way.

The traditional division of teams obscures the interests and attitudes
that these men had in common. They shared a dissatisfaction with the
methods of university scholasticism, and a keen involvement in the questions raised by the new sciences. They also shared, in varying degrees,
an interest in the relation between man's internal ideas and the physical world outside him. Descartes's achievement was to play a singularly
important part in developing each item on this fresh agenda, especially
the last one.

---

* See p. 208, below.

# 2

## THE MONSTER OF MALMESBURY
# *Hobbes*

IN 1646 THOMAS HOBBES WAS MATHEMATICS TUTOR TO THE FUTURE King Charles II in Paris, where both men were sheltering from England's civil war. The young prince reportedly found his teacher to be "the oddest fellow he'd ever met." This was one of the nicer things said about Hobbes. The "Monster of Malmesbury," as one pamphleteer called him, became the most vilified thinker in Britain, and had almost no defenders in his own country for about a century after his death in 1679 at the great age of ninety-one. He had been born eight years before Descartes, but outlived him by nearly thirty years.

His reputation fared a little better in parts of continental Europe, but even there the verdicts were usually mixed. For Voltaire, Hobbes was *profond*, yet also *bizarre*. At home some people said that the Great Fire of London in 1666, and an outbreak of bubonic plague a year earlier—Daniel Defoe's "Plague Year"—was God's way of punishing England for tolerating such an impious beast. A few weeks after the fire, a parliamentary committee began to examine "such books as tend to Atheism, Blasphemy, or Profaneness," including Hobbes's best-known treatise, *Leviathan*, which had been published in 1651. He was told that some bishops wanted him dead.

How did Hobbes make so many enemies? Quite apart from his politics, of which more later, there was plenty of provocation in his writings. There were tirades against Aristotle and scholasticism, aimed at the universities,

36

which set many academics against him. There were attacks on theologians, who, Hobbes maintained, claimed to know more about God than mortal minds could grasp. And there was an account of psychology that was widely taken to imply that man is at bottom selfish, which was regarded as a pernicious doctrine, since it was an insult to man's maker and seemed to underwrite immoral conduct. Descartes wrote that Hobbes's moral principles "are extremely bad and quite dangerous in that he supposes all persons to be wicked, or gives them cause to be so."

Hobbes also angered clerics by arguing against the autonomy of the churches, which tended, in his opinion, to lay claim to a dangerous amount of power. He maintained that religious disputes should ultimately be adjudicated by the sovereign of each country, which is one reason why he excoriated Catholicism, a transnational religion with a pope who claimed an authority above that of any king. According to Hobbes, some Protestant groups, too, damaged the stability of the realm. They did this in either or both of two ways: by giving too much latitude to ordinary believers, who were liable to develop dangerous convictions and be disobedient; or by establishing a clerical structure—on the model of the Scottish Presbyterians—which rivalled the orderly hierarchy of appointed bishops, and thereby undermined the authority of the state. Hobbes's own father was a cleric, as it happens: an irascible, semi-literate man, fond of cards and drink, who was excommunicated when Hobbes was a youth, and later disappeared from his parish in north Wiltshire after beating up another clergyman in a churchyard.

Above all, though, it was probably Hobbes's materialism, and what this was taken to entail, that made him an anathema. Like Descartes, and other devotees of the "new philosophy" pioneered by Galileo, Hobbes regarded nature as a machine. But he took this idea further than other philosophers, and maintained that absolutely everything is physical: "the *Universe* . . . is Corporeall, that is to say, Body; and hath the dimensions of Magnitude, namely, Length, Breadth, and Depth . . . and because the Universe is All, that which is no part of it, is *Nothing*; and consequently *no where*." It followed that there was no such thing as an immaterial mind or spirit of the sort that Cartesians believed in. According to Hobbes, a person expires, at least temporarily, when his body does, and his afterlife begins only when his body is resurrected on the day of judgement. This idea, which is some-times called "mortalism," has a long history in Jewish thought, and, as a minority view, in Christianity. It was even held by one pope, John XXII, in the fourteenth century, until his college of cardinals talked him out of it. Hobbes's mortalism is probably the source of the lasting rumour that he did not really believe in an afterlife. Graham Greene, a Catholic novelist who was presumably relying on Catholic propaganda, wrote in 1974 that Hobbes "denied the possibility of any supernatural punishment for vice or reward for virtue." This is not true. At the resurrection, Hobbes's God would have ample opportunity to distribute posthumous rewards and pun-ishments, albeit belatedly.

Hobbes was sceptical of tales about ghosts and witches, and this scep-ticism was itself regarded in some quarters as evidence of irreligion, or at least of insufficient respect for spiritual matters. Denying that there was such a thing as a witch was almost as bad as being one. There were other enlightened thinkers who shared Hobbes's disdain for stories of supernatu-ral creatures stalking the villages of England; but the belief in witches was a powerful force in his day, perhaps because these were unsettled times. A third or more of all the people executed for witchcraft in England between the fifteenth and eighteenth centuries were dispatched in the mid-1640s by Matthew Hopkins, the self-described "Witch-finder General," and his associates, just when Hobbes was working out the consequences of his materialist philosophy.

Hobbes drew the inevitable theological conclusion from his materi-alism. Only matter exists, so even God himself must be a physical being. This made Hobbes an "atheist" to practically everyone except himself; to most other people, a physical God did not really count as a God at all. The belief in a material God is one of the rarest heresies in the history of Christianity. Tertullian (c. 160–c. 220), one of the Latin Fathers of the Church, believed it, and nothing in the Bible contradicts it, as Hobbes pointed out in a futile attempt to render it palatable. The early church councils never ruled on the question, but the notion was abhorrent to all good Christians from at least the thirteenth century, if not before, until the nineteenth century, when the new American religion of Mormonism embraced it. Mormons maintain that the Bible means what it says in the passages that describe man as made in God's image. Their own scriptures state that God the Father (though not the Holy Ghost) "has a body of flesh and bones as tangible as man's." Hobbes did not go quite so far as this: his God was made of a kind of matter that is too flimsy to be apprehended by human sense-organs, which was also the view of Lucretius, the Epicurean Roman poet.

A revived materialism, which sought to update the ancient Greek version of Democritus and Epicurus, was one of Hobbes's two main philosophical innovations. The other was a novel way to see government. Hobbes's method in political philosophy was the opposite of utopianism. Instead of describing a model society, as Plato did in his *Republic*, Hobbes starts by imagining the horrors of a lawless world, in which people are left to fend for themselves and there is no "common Power to keep them all in awe." The result, as he famously wrote, would be "continuall feare, and danger of violent death; And the life of man, solitary, poore, nasty, brutish and short." To avoid this result, Hobbes argued, people must agree to bow to a sovereign authority, preferably a single monarch rather than any sort of assembly, whom they must invest with broad powers. Anything less would lead to hellish consequences. This authority should be absolute, that is, it must enjoy a monopoly of political power, for if sovereignty were instead divided between, say, a legislature, an executive and a judiciary—as conventional wisdom in England and America later dictated that it should be—that would weaken it, and the monarch would be unable to stave off chaos. Thanks to the sophistication with which Hobbes developed his theory of the state, to his emphasis on the consent of the governed, and on the rule of law, he eventually came to be seen as the pioneer of modern political philosophy.

In his *Leviathan*, Hobbes described King James VI of Scotland, who came to the throne of England and Ireland when Hobbes was a student at Oxford in 1603, as "our most wise King." James had written several books about government, one of which is cast in the form of advice to his eldest son, Prince Henry, whom he expected to succeed him. God, James wrote, has "made you a little God to sit on his Throne, and rule over other men." When a king is crowned, as James put it in another book, he becomes a father to his subjects, and has a fatherly duty to look after them. In effect, a king makes a promise to his people "to discharge honorably and trewly the office given him by God over them." But only God himself can act as the judge of whether or not this promise has been kept. A wicked king is sometimes sent as divine punishment for a wicked people, and it is never right for them to resist or depose him, however bad he is.

Hobbes endorsed some aspects of this view of government. He agreed that a king has an obligation imposed on him by God to protect his people and to promote their welfare, and that under no circumstances may they fail to obey him. Yet he also tried to justify such an absolute monarchy in practical terms—that is, to show why it is in the people's own interests as well as in accordance with God's wishes. The aim of his political philosophy was, as he put it in the closing paragraph of *Leviathan*, "to set before mens eyes, the mutuall Relation between Protection and Obedience; of which the condition of Humane nature, and the Laws Divine . . . require an inviolable observation." To establish that divine laws enjoined unconditional obedience to a sovereign, Hobbes drew on the authority of scripture, as he did, at great length, on many topics. But to establish that human nature also required it, he drew on philosophical arguments that do not depend on any theological position. This is why it has been said that his achievement was to disentangle politics and religion, or at least to attempt to do so. Early in the twentieth century, an American philosopher, John Dewey, wrote that in Hobbes's day politics was by common consent "a branch of theology," and that "Hobbes's great work was in freeing, once for all, morals and politics from subservience to divinity."

We should add two qualifications to Dewey's encomium. First, it was not Hobbes's goal to provide a purely secular understanding of politics. Although he believed that theologians and clerics were often a bad influence on statecraft, there is no reason to suppose that he wanted to elbow God himself entirely out of the picture. Hobbes's account of government does not deny the divine right of kings to rule; it just does not rest on it. For him, political authority is legitimate when there is a tacit or explicit pact between citizens, which their God-given gift of rationality leads them to make. Secondly, the idea of a political theory that is based on reflections about the human condition was by no means new to Western thinking. Classical Greek and Roman political thought had been secular in the same way. So Hobbes's "great work" was, in effect, to promote a partly non-theological politics in Christian Europe, not to invent such a thing for the first time. There are similarities between his political theory and the very old idea that the institutions of government arise out of, or can be justified in terms of, some sort of social contract. It is, however, worth noting that in Hobbes's version, the king's subjects must not behave as if there were any form of contract between themselves and the king which they are entitled to enforce. The Hobbesian contract binds only the citizens, who agree that they shall jointly subordinate themselves to a sovereign. It does not bind the sovereign himself. (The nature of social-contract theories will be examined when we come to Locke in chapter 4.)

Hobbes lived through England's civil wars, and several wars of religion on the Continent. Did these terrifying times prompt him to offer a cure that was worse than the disease? Many have thought so. Denis Diderot (1713–1784), the principal editor of the French Enlightenment's *Encyclopédie*, wrote in the 1760s that Hobbes had mistaken the particularly dangerous circumstances of his own day for a universal phenomenon. Hobbes had therefore adopted too grim a view of human nature and proposed too drastic a remedy for it. That is also the gist of some virtuosic invective by Hugh Trevor-Roper (later Lord Dacre), a British historian who died in 2003. Dacre summed up *Leviathan* curtly: "The axiom, fear; the method, logic; the conclusion, despotism."

Hobbes might almost have acknowledged the first part of this trio: he admitted to a timorous disposition. His mother was, he wrote in some autobiographical verse, frightened into labour by the rumoured approach of the Spanish Armada, leading Hobbes to quip that she "Did bring forth Twins at once, both Me, and Fear." Despite this inheritance, though, it must be said that he was intellectually courageous and habitually fierce with his pen. And Hobbes was not the only thinker to be so badly shaken by sectarian conflict that peace came to seem the paramount goal of government, to be secured at almost any cost. When Hobbes was an infant, Justus Lipsius, a classical scholar and political theorist in what is now Belgium, drew a similar conclusion, because of the "many millions of men" who "have bin brought to ruin and do dayly perish" in religious wars.

To the charge of using logic as his method, Hobbes would surely plead guilty as charged, for every philosopher likes to think that he has reached his conclusions via rigorous reasoning. But although no sound argument can be too rigorous to be right, a bad one may fail to persuade precisely because its author tries too hard to be tidy. It was, however, not so much a love of logic *per se* which sometimes led Hobbes astray, but rather a love of one particular form of tidiness, namely Euclid's geometry. Hobbes was bedazzled by what Euclid had achieved in mathematics with the use of simple axioms and strict definitions, and he wanted to do something similar for politics. This is one main reason why he was so often misunderstood. Once Hobbes had convinced himself that a definition made sense and would enable him to deduce the conclusions he wanted, he would employ it regardless of what others were likely to make of his use of terms.

For example, in his first printed political treatise, *De cive*, Hobbes argued as follows for what appears to be the shocking thesis that a ruler is always right.

> Since it has been shown above (articles 7, 9, 12) that those who have obtained *sovereign power* in a commonwealth are not bound by any agreements to anyone, it follows that they can do no wrong to the citizens. For by the definition given in chapter III, article 3, a *Wrong* is simply the violation of an agreement, hence there can be no *wrong* where there has been no agreement.

It is hardly surprising that, 150 years later, Immanuel Kant found the implications of such words to be "quite terrifying," as did many of Hobbes's contemporaries. The passage seems to suggest that a sovereign "may act towards [the citizen] as he pleases," as Kant put it. Maximus, a tyrant in a play by Dryden that was first staged at the height of Hobbes's infamy, in the late 1660s, boasts that rulers such as himself are above censure, because "the world may sin, but not its emperor."

Yet this is not what Hobbes meant. He was making a purely technical point which has confused some people but is not morally outrageous. According to Hobbes, a ruler may indeed be said to be "at fault," for example if his actions "tend to the hurt of the people in general," in which case they are "breaches of the law of nature, and of the divine law." But any such "wrong" is, in Hobbes's usage, done to God, not to the citizens, because it is God's law which is thereby broken, not the citizens' law—even though it is the citizens who are harmed. He did spell this out, but was nevertheless widely misunderstood. Similarly, he wrote that "all men are permitted to have and to do all things in the state of nature," which was taken to mean that there was nothing really wrong with murder, theft, or anything else. In fact he was stating the tautology that nothing would be illegal if there were not yet any laws.

If you seek the truth, wrote Hobbes, it is vital to define your terms, or else you will find yourself "entangled in words, as a bird in lime-twiggs; the more he struggles the more belimed." Unfortunately, he seems to have paid too little attention to the risk of beliming his own readers, as one of his arch-enemies noted:

> Mr Hobs is very dexterous, in Confuting others, by putting a new Sense upon their Words, rehearsed by himself; different from what the same Words signifie with other men. And therefore, if You shall have occasion to speak of *Chalk*; He'll tell you that by *Chalk*, he means *Cheese*: and then, if he can prove that what You say of *Chalk*, is not true of *Cheese*; he reckons himself to have gotten a great victory.

What of Trevor-Roper's suggestion that Hobbes in effect promoted despotism? This is certainly not what the Monster had in mind. Hobbes addressed the complaint that a sovereign with absolute power would tyranically abuse it: his reply was not that such abuse would be worth the price, or did not really matter, but rather that it simply would not happen. A sovereign with unlimited power might, in theory, rob, imprison and kill his subjects at will—but, Hobbes rather lamely asked, "why would he do it?" He could not do so "without violating natural laws and wronging God," and thus putting his own soul at risk of "eternal death." And besides, "there is no reason why he would want to spoil his citizens, since that is not to his advantage." This is not very reassuring. It seems almost charmingly naïve, and is curious to hear from a man so well-versed in history, both ancient and modern. There have been plenty of tyrants to prove him wrong.

Hobbes also made the better reply that, even if a sovereign is not
granted absolute power, but instead just enough to do his job, there is still
some danger that he will abuse it, since "he who has enough strength to
protect everybody, has enough to oppress everybody." In other words, any
effective government has the wherewithal to act despotically, even if it is
not led by a single tyrant. No political system is perfect, Hobbes observed:
"human affairs can never be without some inconvenience." This is a fair
point; but being oppressed by a tyrant who has unlimited power, and an
unlimited reign in which to exercise it, is rather a large inconvenience.
A wise architect of political systems would surely take steps to reduce the
risk of such an eventuality. One effective way to do so is to divide power
between several institutions, which can then moderate the excesses of each
other. As Montesquieu (1689–1755) later put it in his influential *Spirit of the
Laws*: "It has eternally been observed that any man who has power is led
to abuse it. . . . So that one cannot abuse power, power must check power
by the arrangement of things." Hobbes would object that such a division
of powers is a recipe for civil wars. But this does not seem to be true of his
own country, which has been at peace with itself ever since it reined in the
authority of its monarch in 1689.

Some twentieth-century writers have accused Hobbes of advocat-
ing totalitarianism long before it was officially invented in the 1930s. A
"totalitarian" state was characterised by the Italian fascist leader, Mussolini, as one which is not "limited to . . . enforcing law and order, as the
Liberal doctrine would have it," but is "all-embracing," and concerns itself
with "all the manifestations of the moral and intellectual life of man."
Since the 1940s, this overweening type of state has widely been seen as
a form of tyranny that is shared by fascism and communism. Yet Hobbes
seems to have sympathised instead with the spirit of what Mussolini
called the "Liberal doctrine," for he tended to justify most encroachments
on the liberty of individuals in terms of the need to preserve peace. A
good sovereign, according to Hobbes, would protect the freedoms that are
required for the citizens' well-being, and would be careful not to ensnare
them by making too many laws. Hobbes never suggested that the state
should control the arts or entertainment, as bona fide totalitarian regimes
have generally sought to do. And although he wanted the sovereign to

supervise the churches, this measure was intended to reduce the power of zealous factions and interfering clerics, not to impose any particular ideology.

Since Hobbes held that it was the sovereign's job to enforce the laws of God and encourage "the improvement of mankind," the remit of the state did extend beyond matters of national security. Drunkenness, bigamy, incest, homosexuality and "the promiscuous use of women" should be banned, for example, and so should "the superfluous consuming of food and apparel"—which Hobbes seems to have thought would somehow damage a country's wealth. Yet if the regulation of sexual behaviour and intoxicating substances, or the adoption of questionable economic ideas, is taken to be a mark of a totalitarian regime, then every regime has been totalitarian. Although a Hobbesian policy of giving sovereigns a free hand would surely make it harder to resist the rise of a Hitler or a Stalin, the totalitarian goal of an all-embracing state played no part in Hobbes's own thinking. It is easy to put modern labels on his politics, but usually hard to make them stick.

One exception to this rule concerns the equality of citizens. Hobbes was a sort of egalitarian. He criticised the crude belief that "one man's blood [is] better than another['s]," and Aristotle's idea that, as Hobbes put it, "some men are by nature worthy to govern, and others by nature ought to serve." Even if there were such natural differences, Hobbes argued, men would disagree over how they were in fact distributed, so the idea of a natural inequality would lead to quarrels:

> as long as men arrogate to themselves more honour than they give to others, it cannot be imagined how they can possibly live in peace: and consequently we are to suppose, that for peace sake, nature hath ordained this law, *That every man acknowledge [every] other for his equal.*

This was far from what many others believed that nature had ordained. Compare Hobbes's words with, for example, what the *parlement* of Paris proclaimed a century later, on the eve of the French Revolution, in defence of the privileges of nobles: "The infinite and immutable wisdom in the plan of the universe established an unequal distribution of strength and character, necessarily resulting in inequality in the conditions of men within the civil order."

Since nearly all of Hobbes's working life was spent as a tutor, secretary or companion to aristocrats, most of them members of the superbly housed Cavendish family, some people thought that his egalitarianism was an ungrateful cheek. The first Earl of Clarendon, a statesman with two granddaughters who became queens, complained of Hobbes's "extreme malignity to the Nobility, by whose bread he hath been alwaies sustain'd." Clarendon likened Hobbes to the radical "Levellers" for allowing no privileges in government on account of birth, "whereas in all well-instituted governments . . . the Heirs and Descendants from worthy and eminent Parents, if they do not degenerate from their vertue, have bin alwaies allow'd a preference and kind of title to employments and offices of honor and trust."

Hobbes did not seek to level down all differences in wealth or status, though. It was the idea of distinction by right of ancestry to which he objected. His position seems to have been that honours were acceptable insofar as they had been earned and were seen to be distributed fairly. As for economic inequality, since the security of property and the ability of a citizen to "exercise and have the benefit of his own industry" were to be protected by the sovereign, it is reasonable to infer that Hobbes saw nothing wrong with being rich. But he was also sympathetic to the plight of the very poor: he insisted that those who are unable to work should be supported by the state, and not have to rely on private charity.

ALTHOUGH HOBBES sought to outlaw dissolute behaviour, his reputation might lead one to think he had instead encouraged it. There are several stories of repentant sinners blaming him for their downfall. Daniel Scargill, a young Cambridge don who was dismissed from his fellowship in 1669, recited an abject recantation in the university church:

I gloried to be an *Hobbist* and an *Atheist*. . . . Agreeably unto which principles and positions, I have lived in great licentiousness, swearing rashly, drinking intemperately, boasting myself insolently, corrupting others. . . . Oh what height of wickedness had I arrived unto!

It may be doubted whether Scargill was guilty of any wickedness worse than embroidering a confession to win reinstatement, but there were genuine sinners who sang the same tune. John Wilmot, the second Earl of Rochester, led an exceptionally debauched life. In addition to much brawling and the sexual adventures celebrated in his unusually explicit lyric poems, he once claimed to have been drunk continuously for five years. He was briefly imprisoned in the Tower of London for abducting an heiress, whom he subsequently married, and at one stage pretended to be a gynecologist, so that he could molest even more women than he had managed to seduce by conventional means. When he began to succumb to the cumulative effects of his frequent bouts of venereal disease and alcoholism, expiring at the age of thirty-three, Rochester renounced his former life and penitently embraced religion on his way out. According to a sermon preached at his funeral, Rochester told his mother's chaplain that "that absurd and foolish Philosophy . . . propagated by the late Mr Hobbs, and others, had undone him."

This was, of course, just the sort of thing that chaplains liked to hear. Hobbes was seen not merely as an atheist, but as the arch-atheist of his day. And atheists, it was generally held, were bound to lack moral fibre and to sow the seeds of vice. There was an intellectual scandal when, a few years after Hobbes's death, Pierre Bayle suggested that it was possible for unbelievers to be decent and virtuous.* Hobbes did not in fact advocate a godless society, and he may well have shared the conventional opinion that such a thing would be disastrous. Most people, however, believed that his writings were dangerously irreligious and therefore immoral, so it was gratifying to hear this confirmed from the lips of a dying debauchee. Even Casanova (1725–1798), who regarded himself as a man of sound religion and principles, once warned a young lady against reading the pernicious works of Hobbes.

"Fill yourselves with costly Wine and Oyntments . . . oppresse the

---

* See chapter 5, below.

poor righteous man, spare not the Widow"—such were the maxims consonant with Hobbesian atheism, according to one clergyman and botanist, who was an expert on vegetables but had not, perhaps, studied much of Hobbes. There is no reason to think that Rochester paid any close attention to Hobbes's writings, either. Against the poet's bid to lay the blame for his loose living on an elderly philosopher, we can set the simpler story told by Samuel Johnson (1709–1784) in his *Lives of the Poets*. Dr Johnson recorded that Rochester "had very early an inclination to intemperance," and that when he began to habituate the court of Charles II, he "unhappily addicted himself to dissolute and vicious company, by which his principles were corrupted and his manners depraved."

∞

ON THE WHOLE, not even his worst enemies pretended that Hobbes indulged in the vices which his teachings were alleged to promote—though one bishop groundlessly claimed that the philosopher had, like Descartes, fathered an illegitimate daughter. In his old age, Hobbes made some strikingly immodest claims about the importance of his own contributions to science and mathematics; but the only other elements of his biography that may even raise an eyebrow are instances of mild eccentricity. He was, for example, in the habit of singing to himself in bed, because he believed that this would prolong his life. Singing was not the only unusual thing he did in bed: he was also wont to indulge his passion for geometry by drawing triangles on the sheets and on his leg. These curious facts, like most anecdotes about him, come from his close friend and admirer, John Aubrey, a historian and antiquary. Of the 426 biographical sketches written by Aubrey, which became widely known as his "Brief Lives," the one about Hobbes is the least brief.

A wealthy uncle of Hobbes paid for him to begin study at Oxford at around the age of fourteen, by which time he was already proficient in Latin and Greek, thanks to a local schoolmaster. At the university, he was interested in maps, but "did not much care for logick," though in his opinion he succeeded in mastering the subject nonetheless. He came to regard Aristotle, whose ideas were prominent in the curriculum, as "the worst Teacher that ever was." Hobbes evidently impressed some of his own teachers, though, because upon leaving Oxford in 1608, he was offered a post for which he had been recommended by the head of his college, as tutor and companion to William Cavendish, the future second Earl of Devonshire. Thus began a career of attachments to noble families which gave him leisure, and exposed him to libraries, intellectual society and British political life, and enabled him to travel in continental Europe.

In the 1620s, his Cavendish connections also led to involvements with colonial companies that had interests in Virginia and Bermuda, and to some secretarial and translation work for Francis Bacon, the polymathic Lord Chancellor and champion of scientific research. At the time of his dealings with Bacon, though, Hobbes did not yet show much interest in scientific matters and seems not to have developed his philosophical ideas. In the 1620s, and before, his work was literary and historical, with a little politics.

His first book, published in 1629, when he was forty, was a translation of Thucydides's history of the Peloponnesian War, which had been fought between Athens, Sparta and their allies in 431–404 BC. In a prefatory essay to his translation, Hobbes wrote that Thucydides preferred government when it was "democratical in name, but in effect monarchical," as it had been under Pericles. Thucydides did not like democracy, because it left the people prey to "demagogues" who led them into a mess of inconsistent resolutions. But neither was he fond of rule by "the few"—that is, of aristocratic government—since the few tended to be riven into all too many factions, which led to sedition.

In an autobiographical Latin poem, Hobbes later wrote that Thucydides (in the ungainly words of a translator)

> . . . says Democracy's a Foolish Thing,
> Than a Republic wiser is one King.

Thus the politics of the ancient historian, as Hobbes understood them, were similar to his own. Hobbes also noted that anyone in Athens who gave the people good advice was rewarded with unpopularity, which is what he came to feel about the ungrateful English commonwealth. Another foreshadowing of his own fate came in what he wrote about Anaxagoras, a Presocratic philosopher of whom Thucydides was said to have been a disciple: "[his] opinions, being of a strain above the apprehension of the vulgar, procured him the estimation of an atheist . . . though he were none. . . ."

The next year, Hobbes had a sort of revelation, or so he made it sound in a tale he told Aubrey. Hobbes was in Geneva in 1630, accompanying the son of a Nottinghamshire landowner on a continental tour, when he accidentally came across geometry, supposedly for the first time. He found a copy of Euclid's *Elements* in a gentleman's library, lying open at the 47th proposition of book 1:

> He read the proposition. "By G—," sayd he, "this is impossible!" So he reads the demonstration of it, which referred him back to such a proposition; which proposition he read. That referred him back to another, which he also read . . . [and so on] . . . at last he was demonstratively convinced of that trueth. This made him in love with geometry.

Two and a half centuries later, Bertrand Russell (1872–1970) described a similar bolt from Cupid: "At the age of eleven, I began Euclid, with my brother as my tutor. This was one of the great events of my life, as dazzling as first love. I had not imagined that there was anything so delicious in the world." Unlike Russell—who one may suspect knew Aubrey's story and was echoing it—Hobbes certainly did come to geometry rather late in life. But the striking tale of his sudden enchantment in 1630 must have been somewhat embellished. The 47th proposition of Euclid's book 1 is Pythagoras's theorem, and although it is plausible that a copy of Euclid might have been purposely left open at its most famous page, it is not credible that a novice would have been able to grasp the complex proof of this theorem at first sight. Besides, there is circumstantial evidence that Hobbes had read some Euclid before this visit to Geneva.

There is no doubt, though, of the unique importance that Hobbes came to attach to geometry. Geometry is "the Mother of all Naturall Science," as he later put it in *Leviathan*, because "Nature worketh by Motion; the Ways, and Degrees whereof cannot be known, without the knowledge of the Proportions and Properties of Lines, and Figures." This is what Galileo had argued in 1623. Galileo's famous statement that the book of nature is "written in the language of mathematics" went on to specify that the characters of this language "are triangles, circles, and other geometric figures without which it is humanly impossible to understand a single word of it."

According to Hobbes, geometry also deserves most of the credit for the gifts of technology and thus of civilisation:

> whatever benefit comes to human life from observation of the stars, from mapping of lands, from reckoning of time and from long-distance navigation; whatever is beautiful in buildings, strong in defence works and marvellous in machines, whatever in short distinguishes the modern world from the barbarity of the past, is almost wholly the gift of Geometry; for what we owe to physics, Physics owes to Geometry.

So enduring was Hobbes's intoxication with geometry that a quarter of a century later he stumbled into a protracted fight that damaged his credibility as a man of science. For over two decades, starting in 1656, he engaged in vituperative exchanges with an Oxford mathematician about an ancient set of geometrical problems that he wrongly believed he had solved or nearly solved. This unhappy episode, of which more later, has been aptly described as "nasty, brutish and long."

After returning to England from his visit to Geneva, and his purported revelation in the library, Hobbes rejoined the Cavendish family in 1631, and his Galilean philosophy began to take shape. In the mid-1630s, he met Descartes's friends Mersenne and Gassendi in Paris, and in 1636 went to Florence and saw Galileo himself, who, as he later wrote, "was the first that opened to us the gate of natural philosophy universal, which is the knowledge of the nature of motion." Of this trip, Hobbes wrote in his verse autobiography:

*To Matter, Motion, I myself apply,*
*And thus I spend my Time in Italy.*

Even the happiness, or otherwise, of mankind could be illuminated by the idea of matter in motion: "there is no such thing as perpetuall Tranquillity of mind, while we live here; because Life it selfe is but Motion, and can never be without Desire, nor without Feare." God had something better in store for the righteous in heaven, but here below it was all buffeting and collision, both outside our heads and in them.

By the late 1630s, Hobbes had formed his plan for a philosophical system that would begin with the physics of motion, proceed to psychology and the analysis of language, and end with politics. His first scientific work sought to give a materialist account of the workings of the mind in terms of the internal motions of the brain and body, which he later summarised in *Leviathan*:

> As, in Sense, that which is really within us, is . . . onely Motion, caused by the action of externall objects . . . to the Sight, Light and Colour; to the Eare, Sound; to the Nostrill, Odour, &c: so, when the action of the same object is continued from the Eyes, Eares, and other organs to the Heart, the reall effect there is nothing but Motion, or Endeavour; which consisteth in Appetite, or Aversion, to, or from the object moving . . . the appearance, or sense of that motion, is that wee either call *delight* or *trouble of mind*.

He described reasoning as a form of "computation," which excited Leibniz and has led some to suppose that he anticipated the popular modern conception of the mind as a computer, which in a limited sense he did. What he meant was that reasoning somehow involves the addition and subtraction of ideas—a crude notion that he did not develop. He was particularly proud of his work on optics and visual perception, which was not published until several decades later. It has been suggested that if only he had published this work earlier, he might have shared more of the credit that went to Descartes for advancing the "mechanical philosophy."

Hobbes and Descartes did not think much of each other as philosophers. One bone of contention between them concerned the limits of mechanical explanation. Hobbes did not think that there were any. Descartes, as we have seen, believed that mechanical explanation stopped short of the thinking self, which was beyond the reach of physics. Hobbes was one of the thinkers invited to comment on Descartes's *Meditations*. Descartes's published responses to Hobbes's objections were exasperated and dismissive, and his private comments were even more blunt: "His most recent arguments . . . are as bad as all the other ones I have seen from him." For his part, Hobbes once remarked that Descartes was a great geometer, but "his head did not lye for philosophy."

Hobbes was convinced that the methods of the mechanical philosophy could be used to shed light not only on the mind but also on politics:

> as in an automatic Clock or other fairly complex device, one cannot get to know the function of each part and wheel unless one takes it apart . . . so in investigating the right of a commonwealth and the duties of its citizens, there is a need, not indeed to take the commonwealth apart, but to view it as taken apart, i.e. to understand correctly what human nature is like.

The workings of human nature were in some respects as predictable and uniform as the behaviour of inanimate objects, according to Hobbes. For example:

> each man is drawn to desire that which is good for him and to avoid what is bad for him, and most of all the greatest of natural evils, which is death; this happens by a real necessity of nature as powerful as that by which a stone falls downward.

By understanding such necessities of nature, it should be possible to see what sort of government would work best—for "the skill of making, and maintaining Common-wealths, consisteth in certain Rules, as doth Arithmetique and Geometry." If moral and political philosophers would only follow the lead of natural philosophers and mathematicians, one of the main problems of politics, which is the avoidance of civil war, could be solved:

if the patterns of human action were known with the same certainty
as the relations of magnitude in figures . . . the human race would
enjoy such secure peace that (apart from conflicts over space as the
population grew) it seems unlikely that it would ever have to fight
again.

Hobbes's passing remark about population growth is uncharacteristic.
It is one of the few places in his works in which he showed much awareness
of material conditions as a potential cause of civil strife. He usually wrote
as if civil wars were always the result of mistaken political beliefs, which is
one reason why his remarks about good government seem overly abstract.
He generally claimed that such wars break out because people fail to appreciate why they must never resist the sovereign authority that protects them;
if only they understood human nature aright, they would live peacefully.

Hobbes's claim that a scientific grasp of human nature could put an
end to most civil wars is in one respect even more extravagant than Descartes's prediction that science would abolish all disease within his own
lifetime. Descartes did not go so far as to say that all the requisite medical
knowledge was already in place: his claim was that the rate of progress in
medicine was so great that all cures would soon be found. Hobbes, by contrast, thought that he already knew everything that was needed to procure
peace. All that was required was for people to acknowledge the accuracy of
his picture of human nature, and to act accordingly.

We shall now take a closer look at this picture, and compare it with
what is usually taken to be Rousseau's rival one.

∞

Hobbes's depiction of the unpleasantness of life in the "condition of
mere nature" is to this day regularly contrasted with what Jean-Jacques
Rousseau (1712–1778) is said to have believed a century later about the
gentle ways of the "noble savage." Thus in 2013 one American anthropolo-
gist who lived among the Yanomamo Indians around Venezuela's Amazon
region wrote that their violent raids on each other's villages are "probably

a typical example of what life is like in a state of nature, in the absence of the institutions of the political state," and therefore illustrate that Hobbes was right. Rousseau, on the other hand, is said by this author to have imagined that humans in this state were "blissful, non-violent, altruistic, and noncompetitive" and were "generally 'nice' to each other." As we shall see, this account is somewhat misleading about Hobbes and entirely wrong about Rousseau.

In a similar vein, Steven Pinker, a psychologist, has written in a recent history of violence that there is a constant danger of war and death in "nonstate" societies, just as Hobbes maintained. To support this idea, Pinker draws on archaeological evidence from a small number of prehistoric graveyards, which suggests a higher rate of deaths by violence than is found in many developed countries, and on recent studies of surviving hunter-gatherer societies and other isolated groups, whose way of life is presumed to be similar to that of all our ancestors five thousand and more years ago, before the emergence of state governments. "For centuries," Pinker writes, "social theorists like Hobbes and Rousseau speculated from their armchairs about what life is like in a 'state of nature.' Nowadays we can do better."

It is true enough that the studies available to thinkers in today's armchairs are more informative than the travellers' tales and ancient texts that were browsed by writers in the seventeenth and eighteenth centuries. And Rousseau could indeed be wildly fanciful in his speculations. In the margins of his copy of Rousseau's writings about primitive man, Voltaire made incredulous notes such as "How do you know?" and "How you exaggerate everything!" (Montesquieu was even more inventive than Rousseau: he cited just one case of a mentally defective boy found wandering in a German forest as evidence for his theory that primitive man was very timid.) Still, a little more time spent in armchairs with the books of Hobbes and Rousseau would have shown that excursions to the Amazon or to prehistoric graveyards are largely irrelevant to what these philosophers wrote about the behaviour of mankind. As we shall see, such excursions certainly do not show that Rousseau was wrong and Hobbes was right.

Consider first Rousseau, whose views about the mixed blessings of civilisation will come up again later in this book. He never used any term that can plausibly be translated as "noble savage," did not idealise man in his first "state of nature," and in fact largely adopted Hobbes's view of mankind just before the birth of modern societies as quarrelsome, sometimes bloodthirsty and largely motivated by self-preservation. Rousseau was not always consistent, and confusingly used the expression *état de nature* rather loosely. It is not clear quite when the myth of his peaceful "noble savage" took hold, but it is not hard to see how a hasty reading of his *Discourse on the Origin of Inequality* (1755) could give rise to it.

Rousseau did believe that some economic and technological developments had come at a considerable cost to man's well-being, and in certain respects amounted to a step backwards. But there are large differences between his views and the ancient Greek myth of a Golden Age of mankind, with which they are often confused. The oldest written version of this myth is found in the works of Hesiod, who described the first "golden race" of men as living "without sorrow of heart, remote and free from toil and grief," making merry and dwelling in peace. During this time, as the Latin poet Ovid later put it, "men of their own accord, without threat of punishment, without laws, maintained good faith and did what was right." In the subsequent generations of the Silver and Bronze eras, according to this story, men got steadily fiercer and eventually reached the "Iron" period, when "all manner of crime broke out." This notion of an idyllic phase at the dawn of man's history, when people were simple, happy and virtuous, seems to have informed the sentimental depiction by some later Europeans of the inhabitants of the New World and other recently explored places. In a satirical magazine article in 1853, entitled "The Noble Savage," Charles Dickens ridiculed such romanticised accounts of North American Indians, bushmen and Zulus. He presented them as in fact venal, bloodthirsty, foolish, comic and doomed. It seems to have been this ironically titled tirade by Dickens which first gave the term "noble savage" its wide currency. (The origin of the expression probably lies in a travel book two centuries earlier, which noted that the "savages" in Canada were "truely Noble" because all the men engaged in hunting—a pastime reserved in Europe for the aristocracy.)

One of the earliest suggestions that the ways of savages might not be so much worse than European life, and might even in some respects be better, had come in an essay by Montaigne (1533–1592), in which he mused on the peoples he read about in accounts of the New World, and on three Brazilian cannibals he had met in the company of the king of France in Rouen in 1562. In general they seemed to Montaigne to be barbarous "only in that they have been hardly fashioned by the mind of man, still remaining close neighbours to their original state of nature." As for the practice of eating enemies killed in war, what saddened Montaigne was that "while judging correctly of their wrong-doings we should be so blind to our own," because Europeans "surpass them in every kind of barbarism." Europeans, for example, burn people alive for heresy. One of the cannibals, noted Montaigne, was shocked to see that in France there were people "bloated with all sorts of comforts" while others were "begging at their doors." This sort of inequality was one aspect of so-called civilised life that led Rousseau to argue that it was not so superior after all.

Things began to go seriously wrong for mankind, Rousseau suggested, with the first enclosure of land—that is, when some ground was taken as private property—and especially when agriculture and metallurgy were developed, thus increasing the opportunities for some people to accumulate more goods than others. The result was a disaster from which we seem unable to recover: "There arose between the right of the stronger and the right of the first occupant a perpetual conflict which ended only in fights and murders. Nascent society gave place to the most horrible state of war. . . ." This unhappy stage in the development of humanity is, according to Rousseau's scheme of things, the last of four discernible phases that unfolded before man took the step of subjecting himself to the authority of a state. Because there is as yet no proper government, life at this relatively late stage still counts as being in a "state of nature" in Hobbes's special sense of that term. But it does not reflect what Rousseau took to be the natural state of man. Unlike the "war of all against all" which Hobbes took to be an inevitable consequence of attempts to live without the benefit of a common authority, Rousseau's "horrible state of war" is the result of "a multitude of passions which are the product of society"—that is, of economic developments that were an unfortunate accident of history.

Rousseau did not think that man was benign and peaceful right up until the time when farming, metal tools and the accumulation of wealth came along and ruined everything. And although he did believe that our earliest human-like ancestors were physically healthier and in some respects happier than we have ever been since, and that these creatures did not on the whole get into fights, he did not idealise them or wish we could go back to their ways. Both misconceptions are the result of failing to distinguish between the various phases that, according to Rousseau, preceded modern society—which is easy enough to do, because he sometimes weaves between them without clearly marking his path.

Rousseau's first phase is one of pure animality, in which each man is largely solitary, deeply stupid, and differs from other animals only in having the capacity for self-improvement. He lives in the moment, with only the slightest forethought or memory, so he is largely untroubled by fears or regrets. He is on the whole good-tempered, and, according to Rousseau, has "an innate repugnance at seeing a fellow creature suffer." Yet he cannot be described as virtuous, because he does not know what he is doing. He does not engage in warfare, but this is not because he is a principled pacifist or benevolent moralist. It is merely because he does not feel the need for dealings of any sort with his own kind. He forms no bonds with others and probably does not recognise any of them individually. Indeed, Rousseau suggests that such a creature would not even be able to spot his or her own offspring, who are presumably produced by sporadic unthinking encounters. It is not surprising that Voltaire wondered how Rousseau could claim to know all of this.

Voltaire wrote to Rousseau and gently made fun of him: "One acquires the desire to walk on all fours when one reads your work." He was quite right that, according to Rousseau, man in his first state of nature did not even walk upright. Having noticed that people come in a variety of shapes, sizes, colours and degrees of hairiness, Rousseau suggested that orangoutans in East Asia and African apes are probably members of the human species who happen to lack the capacity for self-improvement. In other words, the only differences between orangoutans and people is that the former have less potential and more hair.

In Rousseau's second stage, man begins to better himself. He makes some tools, including weapons, and starts to feel rather superior to the other animals who don't. He gathers together in herds, manages to invent language and builds huts. Some rudimentary private property emerges, and families begin to form. Even in this early phase, Rousseau believed, some quarrels would break out. In the next stage, families assemble in villages, and hunt, fish and collect food. They enjoy themselves together in spontaneous dance and song, though a more social life gives rise not only to more fun but also to vanity, scorn, shame and envy. Though it is far from perfect, Rousseau thinks that this third stage—which is, he supposes, the stage reached by some but not all of the primitive peoples discovered by the explorers and colonists of his day—"must have been the happiest epoch . . . and the best for man." He was fond of comparing it favourably with subsequent stages of civilisation, since it is unpolluted by their greed, artificiality and unhealthy lifestyles. Rousseau's critique of modernity sometimes has such a contemporary ring that one half-expects him to advocate yoga. But he was under no illusion that life in this more natural epoch was all sunshine and smiles. With no government except the patriarch of each family to restrain them, pride and jealousy wreaked their terrible effects on people, even before agriculture made things still worse: "revenge became terrible, and men grew bloodthirsty and cruel. This is precisely the stage reached by most of the savage peoples known to us. . . ." So much for Rousseau's supposedly peaceful savage who was generally nice to others.

Rousseau's aim in these "conjectures," as he called them, was to enable man to see himself "as nature made him," by illustrating how the raw essence of humanity may have been diluted by "circumstances and progress." He acknowledged that some sorts of "experiments" were needed to confirm his ideas, but seems to have thought that the rough outlines of his sketch were plausible enough to outweigh any errors of detail.

Hobbes's goals were different. Despite his talk of "the state of nature" and "the condition of meer nature," he had little interest in distinguishing the original characteristics of man from those that were acquired during various stages of social development. Hobbes usually uses "the state of

nature" to mean the condition of being unconstrained by any civil authority, so it is not only ungoverned savages who are in it. The sovereigns of all
countries are also in a state of nature, because they are subject only to God,
not to any global government; and the citizens of a nation in the throes
of civil war may be said to live in a state of nature, too. Hobbes wanted
to convince his readers that mankind is inclined to be obstreperous, or at
least sorely in need of policing, and although he did draw on history and
anthropology to bolster his case, the unfortunate truth could be seen just
as easily by considering modern societies as it can by examining older or
less developed ones.

His first attempt to make this case was in a manuscript circulated in
1640. Since "there needeth but little force to the taking away of a man's
life," it is all too easy to kill someone, even for a weak person to kill a stronger one—for example, by creeping up on him, or poisoning him. Given
that people can be proud and vain, "and hope for precedency and superiority above their fellows," and that they compete among one another
for the things they desire, it is not surprising that mankind has a "mutual
fear of one another." The problem is not so much that everyone is particularly inclined to crime or violence, but that some are, and you never know
where the next threat may come from. As Hobbes put it in a later work,
even if "the wicked were fewer than the righteous, yet because we cannot
distinguish them, there is a necessity for suspecting." Everybody knows this
already, or at least acts as if it is true: "On going to bed, men lock their
doors; when going on a journey, they arm themselves. . . ." Even dogs are
aware of the problem, Hobbes remarks, since they bark at strangers during
the day and at everybody during the night.

In order to protect ourselves and our property, it is sometimes necessary to strike first. So if there were no authority to keep the peace, the
result would be "a war of every man against every man." How bad would
this get? Hobbes is usually careful to say that being in a state of war does
not necessarily mean constant mayhem. In fact, on his understanding of
the term "war," its nature "consisteth not in actuall fighting; but in the
known disposition thereto, during all the time there is no assurance to
the contrary." In other words, it is the continuing threat of violence, not
necessarily bloodshed itself, which qualifies as a state of war. He compared

the situation to "foul weather," which may not consist in actual downpours "but in an inclination thereto of many days together"—a state of the elements that is particularly familiar in Britain.

Strictly speaking, then, Hobbes's theory of what life would be like without government does not entail any particular level of violence, just the threat of it. Yet the end of his most famous passage implies that the bloodshed would be so bad that many or even most people would die young. At a time when

> men live without other security, than what their own strength, and their own invention, shall furnish them withal . . . there is no place for Industry; because the fruit thereof is uncertain: and consequently no Culture of the Earth; no Navigation, nor use of the commodities that may be imported by sea; no commodious Building . . . no Knowledge of the face of the Earth; no account of Time; no Arts; no Letters; no Society; and which is worst of all, continuall feare, and danger of violent death; And the life of man, solitary, poore, nasty, brutish, and short.

Hobbes got rather carried away here and was over-egging his pudding. He offered no compelling reason to believe that in the absence of a common authority, crime and civil warfare would generally be bad enough either to cause a large number of deaths directly or to make all economic development impossible.

To bolster his case, Hobbes wrote that "the savage people in many places of *America*" have no government except within families, and consequently "live at this day in that brutish manner, as I said before." But this was a rather selective use of the evidence available to him. Some accounts of Native Americans did indeed depict violent chaos and no government, but others reported no government and yet no chaos either, and still others reported that the savage Americans did have forms of government after all, though this did not necessarily make them peaceful. One of the most widely read descriptions asserted that they were ruled by "Petty Princes, or Kings," yet regularly murdered each other nonetheless.

A survey of recent hunter-gatherers and nomads who have no "central-

ized authority, standing armies, or bureaucratic systems" concludes that
they "have lived together suprisingly well . . . without a particular propensity to violence." There is, of course, room for debate about exactly how
much fighting counts as a notable propensity to violence: it might still
be true that such people would live even more peacefully under the conditions of a modern state. It is not surprising that colonial powers which
have sought to pacify weaker native populations have generally succeeded
in reducing the amount of everyday bloodshed—though usually only after
demonstrating their own superior ferocity.

Hobbes had an answer to those who were unconvinced by his foray
into anthropology:

> But (someone will say) there never was a war of all against all. What?
> Did Cain not kill his own brother Abel out of envy—a misdeed so
> great that he would not have dared to commit it if there had then
> existed a common power capable of avenging it?

This is a curious use of the biblical story of Cain and Abel, and would
hardly prove Hobbes's point even if the tale were true. Cain killed his
brother because they had both made offerings to God, and God accepted
Abel's sacrifice but rejected Cain's. Cain knew that God had power over
him, and would disapprove of the murder, since otherwise he would not
have made a sacrifice in the first place, or tried to conceal his deed. Pre-
dictably, God soon found out and punished Cain. So there was in fact an
authority capable of avenging the killing, yet Cain did it anyway. Also,
the murder was prompted by what appeared to Cain to be an infuriatingly
capricious decision by his all-powerful sovereign. So the political moral of
the tale seems to be the opposite of what Hobbes had in mind.

HOBBES WAS OFTEN accused of depicting man as fundamentally evil.
On the face of it, it is odd that he should have been criticised in this way,
since that is what every type of Christian already professed to believe. For
members of the Church of England, the doctrine of original sin was codi-
fied by the ninth of their "39 Articles" of 1563:

> Original Sin . . . is the fault and corruption of the Nature of every
> man, that naturally is ingendered of the offspring of Adam; whereby
> man is very far gone from original righteousness, and is of his own
> nature inclined to evil. . . .

Hobbes's offence was presumably to have presented the offspring of Adam
as in some way the wrong kind of bad. Certainly his picture is not particularly Christian, since Jesus is given no paramount role in rescuing man
from his wretched state. However, Hobbes does offer hope of a return to
original righteousness; indeed, it is precisely in order to scare us into seeing
where salvation can be found that he raises the spectre of a "war of all
against all." Man may have a powerful urge to quarrel with his fellows, but
he also has a yearning for peace, according to Hobbes. This is because he
naturally seeks to preserve his own life, and the God-given gift of reason
enables him to see that this is not possible in a state of war:

> he . . . that desireth to live in such an estate . . . contradicteth himself.
> For every man by natural necessity desireth his own good, to which
> this estate is contrary. . . . [R]eason therefore dictateth to every man
> for his own good, to seek after peace, as far forth as there is hope to
> attain the same. . . .

Thus the popular image of Hobbes shows only one side of him. He is
remembered as a man who warned that without strong government, life
would be nasty, brutish and short. But he also maintained that our rationality and desire for self-preservation would bring us to seek peace, and
thereby make life pleasant, civilised and long.

∞

HOBBES WAS SO CAPTIVATED by the idea that every person naturally
"desireth his own good" that he interpreted many of our feelings and
actions as somehow self-centred even when they do not appear to be
so. For example, he defined "pity" as "imagination or fiction of future

calamity to ourselves, proceeding from the sense of another man's present calamity." Does this mean that when we pity someone else, it is
really ourselves for whom we feel sorry—that our emotion amounts
only to displeasure at the thought that the other person's misfortune
may eventually befall us, too? Hobbes did seem to believe that the force
of our emotion is somehow caused by a thought or feeling about ourselves, which is questionable. His theory appears to imply that if we
were sure that some disaster could never happen to us, then we would
not be sorry for its victims, which does not seem to be the case. Hobbes
could perhaps reply that, even if we soberly calculate that some misfortune is quite certain never to befall us, we cannot entirely extinguish the
thought of its doing so, and that it is this fact which, unbeknownst to
ourselves, somehow generates the emotion of pity. It is hard to see how
such a theory could be refuted, but it is equally difficult to imagine how
it could be verified.

We can fairly say that Hobbes's account is egoistic in the sense that it
seeks to explain pity as somehow arising from a concern for ourselves. But
it should be noted that he is proposing an explanation for the feeling of
compassion, not denying that it exists, or suggesting that we ought not to
feel it. Aubrey told an intriguing story about a poor and infirm old beggar
whom Hobbes met on a London street. Beholding him with eyes of "pitty
and compassion," Hobbes gave the man sixpence, whereupon he was questioned by a cleric:

> Sayd a Divine . . . that stood by—"Would you have donne this, if it
> had not been Christ's command?"—"Yea," sayd he.—"Why?" quoth
> the other.—"Because," sayd he, "I was in paine to consider the miser-
> able condition of the old man; and now my almes, giving him some
> reliefe, doth also ease me."

Perhaps the cleric's query was framed to elicit an admission from Hobbes
that would undermine the theory of human selfishness that was widely
attributed to him. If so, it is not clear whether or not the attempt succeeded. The only thing we can safely conclude from his reported reply is
that he was a man who felt compassion and liked to relieve suffering.

Still, he evidently also liked to offer analyses of our behaviour and emotions in terms of thoughts about ourselves, and it may be wondered why. What inclined him to believe that "all society . . . is a product of love of self, not of love of friends," and that "all the heart's joy and pleasure lies in being able to compare oneself favourably with others and form a high opinion of oneself"? Hobbes's cynicism extended even to laughter, which was to be explained as "nothing else but" a sudden feeling of superiority. In part he was led to such unflattering and simplistic generalisations by his desire to set psychology on a scientific footing. Simplicity is a virtue in science: if laughter and all our other pleasures can be traced to a single cause, so much the better. The powerful force by which "each man is drawn to desire that which is good for him and to avoid what is bad for him," which Hobbes had compared to the force of gravity, seemed to him to provide the most economical and best-confirmed explanation of our psychology. It was therefore a suitable cornerstone for the mechanical science of human behaviour that he sought to provide. The workings of the mind could thus neatly be revealed as a series of pushes and pulls inside an apparatus that was built above all to look after itself.

In the final decades of the seventeenth century, many critics countered with a sunnier interpretation of human nature. They portrayed man as primarily driven by fellow-feeling, not self-interest. Such writers cited acts of generosity and selfless behaviour among adults, children, wild and domesticated animals, and even insects, to paint a more benevolent picture of the living world than one will find in the pages of Hobbes. Some of these tales are so maudlin that they might have made even the creator of Tiny Tim and Little Nell wince. If there had been modern newspapers in Hobbes's England, we may imagine these sentimental moralists being drawn especially to the accounts of firemen rescuing kittens, while Hobbes turned grimly to the crime reports.

A half-century later, the Scottish philosopher David Hume concluded that both parties were misguided. It was fruitless to dispute whether benevolence or self-love "prevail in human nature," he argued, since the question is too vague. Exactly how selfish or altruistic does man have to be for selfishness or altruism to "prevail"? Hume's point applies just as much to recent writers who draw on biology to conclude that man is purely or mainly selfish by nature. For example, the zoologist Richard Dawkins wrote in *The Selfish Gene*,

> Be warned that if you wish, as I do, to build a society in which individuals cooperate generously and unselfishly towards a common good, you can expect little help from biological nature. Let us try to *teach* generosity and altruism, because we are born selfish.

Everyone can agree, Hume wrote, that there is "some particle of the dove, kneaded into our frame, along with the elements of the wolf and serpent," so why insist that we must at bottom be just one of them? Both the crime reports and the uplifting tales are true, and there is no clear sense in which either reveals a deeper truth than the other. Besides, people appear to vary widely in their degrees of selfishness, an interesting fact which is obscured by the theory that everyone is really seeking self-gratification all of the time.

Hume argued that self-interest did not in fact provide a simple explanation of human psychology but rather a convoluted one. He aptly characterised Hobbes's type of theory as the idea that "whatever affection one may feel, or imagine he feels for others, no passion is, or can be disinterested." According to this way of thinking, even sincere friendship or benevolence are forms of self-love, since "unknown to ourselves, we seek only our own gratification." But, Hume pointed out, the most economical way to account for the gratification that we obtain from our benevolent actions or friendships is to acknowledge the simple fact that we sometimes take pleasure in the well-being of others. Recall the tale of the beggar. Hobbes said he felt better once he had handed over sixpence, because reducing the beggar's suffering thereby eased his own discomfort. But why would he have felt any discomfort in the first place if he had been concerned only for his own gratification? Hobbes might answer that he had been pained at the thought of being reduced to penury himself, but this is a needlessly complicated explanation.

HOBBES'S ACCOUNT of psychology was in one sense selfish, but his moral philosophy enjoined us not to be. He held that there are "Immutable and Eternall" moral principles which oblige us to be good to others. Hobbes listed twenty-one such principles in his *Leviathan*. The upshot of them all, for the benefit of those who cannot study them in detail, he handily summarised as *"Do not that to another, which thou wouldst not have done to thyselfe."* This is one form of a dictum, known as the Golden Rule, that is found in almost every religious and ethical tradition in recorded history.

These moral rules are the "laws of nature," which have a different status from the laws that communities invent for themselves, according to Hobbes. The idea that there are two kinds of rules of conduct, man-made ones and something higher, is a very old one, which Aristotle accepted: "For there really is, as everyone to some extent divines, a natural justice and injustice that is common to all, even to those who have no association or covenant with each other." It is this sort of "law of nature," wrote Aristotle, to which Antigone in Sophocles's tragedy was referring when she spoke of

> . . . the unwritten unalterable laws
> Of God and heaven. . . .
> They are not of yesterday or to-day, but everlasting,
> Though where they come from, none of us can tell.

Nowadays, the term "law of nature" means something rather different. It is used almost exclusively to refer to scientific generalisations such as Newton's laws of motion. This scientific sense of the term is older than modern science itself: Roman writers in the first century BC already described physical processes and events as bound by laws. Thus Lucretius wrote that iron is attracted to magnets by a law of nature. In Hobbes's time, when both senses of the term "law of nature" were in use, scientific laws began to be formulated precisely, and were often said to have been fixed by God. As Robert Boyle, a leading member of the Royal Society, put it in 1674: "God . . . established those rules of motion, and that order among things corporeal, which we call the laws of nature." Boyle himself discovered a rule that still bears his name, relating the pressure, volume and temperature of gases. It is presumably because both types of law were regarded as imposed by God on His creation that it seemed appropriate to call them all "laws of nature."

But there is, of course, a glaring difference between the behaviour of gases and the behaviour of people. Gases invariably obey Boyle's Law, but people frequently break the "unalterable" natural laws of morality. So in what sense do these moral laws of nature exist? One clumsy answer is that both scientific and moral laws describe how things ought to behave—it is just that people are more disobedient than gases. This now sounds like a joke, but Montesquieu, for one, seems to have believed something like it. He wrote that "the intelligent world is far from being as well governed as the physical world." Since people are liable to error and have the gift of free will, they regularly go astray and do not consistently act in accordance with the laws which God laid down for them. Even beasts "do not invariably" observe their natural laws, according to Montesquieu, though they seem to be an improvement on people in this respect. Plants, however, are very well-governed: they "better follow their natural laws." In other words, cabbages are more law-abiding than kings.

Hobbes did not get into any such muddle. His moral laws of nature deal with "what conduceth to the conservation and defence" of human life, that is, with the most effective means of self-preservation. For example, given the brutish tendencies of one's fellows, it is just a fact, or so he believed, that the likeliest way to stay alive is to make peace rather than war. And so, "the first, and Fundamentall Law of Nature . . . is, *to seek Peace, and follow it.*" The other twenty maxims in Hobbes's list concern the kinds of behaviour that tend to promote peace, such as keeping your promises and dealing fairly with others, and with the social arrangements that are best suited to encourage harmonious living. He referred to these maxims as "Conclusions, or Theoremes" and held that they may be "found out by Reason." In each case, he gave arguments to show why each type of conduct is required for peace, and he often derived one law from another, just as Euclid deduced his theorems of geometry in part from preceding theorems. Hobbes's demonstrations are not always watertight, but then neither were Euclid's. The result was, purportedly, a corpus of knowledge about the recipes for peace and survival.

This knowledge was solid enough to be called a "science," or so Hobbes believed, but he also referred to its theorems as "precepts," i.e., commands, and he usually stated them in the form of injunctions. It appears that each moral "law of nature" may be considered in either of two ways: as a statement of how things are (e.g., "keeping your promises is conducive to peace") or as an order (e.g., "you must keep your promises"). Considered as statements, these laws would be true in the same way that Boyle's Law, or any other accurate generalisation, is true: promise-keeping is conducive to peace. But considered as orders, they are, of course, not always followed: people sometimes break their promises.

According to Hobbes, one should, strictly speaking, call something a "law" only if it has been commanded by someone in authority. He wrote that his precepts had in fact been so commanded: they "are the same as the precepts which have been promulgated by God's own Majesty as the *laws of the Kingdom of heaven* through our lord *Jesus Christ* and the holy *Prophets* and *Apostles*." Hobbes took himself to have shown that the traditional virtues such as "*Justice, Gratitude, Modesty, Equity, Mercy*" are the "Means of peace," and thereby worth practising if you want to thrive. But he also took pains to establish that all his moral rules could be found in the Bible.

Given the existence of such rules, which we are told are discoverable by reason and supported by scripture, one would think that there are definite answers to ethical questions. Murder, for instance, is presumably just wrong. Yet sometimes Hobbes seemed to say that nothing is really good or bad but merely appears to individuals to be so. For example, in an early part of *Leviathan*, he wrote that

> whatsoever is the object of any mans Appetite or Desire; that is it, which he for his part calleth *Good*: And the object of his Hate, and Aversion, *Evill* . . . [T]hese words of *Good, Evill* . . . are ever used with relation to the person that useth them: There being nothing simply and absolutely so. . . .

This seems to sit uneasily with the idea that there are moral laws of nature, so it might be thought that Hobbes was only pretending that a deity had established such laws. Perhaps they were a "noble lie" of the type discussed by Socrates in Plato's *Republic*: a harmless myth which will make the common people "more inclined to care for the state and one another," as Soclates put it. However, a noble lie will not work unless its falsehood remains a secret from those it is intended to deceive. Why would Hobbes reveal the shocking truth that nothing is really good or bad, and then a few chapters later apparently try to convince his readers of the opposite?

The answer is that Hobbes did not believe any such shocking truth. When he wrote that nothing is "simply and absolutely" good or evil, he did not mean that good and evil do not exist. He was trying to explain how we ordinarily use these terms, and how our minds work. Just before this passage, Hobbes notes that different people have different likes and dislikes, and that, because our bodies are constantly changing, the same things can occasion different desires and aversions in the same person at different times. In his view, the various phenomena that affect us do so by causing motions in our bodies, which are manifested as perceptions, desires and aversions. These interactions are complex, and we should not think of desirability or undesirability as somehow inherent in external objects and states of affairs. Just as the appearance of redness does not itself reside in a fruit, but is rather an effect of the fruit's matter on our sense-organs, so the fact that we find something desirable (and thus call it good) should be understood as a complex interaction between ourselves and our environment. Many questions can be asked about this theory of mind and language, but there is no reason to think that it conflicts with his account of the moral laws of nature. What is ultimately beneficial to people is peace, whether they realise it or not, and Hobbes's hope was that once they see that this is true, they will come to desire peace, and call it good.

WE ARE NOW in a position to see what is correct, what is questionable and what is mistaken in the longest-standing criticisms of Hobbes's ethical doctrines. In 1683, four years after his death, Oxford University issued a decree condemning twenty-seven "impious doctrines" and the "pernicious" publications that defended them. Copies of Hobbes's *Leviathan* and *De cive* were ceremonially burned in a quad, together with some two dozen works by other authors, while a crowd of scholars stood by the bonfire and hummed their approval. This seems to have been the last large public book-burning at Oxford. Here are two of the doctrines attributed to Hobbes in the decree:

> Self-preservation is the fundamental law of nature, and supersedes the obligation of all others, whenever they stand in competition with it.

> In the state of nature, there is no difference between good and evil, right and wrong; the state of nature is a state of war, in which every man hath a right to all things.

It is true enough that self-preservation is, for Hobbes, in one sense the foundation of the various moral laws of nature: once you accept that people want to stay alive, everything else supposedly follows. But although he begins with a selfish premise, he ends up with the unselfish Golden Rule, "do not that to another, which thou wouldst not have done to thyself"—or, as God put it to Moses, and Jesus echoed to his disciples, "thou shalt love thy neighbour as thyself." Hobbes does argue that you are always entitled to defend your own life; this is the one right which is not ceded to a sovereign authority when you agree to be bound by government. But once we have made such an agreement, this right does not entitle us to do whatever we fancy will make us safer, such as launching pre-emptive attacks, since it was precisely to avoid such a war of all against all that Hobbes advocated submission to a sovereign's laws. So it does not seem to be true that self-preservation trumps every other consideration for Hobbes.

As for the "state of nature," it is by definition the predicament in which there is no effective government to regulate behaviour, so everyone will do what he likes, or so Hobbes pessimistically assumed. The idea that bad behaviour would be rampant in a Hobbesian state of nature was a popular theme of stage comedies at the time: "in matter of women, we are all in the State of Nature," scoffed one stage drunkard, "every Man's Hand against every Man. Whatever we pretend." It was perhaps to emphasise the chaos of such a state that Hobbes noted that "the notions of Right and Wrong . . . have there no place." This was a rather misleading way for him to put it, though, since God's laws are eternal, according to Hobbes, and therefore must apply in all situations. So, strictly speaking, there is a difference between right and wrong in the state of nature; it is just that nobody takes any notice of it.

In a book published six years after the Oxford decree, John Locke, who was mindful of the furore caused by Hobbes's writings, was careful to state explicitly that "the state of nature has a law of nature to govern it, which obliges everyone." Hobbes would have saved himself much trouble if he had written as plainly as this, since this was his view, too. He presumably neglected to spell it out because he wanted above all to scare people by stressing the anarchy that would prevail in the absence of government.

A third "impious doctrine" listed in the decree was that "Possession and strength give a right to govern, and success in a cause or enterprise proclaims it to be lawful and just. . . ." This charge may originally have been laid at Hobbes's door because of his apparent withdrawal of support for the Royalist cause in the English civil wars once that cause was lost. In *Leviathan*'s last pages, which he wrote in the latter part of 1650, a year and a half after the execution of Charles I, Hobbes indirectly addressed the vexed question of loyalty to the Cromwellian regime. Must one obey a usurper once he has overthrown the sovereign authority? It was clear from his earliest political writings, and reiterated at the end of *Leviathan*, that allegiance is the price to be paid to whoever is capable of protecting the citizens. According to Hobbes, a new authority should be obeyed once the usurpers are unassailably in charge and therefore in the best position to keep the peace. In 1650, it was the regime that had killed the king which was in this position. But it does not follow that, for Hobbes, the success of a rebellion retroactively justifies an act of regicide, or any other sins of the past. Allegiance to a regime does not require one to approve of the way in which it came to power; indeed, as Hobbes noted, "there is scarce a Common-wealth in the world, whose beginnings can in conscience be justified."

Hobbes did not endorse any general principle to the effect that might makes right. Except in one very special case, might does not even give the right to govern, because strictly speaking it is the consent of the people which confers legitimacy on a regime. Sovereignty, as Hobbes put it in *Leviathan*, "ariseth from Pact." Once the Cromwellian regime had the might to fulfill the duties of government, it was rational for people to consent to be ruled by it. Thus strength is a necessary precondition of the right to govern, but it is not ordinarily a sufficient one. The special exception is the case of God. Hobbes wrote that God's right to reign over men—apart from the Jews, with whom He had made an explicit pact—"is to be derived . . . from his *Irresistible Power*."

∞

AT THE BEGINNING of 1652, the year after *Leviathan* had been published, Hobbes returned to England from more than a decade of voluntary exile in France. His first new publication was a largely scientific tract, *De corpore* ("Of body"), much of which had been written long before. As well as science, it contained mathematical work, some logic, and some metaphysics, in the Aristotelian sense, which means the treatment of fundamental concepts that are used to describe the world, such as cause, effect, identity, space and time. There was material on motion, gravity, optics, sense-perception, animals, stars, heat, the weather and other topics. The twentieth chapter, on geometry, was an intellectual disaster. Everything else in the book has long been forgotten.

In *Leviathan*, Hobbes had posed a rhetorical question: "who is so stupid, as both to mistake in Geometry, and also to persist in it, when another detects his error to him?" This remark turned out to be rather unfortunate, as John Wallis, an eminent mathematician, gleefully demonstrated. Wallis was a Presbyterian, a university man, and formerly active on the anti-Royalist side in the civil war—and thus three times an enemy to Hobbes. The tone of the exchanges between Hobbes and Wallis may be gauged from the titles of some of them: "Markes Of the Absurd Geometry, Rural Language, Scottish Church-Politicks, And Barbarismes of John Wallis," "Due Correction for Mr Hobbes. Or Schoole Discipline, for not saying his Lessons right." Six years into this battle, Wallis explained to a friend why he devoted so much energy to teaching Hobbes a lesson. It was because Hobbes had attacked the universities and clergy, "as though the Christian world had not sound knowledge . . . and as though men could not understand religion if they did not understand Philosophy, nor Philosophy unless they knew Mathematics." So it was time for a mathematician to show him "how little he understands the Mathematics from which he takes his courage."

Hobbes said that Wallis was fighting him on behalf of "all the ecclesiastics of England," which was not far from the truth. Hobbes's treatment of "squaring the circle" provided these enemies with a golden opportunity. This ancient challenge involves constructing a square equal in area to a given circle, using only an unmarked ruler and a set of drawing-compasses. To be a circle-squarer was already regarded as a bit of a joke in Athens in the fifth century BC, not because the task was already known to be impossible, but because it was infamously addictive. Circle-squaring crops up in Aristophanes's comedy *The Birds*, and Anaxagoras, the reputed teacher of Thucydides, was said to have kept himself happy in prison by toying with it. Dante mentioned the intractability of the problem in his *Paradiso*, though perhaps he should have included it instead in his accounts of hell or purgatory. In 1755, the French Royal Academy was so overwhelmed with proposed solutions that it resolved to examine no further attempts.

In 1882, it was finally proved that no circle can be squared, but the challenge had produced plenty of valuable work, as well as immeasurable dross. In Hobbes's time, some serious mathematicians still thought it could be done, though Descartes, Fermat, and many others disagreed. Hobbes was by no means mad to try it. Yet, as he dug himself ever deeper into mathematical absurdity while attempting to rebut the merciless Wallis, he acknowledged that it was starting to look that way: "either I alone am insane, or I alone am sane. There is no third alternative, unless, as someone might say, we are all insane."

One point of interest in this otherwise unedifying episode is that it was partly Hobbes's philosophical views that led him astray. Wallis recognised the power of algebra in geometry, but Hobbes—like many others at the time—thought that this new-fangled approach, which had been pioneered by Descartes, was too abstract to be legitimate. He ridiculed the symbolic notation of the new geometry, the pages of which look "as if a hen had been scraping there." The key failing of contemporary geometry, as Hobbes saw it, was that it had lost its focus on the practical applications which make the science valuable, and was instead insisting on superfluous degrees of precision. Some of Hobbes's "quadratures," or recipes for squaring the circle, were accurate enough for all practical purposes, or so he believed. So what did it matter if they could not satisfy the irrelevant standards of squigglers like Wallis?

Yet Euclid's geometry had been fundamentally abstract, too, and if Hobbes had ever really understood this, his attempts to defend himself and his philosophy now made him forget it. Euclidean geometry does not deal with material objects but with abstractions. Thus Euclid defined a "line" as "breadthless length," even though no physical thing can be so thin as to have no breadth at all. For Hobbes, only matter is real, so if points or lines are not pieces of matter, they do not exist. To make sense of geometry, it was therefore necessary to interpret Euclid's notions in a way that rendered them compatible with this crude form of materialism. Under the strain of attempting to do so, Hobbes's grasp of geometry disintegrated. In one of his last letters on mathematics, he even began to doubt Euclid's proof of Pythagoras's theorem—the very deduction that had enraptured him in Geneva thirty-four years earlier. Thus Hobbes's career in geometry may be said to have come full circle.

HOBBES was not invited to join the Royal Society, which was founded in 1660, even though he had better scientific credentials than some of those who were elected. The war with Wallis, who was a prominent member, cannot have helped, but Hobbes would have been unwelcome for other reasons. His general notoriety would have been a liability for the fledgling society, since some of its critics said that its emphasis on observations and experiments encouraged irreligion. A focus on the senses could, according to these conservatives, divert one from thoughts of a higher, spiritual plane. To deflect such charges, it would be safer not to associate with the infamous Hobbes.

Hobbes was, anyway, unimpressed by the society's approach to the knowledge of nature, which he took to be naïve and haphazard. He disparaged laboratory experiments, which were too easy to misinterpret and often a waste of time. "They display new machines," he scoffed—referring to Boyle's apparatus for the investigation of atmospheric pressure—"in the way that they behave who deal in exotic animals which are not to be seen without payment." It is Hobbes who was responsible for the mischievous tale that the death of Francis Bacon was the result of "his Lordship . . . trying an Experiment." Hobbes told Aubrey, who recorded it for posterity, that during a coach ride to Highgate on a wintery day, Bacon suddenly had an idea and got out to see whether stuffing a chicken with snow would help to preserve its flesh, as a result of which he caught a chill and died. This story, which is still repeated in countless histories, seems to have been made up. Bacon did take a turn for the worse after a coach journey, and he did have an interest in refrigeration. But his final illness began before this trip, and he had already established that meat could be preserved by cold, so he would have had no need to procure a chicken on the road that day.

In Hobbes's time, and long afterwards, the term "experiment" covered casual observations of nature as well as contrived trials in a controlled environment. Hobbes, unlike some, could not see much of a difference between the two. He wrote that "to have had many experiments, is that we call *experience*, which is nothing else but remembrance of what antecedents have been followed by what consequents." Active empirical research was far from useless; indeed, he had done a fair bit of it himself. But it was overrated and sometimes misinterpreted by Boyle and his ilk. As far as Hobbes was concerned, learning by experience did not on its own count as rational knowledge. Part of the trouble with the Royal Society was that it did not pay enough attention to this fact. Also, the society was ignoring his own valuable work, and therefore failing to progress beyond it.

&#8734;

WHEN HOBBES's immediate successors in British philosophy built on his ideas, they felt obliged to deny that they were doing so. It was common practice to denounce Hobbes and then copy him, as one poet noted when he wrote of those who

> . . . both condemnd and stole from Hobs
> Like a French thief that murthers when he Robs.

Locke and Hume would rightly have denied that they were full-blown
"Hobbists," but they were certainly rather Hobbish. Echoes of the Monster's work abound in theirs.

Locke claimed not to have read much Hobbes, and mentioned him
only once, disapprovingly, in his long *Essay Concerning Human Understanding* of 1690. But he shared enough of Hobbes's rationalist approach to
religion for one Calvinist critic to claim that Locke "took Hobbes's Leviathan for the New Testament, and the Philosopher of Malmesbury for our
Saviour." In a work on political authority which Locke wrote in his twenties but never published, he described the "state of nature" in unmistakably
Hobbesian terms: "no peace, no security, no enjoyment, enmity with all
men and safe possession of nothing, and those stinging swarms of misery which attend anarchy and rebellion." The sovereign authority of each
nation, he wrote, "must necessarily have an absolute and arbitrary power
over all the . . . actions of his people," except those covered by God's own
laws. There is little need to worry about tyranny, the young Locke continued in a Hobbish vein, since it would not be in a sovereign's interest to
abuse his power.

Even among Locke's later political ideas, there are significant traces of
Hobbish thinking. What he seems most to have picked up from Hobbes,
though, was an interest in the workings of language, and a belief that pursuing it could shed light on other parts of philosophy. In particular, both
men maintained that some traditional puzzles are merely confusions mas-
querading as problems, which appear to be substantive only because people
do not pay enough attention to how words get their meanings. This idea
was far from new in the history of philosophy—it is found in Plato's time
and in every subsequent period—but Hobbes made much more of it than
most, and Locke followed his example.

Hobbes argued, for instance, that the notion of "free will" was a mis-
nomer, not because human freedom does not exist, but because it is not
the "will" which may properly be said to be either free or unfree. The only
coherent sense of freedom, according to Hobbes, is that in which some-

one may be said to be "free from being hindered by opposition." It follows that some of my actions are free and others are not, because sometimes people, or adverse circumstances, get in my way and sometimes they do not. There is no need to agonise over whether or not the will itself is free, because the question is confused. Hobbes confidently pronounced that a "*free-Will,*" as well as a "*round Quadrangle*" and "*Immaterial Substances,*" are "words whereby we conceive nothing but the sound" and are therefore "*Absurd, Insignificant,* and *Non-sense.*" Locke echoed him: "it is as insignificant to ask, whether Man's *Will* be free, as to ask whether his Sleep be Swift, or his Vertue square: *Liberty* being as little applicable to the *Will,* as swiftness of Motion is to Sleep, or squareness to Vertue."

Absurd or nonsensical language, Hobbes wrote, consists of words "without anything correspondent to them in the mind." Philosophers are particularly prone to absurdity, he wrote, mainly because they neglect to lay out their definitions in the fashion of geometers. But exactly what sort of correspondence between words and ideas is required for meaningful thought or speech? Hobbes did not have a great deal to say about this, except that our sensory experience plays some role in generating all of our concepts: "there is no conception in a mans mind, which hath not at first, totally, or by parts, been begotten upon the organs of Sense." This vague principle, however, was a commonplace in medieval thought, and was endorsed by the same scholastic philosophers who were the main producers of alleged nonsense. Locke later tried to explain the principle in more detail.

The most significant use that Hobbes made of this principle about meaning was a theological one. Since we are not aware of God through our sense-organs, we can have no proper conception of Him in our minds (though we know that He exists, because somebody must have made the world). It follows that we cannot meaningfully attribute any qualities to Him in the ordinary way. When we say that God is merciful or wise or good, this is our way of praising Him: "the Attributes we give him, are not to tell one another *what he is,* nor to signifie our opinion of his Nature, but our desire to honor him with such names as we conceive most honorable amongst our selves." This was a radical theory of the religious use of language, and naturally it did not go down well.

In the second half of the eighteenth century, Hume wrote in his *History of England* that Hobbes was then "much neglected," and sounded almost sorry about this fact. He praised Hobbes's clear style and noted his bold opinions, though he also felt obliged to repeat the conventional wisdom that his ethics was suited only to "encourage licentiousness." This prudent attempt to dissociate himself from the Monster was not altogether successful. Dr Johnson, and an anonymous pamphlet opposing Hume's candidacy for a professorship in Edinburgh, still marked him down as a "Hobbist." Hume mentioned Hobbes fairly often in his philosophical works, always to disagree with him, and his criticisms were penetrating. What he never did was acknowledge how much the structure of his own intellectual enterprise was in the spirit of Hobbes. Both attempted the novel project of constructing a science of man. Hume's magnum opus largely follows the plan of the first two parts of *Leviathan*, and of another early work of Hobbes's: it begins with an account of the senses and the intellect, then deals with emotions and action, and proceeds to morals and politics. Hume even took the title of his *Treatise of Human Nature* from a book by Hobbes. The two men shared the view that morals and politics should be investigated by the best scientific methods, though they differed markedly in their ideas of what those methods were. Hume had no crush on geometrical-style proofs and definitions.

Unlike Locke, Hume did not follow Hobbes into a detailed examination of the workings of language (though his investigation of the mind did lead him to the Hobbist conclusion that philosophers tend to spout nonsense when their concepts are insufficiently anchored in experience). Nor did Hume's *Treatise* have anything corresponding to the long third part of *Leviathan*, which is about religion. In other books and essays, though, Hume wrote a great deal about God and Christianity. As we shall see in chapter 7, Hume did so under a disguise of piety, though in truth he was an "enemy to religion"—which, to reassure readers of his own respectability, is what he called Hobbes.

IT HAS BEEN well said by a modern commentator that "Hobbes felt passionately about religion—other people's religion." Hobbes was often agitated by the frightful effects and ridiculous elements of what he took to be mistaken religious views. The polemical intensity of his tirades against the papacy (which he called "the *Ghost* of the deceased *Romane empire*, sitting crowned upon the grave thereof") and against the Catholic Church in general is matched in philosophical literature only by the sallies of the nineteenth-century German pessimist, Arthur Schopenhauer, on the subject of his hated rival, Hegel. No such fire animates Hobbes's professions of his own faith, frequent though they are. Although there is no reason to doubt the sincerity of his avowed fealty to the Church of England, he does not seem to have been particularly pious. One cannot imagine him as a martyr, a spiritual ascetic, or even as a wayward lowly parson like his father.

There is some truth to the idea that he was an enemy of religion, but only in the sense that Luther, Calvin and Jesus himself were all enemies of religion. That is to say, Hobbes was a reformer who rejected some of the dogmas of his day and proposed new ideas instead. Many religious pioneers are at first hailed as heretics or worse. Luther and Calvin were described by some Catholic writers as "atheists," which is what some Romans and other pagans in the first three centuries of our era called all Christians. One Roman emperor speculated that the Christians got their "atheism" from the Jews.

Many of the opinions which in seventeenth-century England got Hobbes vilified as an infidel would not even raise an eyebrow in most Christian congregations today. Quite the reverse. Nowadays it is people who believe in witches, and not those who question their existence, who are more likely to be ushered out of an English church. Hobbes's historical approach to biblical scholarship would today earn him the enmity only of the most extreme fundamentalists; and his idea that religious authorities should not be permitted to exert any coercion over the general population is firmly accepted in most developed countries. His rationalist attitude to miracles and prophecy would attract criticism from some believers, but also wide agreement among others. Some Christian groups, including the Seventh-Day Adventists, now espouse the same "mortalism" as Hobbes—that is, the notion that life after death begins only with the resurrection of the body—though this remains a minority view. His opinion that God Himself has a physical body is shared only by Mormons, but they are more commonly regarded by their critics as eccentric rather than as covert atheists.

Thomas Paine (1737–1809) once wrote that "all of us are infidels according to our forefathers' belief." On the evidence of his published writings, Hobbes was no unbeliever, merely ahead of his time, and independently minded. But did he privately mean what he publicly wrote? If Hobbes did have doubts about the existence of God, he would have had every reason to conceal them. To deny God was to blaspheme, which could in theory have earned him the death penalty, possibly in the form of being burned at the stake. The last religious incineration in England took place when Hobbes was a young man, in 1612, and the threat of the stake appears to have remained in law until two years before his death. Some form of severe punishment would, at any rate, have been a distinct possibility, despite the royal protection he enjoyed in later years from his former pupil.

But it is one thing to note that Hobbes would have hidden his atheist opinions if he had any and quite another to establish that he was in fact an atheist. There is no good reason to think that he was. None of his friends or acquaintances recorded any such impression, though there are stories of his disdain, in some circumstances, for the attentions of priests. If Hobbes sought to conceal his real views about God in order to enjoy a more sympathetic reception, the attempt not only failed to achieve its desired effect but was also bizarre in its execution. Why would a man who sugared his religious ideas to make them more palatable insist that God had a physical body—an idea which almost nobody would be able to stomach?

To determine whether Hobbes was a secret atheist, it is first necessary to clarify what is meant by "atheism," since the term was used rather freely in his time. In *The Atheist's Tragedy*, a play by Cyril Tourneur which was first performed in London in the first decade of the seventeenth century, the villain of the title, Baron D'Amville, is a treacherous and avaricious cynic who believes that men are no better than beasts, that fate is more powerful than providence and that his own share of eternity lies solely in the flourishing of his descendants. He is also a murderer, an attempted rapist, and an accidental suicide; but he never gets round to denying the existence of God. There are in fact no indisputable cases of anyone doing so persistently in Hobbes's England. Robert Burton could not name any in his lengthy treatment of the subject in *The Anatomy of Melancholy*, published in 1621, though he mentioned many suspect foreign infidels, of whom there were allegedly fifty thousand in Paris alone, according to one of his sources.

In his essay "Of Atheisme," Francis Bacon pronounced it incredible that "this universall Frame, is without a Minde," and he thought that nobody else really believed such a thing either, even if they claimed that they did. Let us take it that an atheist, in the sense worth discussing, is someone whose settled opinion is that the universe has no intelligent creator. It was not until about a century after Hobbes's death that the first known confessions of atheism in this sense were published in English or French, and even these were not issued under their authors' real names. There were, however, people in Hobbes's day who confessed that they had in the past suffered some doubts about the existence of God; such confessions were always accompanied by assurances that these doubts had been overcome. Thus John Bunyan, the Puritan author of *The Pilgrim's Progress*, admitted in his *Grace Abounding* (1666), which was issued "for the support of the weak and tempted," that in his darkest days he had had blasphemous thoughts which "stirred up questions in me, against the very *being* of God." We cannot, of course, rule out the possibility that Hobbes sometimes had such questions too; but it is reasonable to assume that his settled view was as he stated it in *Leviathan*, namely that the world requires a cause:

> he that from any effect hee seeth come to passe, should reason to the next and immediate cause thereof, and from thence to the cause of that cause . . . shall come at last to this, that there must be . . . one First Mover; that is, a First, and an Eternall cause of all things; which is that which men mean by the name of God.

In Hobbes's time, an inference from the existence of the world to the existence of God would have seemed all but irresistible to anyone who liked to follow logical arguments all the way to their conclusions. It was not until over a century later that powerful reasons to doubt this train of thought began to circulate, most notably in Hume's posthumously published *Dialogues Concerning Natural Religion*. There are no signs that Hobbes noticed any of the flaws in theological reasoning that were later exposed by Hume.

We should, however, consider the possibility that Hobbes was an atheist without realising it. Does his material God count as a real God? Boyle, for one, did not see how it could: "how a thing material can create matter and have an Infinite Power, I confess I do not understand." If belief in a physical God qualifies as atheism, then Hobbes was indeed an atheist even if he sincerely believed that he wasn't.

There is another conception of God that is even more unorthodox than Hobbes's official view, and which some people suspect that he secretly shared. This is Spinoza's theory that God and nature amount to the same thing. Hobbes explicitly rejected this idea: "by the name *God* is meant the *cause of the world*; and those who say that the world is God, are saying that there is no cause of the world, i.e. that there is no God." Despite this official denial of Spinozism, much has been made of a private remark that may seem to give the game away and reveal Hobbes as a covert Spinozist. Hobbes read Spinoza's infamous *Tractatus theologico-politicus*, which was published in 1670, and told Aubrey that Spinoza had outdone him, and that he himself "durst not write so boldly."

Spinoza's *Tractatus*, which was influenced by some of Hobbes's work, went much further than Hobbes in its textual criticism of the Bible, its scepticism about prophecy and miracles and on other religious matters. There were several topics on which Spinoza pronounced more boldly than Hobbes and about which Hobbes may secretly have agreed with him. A likely case in point is the frequency of miracles. Spinoza argued robustly that the idea of miracles made no sense and that therefore there never were any. Hobbes wrote that they used to happen in biblical times but had ceased with the deaths of the apostles. This abrupt end to supernatural activities was a common tenet among Protestants, while Catholics typically claimed that miracles continued apace up to the present day. Hobbes may well have privately doubted all miracles but believed that he could not get away with denying the ones in the Bible. The trouble with the theory that it is Spinoza's identification of God with nature to which Hobbes was referring is that Spinoza himself largely held back this doctrine until his posthumously published *Ethics*, which Hobbes never saw. One brief passage in the book that Hobbes read does imply the doctrine, but that is all. The claim that this is what Hobbes also believed but dared not write is therefore a flimsy one.

Spinoza is the subject of the next chapter. He shared Hobbes's admiration for geometry, though this did him considerably less harm than it did Hobbes. Both men were condemned by their contemporaries, and by several subsequent generations. But although Spinoza was once at least as vilified as Hobbes, he came eventually to be regarded by many as one of the most lovable of philosophers. Hobbes has not won such affection.

# 3

# A BREEZE OF THE FUTURE
## *Spinoza*

By the decree of the Angels and the word of the Saints we ban, cut off, curse and anathemize Baruch de Espinoza. . . . Cursed be he by day and cursed by night, cursed in his lying down and cursed in his waking up, cursed in his going forth and cursed in his coming in; and may the Lord not want his pardon, and may the Lord's wrath and zeal burn upon him. . . .

We warn that none may contact him orally or in writing, nor do him any favor, nor stay under the same roof with him, nor read any paper he made or wrote.

WITH THESE WORDS, PRONOUNCED ON 27 JULY 1656, THE PORTUGUESE-Jewish community of Amsterdam excommunicated Spinoza. He was then twenty-three years old, the son of a fruit-merchant, and once regarded as a promising biblical scholar. The Amsterdam synagogue was fond of excommunications and issued them frequently, sometimes in response to relatively minor misdeeds. Two friends of Spinoza's were similarly cursed and cast out in the same week. But the curse on Spinoza was the fiercest excommunication ever issued by the congregation.

This Jewish community had a past that made its members especially sensitive to any apparent challenge. They were former Marranos—Jews who had for generations been obliged to live as Christians in their native

Spain and Portugal, and who had come to Amsterdam at the end of the sixteenth century to live openly as Jews once more. Much of their knowledge of Jewish law and tradition had been lost during the years when their ancestors had been forced to practise their religion in secret. Indeed, by the time they escaped to the relative freedom of the Netherlands, their earnest attempts to become good Jews were hampered by the fact that many of them had all but forgotten what this entailed. Very few of the Amsterdam congregation could even read Hebrew (Spinoza was one of those who could).

In effect, the Amsterdam Jews were new to Judaism, so they had the zeal of recent converts. They were quick to condemn any of their number whose behaviour seemed to threaten the recently regained faith. In this respect their rabbis almost mirrored the Spanish and Portuguese Inquisitions which had kept a close watch on their ancestors. The Inquisitors had rightly suspected that many of the "New Christians" (i.e., converted Jews) were privately persisting in their old religion. In a similar spirit, the Amsterdam synagogue now kept a sharp eye out for irregularities among the New Jews. Although it busied itself with some offences that were merely trivial, such as talking during services, there was no shortage of serious heresies to be dealt with, too. It is perhaps not surprising that the culture of Marranism, with its peculiar mixture of Christianity and Judaism, and its tradition of intellectual subterfuge, should prove to be a seedbed of unorthodox ideas.

ONE EXAMPLE of the nonconformity bred by the contorted history of the Marranos is the case of Uriel Da Costa, who committed suicide when Spinoza was eight. "There are people who always proclaim: 'I am a Jew,' 'I am a Christian,'" Da Costa said. "Yet he who pretends to be neither is preferable by far." Da Costa had some difficulty deciding what it was best to be. First he was a Christian (of Marrano blood), then he became a Jew, but he quickly grew dissatisfied with the rediscovered religion of his ancestors. He refused to recognise the authority of rabbis and of Jewish law, and denied that there was an afterlife. After being excommunicated by the synagogue, he broke down and recanted his heresies. But then he rebelled again, was punished once more, and embraced Judaism yet again before killing himself in a fit of despair and perhaps insanity. Little more is known of his evidently ambivalent opinions, but whatever exactly it was that he believed, his behaviour shocked Spinoza's community and made it even more nervous than it already was.

Another rebel member of the Amsterdam Marrano community, who was closer to Spinoza in age, in spirit, and probably in mental stability, was Juan de Prado, a Spanish-born doctor who was excommunicated in the same week as Spinoza. He was about ten years older than the young philosopher and met to discuss religious subjects with him. Like Da Costa, Prado could not decide where he belonged. When in Christian Spain, he risked his life as a secret Jew; later, when among Jews in Amsterdam, he lived as a secret unbeliever. When his religious scepticism got to be too much for the synagogue and he was banned, Prado pretended to recant his heresies and become a pious Jew again. Thus, like a true Marrano of old—but unlike Spinoza, who bravely made no attempt to disguise his opinions—Prado kept his true beliefs hidden from public view. This reticence was understandable, for he shockingly believed that God is in some sense identical with nature, or at least identical with a part of nature. He also maintained that it is unnecessary to practice the Jewish or indeed any religion in order to be saved. Spiritual salvation lies in the knowledge of God and has nothing to do with following the rules of rabbis or endorsing superstitious dogmas. Moreover, much of the "history" in the Bible is downright false, according to Prado. For one thing, the world has always existed and was therefore not created.

Three years after Spinoza and Prado were excommunicated by the synagogue, a spy who worked for the Spanish Inquisition reported back to his masters about them. (The Inquisition took a lively interest in Marranos even after they had gone abroad.) These renegade Jews, the spy wrote, dare to say that the soul dies with the body. They also say, he reported, that "God exists, but only philosophically." This enigmatic idea is what the spy claimed to have picked up from a discussion group attended by the two men. But what can it mean to say that God exists "only philosophically"?

For the spy, who was a monk, it presumably meant that the God which these men talked about was unlike the God of traditional religion because

He was unduly abstract and impersonal. Spinoza's God was indeed an unfamiliar and in some ways distant entity. Like Aristotle's lofty Prime Mover, He took no interest in human affairs. But the spy was wrong if he thought that God therefore played only a peripheral role in Spinoza's universe. Far from it: God played the central role. To learn about the world, for Spinoza, is to learn about God, because "all things are in God." And "the love of God is man's highest happiness and blessedness." A century after Spinoza's death, a German Romantic poet aptly described him as "a God-intoxicated man." This was no exaggeration. How Spinoza's obsession with God can be squared with his uncompromising attack on conventional religions will become clearer later.

It was not at all clear to most of Spinoza's contemporaries, who generally regarded his views as an irreligious abomination. "I do not differentiate between God and Nature in the way all those known to me have done," wrote Spinoza. This sort of statement eclipsed everything else he said about God and made him simply an atheist in most people's eyes. Until Spinoza was rediscovered by some late eighteenth-century German writers, whose reverence for nature led them to count him as a spiritual ancestor, he remained largely a philosophical outcast. Most European thinkers who mentioned him spoke in terms that might almost have been borrowed from the harsh and histrionic decree of the Amsterdam synagogue. Thus the entry on Spinoza in Bayle's influential *Historical and Critical Dictionary*, which was published twenty years after Spinoza's death, calls his main work on religion "a pernicious and detestable book." It also describes his philosophy as "the most monstrous hypothesis that could be imagined."

Yet not even Spinoza's biggest enemies could deny his personal virtue. His kindness and nobility of character were legendary. Bertrand Russell was not alone in regarding Spinoza as "the noblest and most lovable of the great philosophers." Indeed, the worst thing anyone has ever found to say about Spinoza's conduct is that he sometimes enjoyed watching spiders chase flies. People in the seventeenth century found it somewhat paradoxical that a notorious "atheist" could also be a good man; but there was no denying that this is what Spinoza was. Bayle noted, "Those who were acquainted with him . . . all agree in saying that he was social, affable, honest, obliging, and of a well-ordered morality."

A romantic myth has grown up around the story of Spinoza's life. It is commonly said that he was forced to earn his living by grinding lenses, subsisting as a humble craftsman while he pursued his solitary quest for truth. In fact, Spinoza lived comfortably, albeit modestly, on grants and pensions from his few devoted admirers and pupils. Like many others of his time who were interested in optics and experimental science, Spinoza did manufacture some of his own instruments; but his lens-making was primarily a scientific pursuit rather than a commercial one. Descartes had dabbled in lens-grinding too. Spinoza's instruments, though, were of famously high quality, and his practical expertise provided one reason among many why devotees of science and the "new philosophy" from all over Europe sought him out.

In 1673 the University of Heidelberg offered Spinoza, as a man of "exceptional genius," a chair in philosophy, on condition that he not misuse the position to "disturb the publicly established religion." Spinoza could not accept this restriction, and declined the honour (the university was anyway closed shortly afterwards by the occupying French forces). Although he had been cast out by the Amsterdam synagogue, and later almost universally reviled in print, there were some people who recognised Spinoza's remarkable mind and who were eager to know more of his thoughts, even if few could go all the way to accepting them.

∞

AT THE AGE of sixteen, Spinoza disappointed his community by abandoning higher studies in scripture and theology. He had to help manage his father's business, and his intellectual interests were already turning to the world outside the synagogue. A couple of years later he enrolled in a Latin school where he could learn to read the literary classics and the latest scholarly works by non-Jews. His teacher was Francis van den Enden, an ex-Jesuit who had become a doctor and a keen Cartesian—Descartes had spent most of the last twenty years of his life in the Netherlands and his ideas were much discussed there. With the encouragement of Van den Enden, Spinoza shifted his studies towards science, particularly mathemat-

ics and optics. The writings of Descartes and the other pioneers of the
new physics held a much greater attraction for him than the rabbinical
commentaries to which his community tried to steer him. Spinoza was
also soon mixing with the members of various dissident Christian groups
that were collectively known as Collegiants. These small sects, which were
sometimes little more than discussion groups, typically rejected all religious ceremonies. They dismissed the authority of the established churches
and many, or even all, traditional dogmas. Their religion focussed on the
uplifting effects of reading scripture, the virtues of religious freedom and
the desirability of separating church and state. Spinoza met many of the
people who became his closest friends through these groups, and he saw
even more of them after his banishment.

Four years after his excommunication, Spinoza moved to a small town
near Leiden, where he may have studied at the university. By this time,
drafts of some of his philosophical writings were creeping into circulation,
and he was already becoming famous for his microscopes and telescopes as
well as for his alleged atheism. In 1661 he was visited by Henry Oldenburg,
the first secretary of London's Royal Society, who was busy forging links
between Europe's scientific pioneers. This meeting was the beginning of
Spinoza's lifelong involvement with leading figures in the world of science.
In addition to his work in optics, in which he collaborated with Christiaan
Huygens—who founded the wave theory of light, invented the pendulum
clock and discovered the rings of Saturn—Spinoza conducted experiments
in hydrodynamics and metallurgy. He pursued a long correspondence, via
Oldenburg, with Robert Boyle on practical and theoretical issues in chemistry. He also took an active interest in the recently developed mathematics
of probability, and was an eager observer of nature through the magnifying
instruments he made. The depth of his devotion to science may be gauged
from the fact that at the time of his death about one-third of the books in
his personal library were scientific or mathematical works.

Like Descartes and Francis Bacon, Spinoza was convinced of the practical value of the new science. "Mechanics," he wrote in an early essay,
"is in no way to be despised," since it enables us to "gain much time and
convenience in this life." However, for Spinoza the ultimate benefits of
scientific study were spiritual. To acquire the highest sort of knowledge was

to reach nothing less than a state of blessedness, and the study of nature was in effect the study of the divine. "The greater our knowledge of natural phenomena," he later wrote, "the more perfect is our knowledge of the essence of God."

Soon after his excommunication, Spinoza began to write a sort of reply to the synagogue that had cursed him. This manuscript grew to become the *Tractatus theologico-politicus*, a revolutionary work which, unlike his better-known *Ethics*, is comprehensible to people who are not well-versed in philosophy. The *Tractatus* has been largely ignored by recent philosophers, probably because so much of it is about the Bible. This is a pity because the book is not only a landmark in Western thought but also an invaluable introduction to Spinoza's philosophy.

The *Tractatus* contains, among other things, a critical examination of scripture and a defence of what Spinoza took to be its true message. This message was a moral one, he argued, and nothing else: "God through His prophets required from men no other knowledge of Himself than is contained in a knowledge of His justice and charity—that is, of attributes which a certain manner of life will enable men to imitate." Unfortunately, this truth had been lost sight of and religion had become "a tissue of ridiculous mysteries." To know and love God, Spinoza insisted, does not require the performance of any ceremonies, nor belief in any supernatural dogmas, nor the acceptance of any allegedly historical narratives in the Bible. It only requires "the practice of justice and love towards one's neighbour."

Spinoza treated the Bible as a collection of documents that reveal as much about their authors as about anything else, and which are accordingly to be examined with the tools of a literary critic and historian. What such examinations show is that the tales in the Old Testament were invented largely in order to encourage the Hebrews to adopt certain values. Thus the five books of Moses were "calculated to instil with efficacy, and present vividly to the imagination the commands of God." They were written in the form of colourful stories (such as the one about Moses receiving his tablets of stone) because scripture is "adapted to the needs of the common people." As for the ceremonial regulations and other rules that orthodox Jews live by, Spinoza argued that their original purpose was to give the Jews a sense of identity and a system of laws after the liberation from Egypt, when they were uncultivated slaves. These regulations filled a vacuum in desperate times, but they are no longer binding today. According to Spinoza, the prophets may sometimes have believed that they were revealing more than just moral messages and useful guides for life. But whenever they stray into predictions of the future, or speculative theological matters, or tales of miracles, we are at liberty to ignore them, for these men "were endowed with unusually vivid imaginations, and not with unusually perfect minds." The same goes for the authors of the New Testament.

Spinoza seems to have been the first person to argue comprehensively and in detail that "the Word of God is faulty, mutilated, tampered with, and inconsistent" because it has been relayed to us via mere human beings. A few earlier thinkers had noticed the odd problem here and there which seemed to cast doubt on the authority of the Bible. In the eleventh century, a Jewish doctor in Moslem Spain, called Isaac ibn Yashush, noticed that some of the descendants of Esau mentioned in chapter 36 of Genesis, which is supposed to have been written by Moses, had in fact been born long after Moses died. This piece of research merely earned its discoverer the title of "Isaac the blunderer." Closer to Spinoza's own time, Luther and Hobbes had acknowledged that because the death of Moses is described in the book of Deuteronomy, he cannot really have written it. But Luther insisted that Moses had at least written a great deal of the words attributed to him, and did not raise many other objections. Hobbes was more sceptical, and apparently a significant influence on Spinoza. A critic of the Bible who was more radical than Hobbes was Isaac La Peyrère (1596–1676), a French heretic who believed that the world would soon be run by a Jewish messiah acting in partnership with the king of France. La Peyrère was apparently of Marrano origin and probably met Spinoza. He argued that the Bible offered not an account of human history but only an account of the history of the Jews; that there were other men before Adam (in China, for example); and that the flood was merely a little local difficulty in Palestine. Spinoza used many of La Peyrère's criticisms of the accuracy of the Bible, but he was more scholarly and he went farther. While La Peyrère and others cavilled at some biblical narratives, Spinoza dug deep into the foundations of traditional religion.

The basic error behind accepted views of God was, as Spinoza once put it in a letter, "to confuse God's nature with human nature." Anybody who takes the stories of the Bible literally is guilty of this confusion, because many of the tales of both the Old and New Testaments are really just parables designed to communicate a complex message to simple people in terms with which they are familiar. The stories do this by giving God a human personality. For example, the Bible portrays God as someone who lays down laws just like an earthly king, and who promises to bestow rewards on those who obey them, and punishments on those who do not. But the truth of the matter, Spinoza argued, is that God is not remotely like a king or indeed any other sort of person. To suppose that God has any desires—even to suppose that He wants people to behave in one way rather than another, for instance—or that He makes promises, or that He distributes gifts or takes revenge, is to mix up human characteristics with divine ones.

It is, Spinoza acknowledged, often convenient to use human terms when talking loosely of the divine, as he himself did when he sometimes wrote of God's "commands" and of what God "requires" of man. But strictly speaking it is inaccurate: "God is described as a lawgiver or prince, and styled just, merciful, etc, merely in concession to popular understanding, and the imperfection of popular knowledge." In reality, Spinoza explained, God's so-called "decrees" are "eternal truths." What he meant by this is that divine laws are not like human laws but more like laws of nature in the scientific sense. Divine laws cannot be broken, any more than the law of gravity can be broken. People can, though, foolishly attempt to ignore them, in which case the consequences will be just as unfortunate and just as inevitable as the consequences of attempting to walk off a precipice. There are many echoes of Hobbes here.

When God revealed to Adam the evil that would come to pass if he ate the forbidden fruit, Adam wrongly took this to be a command expressing God's fearsome authority. But God was not threatening Adam. He was merely informing him about a fact of nature. According to Spinoza, it is a fundamental truth about the human condition that sin causes suffering and virtue causes bliss. What the Bible calls God's commands should therefore be taken as helpful warnings about what certain actions are bound to lead to.

Blessedness or salvation is the automatic result of living in the right way, not because God whimsically chooses to reward those who follow a particular set of rules, but because living in accordance with what the Bible presents as God's commands—i.e., being just and charitable—is in fact an effective recipe for the highest happiness. This is just a consequence of human nature. We flourish when we are virtuous and suffer when we sin, just as we thrive if we eat nourishing food and die if we eat poison. It follows that the rewards of virtue are reaped during earthly life, not later in heaven. Similarly, the misery of sin is suffered here and not afterwards in hell. Spinoza had a low opinion of those who practise justice and charity merely in order to secure a satisfactory afterlife for themselves. Anyone who is kept from vice only by his fear of punishment, Spinoza wrote, does not really embrace virtue. And besides, there is no afterlife.

Spinoza's determination to purge the divine law of any apparent resemblance to human law led him to deny that anything can be said to be contrary to God's will. It is commonly held that Adam and Eve's original mischief, and indeed all sins, go against the will of God. Similarly, people say that God is angry or sad, or at least disapproving, when His creatures are wicked. But according to Spinoza, this manner of speaking does not make sense: "it would argue great imperfection in God if anything happened against His will, or if He wanted something He could not possess, or if His nature were determined in such a manner that, just like His creatures, He felt sympathy with some things and antipathy to others."

Spinoza's unusual God might seem to present a moral problem. If He does not feel any pity or love towards His creatures, and if nothing that happens can be said to be contrary to His will, does that not make Him somewhat amoral? Perhaps. But the God of traditional religion presents problems of His own and is arguably even worse. For there is undoubtedly a great deal of unmerited misery and pain in the world, yet it seems that He only rarely if ever does anything about it. Unlike Spinoza's God, the traditional God is said to sympathise with the sufferings of His creatures and to abhor evil, so it is all the more incomprehensible that He should allow such unpleasantness to exist. The difficulty of reconciling the existence of evil with God's alleged omnipotence and mercy has, it can plausibly be argued, defeated every orthodox theologian in the history of monotheism. But Spinoza thought he had an answer to the problem: there is, he reasoned, no such thing as evil or suffering from God's point of view, and this explains why God never tries to do anything about it.

Just as nothing can be said to be either contrary to or in accordance with God's will, so nothing is either good or bad from God's perspective, which is to say from the point of view of nature or the universe as a whole:

> nature is not bounded by the laws of human reason, which aims only at man's true benefit and preservation; her limits are infinitely wider, and have reference to the eternal order of nature, wherein man is but a speck. . . . If anything, therefore, in nature seems to us ridiculous, absurd, or evil, it is because we only know in part, and are almost entirely ignorant of the order and interdependence of nature as a whole.

Various things are good or bad from our limited and self-interested standpoint, insofar as they are beneficial or harmful to us. But to expect God to vanquish "evil," or even to disapprove of it, is to confuse His perspective with ours. In a similar vein, Spinoza wrote, "I do not attribute to Nature beauty, ugliness, order or confusion. It is only with respect to our imagination that things can be said to be beautiful, ugly, well-ordered or confused."

In taking this radical stand, Spinoza was not endorsing mere subjectivism. That is, he was not maintaining that good, evil, beauty, ugliness and so on are nothing more than matters of individual opinion, as the Sophist Protagoras apparently did in the fifth century BC. For when Spinoza spoke of goodness and other values as relating to "our" reason, "our" benefit and "our" imagination, he was referring to humanity as a whole. He certainly believed that it was possible to be rational and objective about what was good or bad for humanity, so it was by no means true that anyone's casual opinions were just as sound as anyone else's. His point was rather that one should not confuse human values with the divine point of view. God, or nature, has no use for such categories as good and bad.

This attempt to distinguish qualities that are related to human concerns and human experience from those that are intrinsic to nature is reminiscent of Galileo's view of sensory qualities such as colour, feel and taste. As we have seen, Galileo, Descartes and the other pioneers of the mechanical philosophy sought to purge physics of all but the measurable "primary qualities" (as Boyle called them), i.e., shape, size, position and a few favoured others. According to the new science, only these qualities genuinely belong to material objects. When, by contrast, we judge that something is red, pungent or hot, for instance, we are not describing the object itself but merely describing the way it affects human faculties. Spinoza endorsed this theory and took it further. His list of the qualities which man tends wrongly to attribute to nature includes "good, evil, order, confusion, warm, cold, beauty, ugliness." He sometimes borrowed the dismissive language of the mechanical philosophers to make his theological points, for example when he wrote that "nothing is in itself absolutely sacred, or profane, and unclean, apart from the mind, but only relatively thereto." Thus Spinoza can be seen as carrying the message of the mechanical philosophy beyond the confines of physics into the new territory of religion and ethics.

One key element in Spinoza's critique of traditional religion is his attack on the idea of the "supernatural." Here again his efforts to tear the mask of human personality from the idea of God join forces with a confident enthusiasm in the possibilities of science. He argued that tales of miracles and other forms of divine intervention all make the error of supposing that laws of nature are like human laws and may be contravened at the discretion of the lawmaker. But it is a misunderstanding to think that the laws of nature can be temporarily suspended in this way. They are not like parking regulations. If some event genuinely conflicts with what was previously taken to be a law of nature, then all that follows is that this supposed law was not in fact a law in the first place. Besides, to judge that something is supernatural is to declare that it is beyond the powers of nature. Yet how could anyone presume to know enough about nature's capabilities to reach such a conclusion? As Spinoza put it,

> do we petty men have such an understanding of Nature that we can
> determine . . . what is beyond its power? Since nobody can make such
> a claim without arrogance, one may therefore without presumption
> explain miracles through natural causes as far as possible.

Spinoza did not think he was already in a position to provide natural explanations for every alleged miracle that came along. But he could see no good reason to rule out all such explanations in advance—and, more importantly, the notion of the supernatural did not make sense.

For Spinoza, all genuine scientific laws express truths about God, i.e., about nature. It follows that if God were to seek to "break" the laws of nature in order to impress His creatures with some divine message, He would in effect be attempting to confound Himself. But this is an absurd idea. How can God contravene nature if He is nature?

Spinoza believed that his own view of the matter not only made more sense but also provided a better route to God. He wrote that

> the masses think that the power and providence of God are most clearly displayed by events that are extraordinary and contrary to the conception they have formed of nature . . . : they think that the clearest possible proof of God's existence is afforded when nature, as they suppose, breaks her accustomed order. . . .

Yet surely a "fixed and immutable order of nature," such as Spinoza believed in, would be a more fitting testimonial to a perfect and infinite Being than any amount of resurrected bodies, tidal disturbances in the Red Sea or great balls of fire on Mount Sinai. After all, no amazing event, however extraordinary, could be evidence of literally infinite power. It could only be evidence of extraordinary power, which is a far lesser thing. God is supposed to be more than merely amazing. Moreover, a gullible attitude to fantastic stories can easily lead one astray, for as Moses himself observed, "false prophets" can perform wonders too.

The true object of the miraculous stories narrated in the Bible was, Spinoza argued, "to move men, and especially uneducated men, to devotion . . . not to convince the reason, but to attract and lay hold of the imagination." One should therefore not read too much into the details of these tales, as the orthodox religions now unfortunately do. One should focus instead on the virtue and piety which it was their main purpose to instil. Take the life of Christ, for instance. Spinoza was happy to acknowledge that it "provided an example of surpassing holiness," and that Christ had such a profound understanding of the divine law (that is, of justice and charity) that he could be regarded as "the mouthpiece of God." But Spinoza gave Christ this special place largely on account of his moral teaching and the example he set to others, not because he was the son of God in any supernatural sense. Christ's teachings were divine, but the man himself was not, for no sense could be attached to such a bizarre idea: "As to the . . . teaching of certain Churches, that God took upon Himself human nature . . . they seem to me to speak no less absurdly than one who might tell me that a circle has taken on the nature of a square."

Mohammed, too, taught the divine law and so was a true prophet, though apparently a lesser one than Christ. It does not matter what religion a man professes, or even if he is totally ignorant of all scriptures, so long as he lives in the right way. Indeed, "wherever justice and charity have the force of law and ordinance, there is God's kingdom."

To build God's kingdom it is necessary to organise the state on broadly democratic principles and to allow absolute freedom of speech, and considerable freedom of religion. The whole point of government, Spinoza maintained, is liberty: "the object of government is . . . to enable [men] to develop their minds and bodies in security, and to employ their reason unshackled; neither showing hatred, anger, or deceit, nor watched with the eyes of jealousy and injustice." The state authorities may interfere in religion—indeed, they must do so, since religion is too dangerous to be left in the hands of priests. But state intervention is justified only for the purpose of ensuring that all rites, ceremonies and "outward observances of piety" are in accordance with "the public peace and well-being." People's beliefs must be left an entirely private affair, and neither priests nor churches (nor presumably synagogues, mosques or temples) are to be given any legal powers. Give priests power and they soon start persecuting anyone who disagrees with them. The result is always strife, schism and sectarianism. Spinoza did not, however, advocate a separation of church and state in the form that came to be enshrined in the United States Constitution. Quite the reverse. According to Spinoza, the state should establish and supervise a national religion, though it should be "very simple" and "of a most universal nature." All other peaceful religions are to be permitted, though they must have fewer and less impressive buildings than the established national faith.

The prosperous and relatively peaceful city of Amsterdam was evidence of the benefits of tolerance and diversity. Although the city enjoyed only comparative freedom, as Spinoza knew from personal experience, it was much better than many other places in Christendom, and it showed that liberty of thought need not be a threat to public order. Far from being a danger, intellectual freedom had in fact considerable advantages. Such freedom is "absolutely necessary for progress in science and the liberal arts: for no man follows such pursuits to advantage unless his judgement be entirely free and unhampered." Besides, since it is impossible to extinguish independent thought altogether, any attempts to stifle the public expression of it will have undesirable consequences: "men would daily be thinking one thing and saying another, to the corruption of good faith, that mainstay of government, and to the fostering of hateful flattery and perfidy, whence spring stratagems, and the corruption of every good art."

Spinoza claimed that he had no desire to abolish conventional religions or even to encourage the masses to discard their conception of God as a king-like ruler. Not only would such an aim be inconsistent with his liberal principles of toleration, it would be quite impossible to achieve. The people need their relatively crude images and stories, and if they did not think of God in personal terms, as a being with wishes, emotions and a close involvement with human life, they would probably not think of Him at all. Spinoza's writings were aimed at the few who could appreciate philosophical ideas and so were capable of grasping the unvarnished truth.

His *Tractatus* was accordingly published in Latin, the language of the learned. It was anonymous and gave false information about its publisher, but many scholars and churchmen knew who was responsible for it. Spinoza was most concerned when some friends tried to arrange a Dutch translation in order to reach a wider audience. He believed that such an edition would arouse the anger of the masses and possibly lead to violence. These fears were well-founded. When a friend and follower had unwisely published a Spinozist account of religion under his own name and in plain Dutch, he had been flung into prison, where he died. Even before the publication of the Latin version of the *Tractatus*, Spinoza was aware that theologians were "everywhere plotting against me." When the book came out, a former pupil who had become a Catholic warned Spinoza that if he did not recant his "wretched and insane reasoning . . . the wrath of the Lord will be kindled against you." Spinoza wisely never published the major work, *Ethics*, that gave full expression to his ideas.

∞

THE ONLY BOOK that Spinoza published under his own name was ostensibly about someone else's philosophy: *Parts I and II of Descartes's "Principles of Philosophy," demonstrated in the geometric manner.* As its title suggests, this was a textbook rather than an original treatise, but it was more than just a classroom exposition of Descartes. Sometimes Spinoza used arguments of his own to establish Cartesian conclusions. Occasionally, the conclusions themselves were novel, though in this book Spinoza's few criticisms of Descartes were usually veiled ones. It may seem odd that Spinoza should devote such deferential attention to Descartes when the ideas of the two men were in fact so far apart. With hindsight, their differences appear to be more striking than their similarities; but that is not how it seemed to Spinoza at the time. For him, it was what he shared with Descartes that was more important. In those days, to be modern-minded in philosophy and science was to tread in the footsteps of the pioneering Descartes. Although Spinoza did once refer to "the stupid Cartesians" who had failed to understand him, Descartes himself was the principal modern philosopher to be reckoned with. He was the only philosopher at all to be mentioned in the *Ethics*, except for one passing reference to old Seneca and one to Buridan and his proverbial ass.

Spinoza's *Ethics*, like most of his book on Descartes, was modelled on Euclid's geometry. Each part starts with definitions, which are followed by axioms or postulates, and then chains of supposedly rigorous demonstrations of various theorems. Earlier thinkers had very occasionally tried to squeeze their philosophy into Euclidean form—Proclus in the fifth century was a notable example—but falling in love with geometry seems almost to have been an occupational hazard of seventeenth-century philosophy. As we have seen, Hobbes's infatuation with it did him damage in various ways. Spinoza's case of geometrophilia was less unhealthy, but the infection was real. He wrote of aiming for "the kind of knowledge of God that we have of the triangle," and his letters were packed with questionably relevant geometrical analogies. In the *Ethics*, he announced his intention to "consider human actions and appetites just as if it were a question of lines, planes and bodies." And, like Proclus, but unlike Hobbes, he even laid out his treatise in largely Euclidean format rather than continuous prose.

Spinoza acknowledged that his pseudo-mathematical approach would strike many people as odd. But he argued that it was nevertheless the right one to take: "if men understood clearly the whole order of Nature, they would find all things just as necessary as are all those treated in mathematics." In other words, once people had grasped Spinoza's work they would come to see that the most basic truths about the world, including those about God and even the foibles of human behaviour, can indeed be demonstrated in much the same way that Euclid demonstrated his geometrical theorems. Unfortunately, people did not come to see this at all. Spinoza would have been disappointed to learn that after more than three hundred years of study, even his greatest admirers have to admit that many of his proofs do not work. There are too many gaps, begged questions and disputable assumptions. It is probably fair to say that nowadays few philosophers who agree with Spinoza on some point do so because they have been convinced by a pseudo-mathematical demonstration in the *Ethics*.

Even so, the *Ethics* presents a remarkable challenge to the view that God and nature are wholly separate, and it is packed with intense philosophical reasoning. Juan de Prado, and perhaps other Marrano contemporaries of Spinoza's, had already said that God was nature. So had Giordano Bruno, a heretical friar and occultist who had been burned at the stake in 1600. But nobody before had tried so hard to work out the details of this sort of idea, or to explain its implications for man. The *Ethics* provided the modern West with the first philosophically sophisticated alternative to the world-picture that is shared by Judaism, Christianity and Islam. Moreover, it did so in a way that gave due prominence to the new science.

Spinoza's genius was to take the traditional idea that God is One and infinite and to pursue it to what seemed to be its logical conclusion. This conclusion is that there is no room for a world that is distinct from God. If nature were something altogether different from God, Spinoza reasoned, then it would have to possess some properties that God lacked—but how could an absolutely infinite God possibly lack anything? To put it crudely, a God who is infinite in every respect is bound to fill the world, and cannot be confined to a separate existence, however lofty. Several other lines of thought seemed to Spinoza to lead inexorably in the same direction.

Thousands of times in his youth, Spinoza would have begun his morning prayers with the words "Hear, O Israel, the Lord is our God, the Lord is One." By the time he was an adult, Spinoza had decided that nature and the Lord had to be "One" as well. He was impressed by "the unity which we see everywhere in Nature" (that is, by the way in which everything in it works harmoniously together), and he argued that such unity would be impossible unless all of nature's apparently disparate elements were at bottom "only one, single being." This sounds a little like Parmenides's famously implausible theory that everything is unreal except for "the One."* But the resemblance is merely superficial. Whereas Parmenides said that nothing exists except for an invisible, eternal and unchanging "One," Spinoza happily accepted the existence of everything that the man in the street believed in, except for ghosts and miracles. Parmenides claimed to establish that there were no people, no earth, no stars and no sun. Spinoza's aim was less outrageous but still controversial. He sought to establish that all objects in the world are manifestations or "modes" of a single all-encompassing and divine "substance."

"Substance" and "mode" were technical terms, originating in Aristotelian philosophy and still much used by Descartes and his contemporaries. Roughly speaking, a substance is something that can exist on its own. A cat is a substance, in this special philosophical sense, but its smile is not, because a smile cannot exist without a cat or some other creature with a face, except in Lewis Carroll's *Alice's Adventures in Wonderland*. As we have seen, Descartes held that there were two radically different kinds of substances: physical ones and spiritual ones. Moreover, there were countless substances of each type, according to Descartes, and every substance had countless properties, known as "modes." (This, at least, was Descartes's usual view, though he sometimes wavered from it.) Spinoza,

---

* See *The Dream of Reason*, chapter 4.

however, sought to demonstrate that the best definition of "substance" led to a quite different story. He defined it as something that does not require anything else to explain its existence or nature. According to Spinoza, it follows that there can be only one such substance, and therefore that each tree, person, planet and house is a mode of it rather than a substance in its own right. It also follows that the allegedly fundamental divide between mental and physical, of which Descartes had made so much, is in fact illusory. The universe's single substance has both mental and physical aspects.

Spinoza's account of the relation between mind and matter is aptly known as a "double-aspect theory." When applied to people, it is relatively straightforward, at least on the surface: it entails that mind and body are two sides of the same coin. For example, if we want to describe some piece of human behaviour, we may focus either on the psychological state of the person concerned—i.e., on what he thinks, feels and desires—or else on his physical state—i.e., on what is happening inside his brain and other parts of his body. According to Spinoza, these are merely alternative ways of describing the same chain of events; they are explanations of one thing from two different perspectives. This sort of theory avoids the puzzles inherent in Descartes's idea that the mental and physical realms are fundamentally distinct and yet mysteriously interact. It does, however, have one odd feature. Spinoza seems to have thought that every physical event, and not only those which involve intelligent organisms, can be described in both physical and psychological terms. It was not only brains but also every physical object which had a mental aspect. Yet how can one describe a pile of rocks in psychological terms? What is the mental aspect of a tree? Spinoza insisted that he did not mean to say that inanimate objects can think or have emotions. But he did feel obliged to admit that everything was in some sense animate. What exactly he meant by this remains obscure.

This talk of an animated universe attracted poets in the late eighteenth century, including Goethe and Coleridge, and others who wished to make a religion out of nature. Spinoza's philosophy seemed to recall that of the early Greek thinkers who spoke of all things as alive and "full of gods," so it appeared to provide an excellent excuse for worshipping the landscape.

After all, did he not identify God and nature, and did this not have the delightful consequence that every bird, flower and even worm was a piece of God? Several early commentators thought so. Spinoza holds, wrote one English scholar in 1698, "that the Deity is the whole Mass of Beings or of Matter in the Universe." In 1705 another British writer coined the term "pantheist" to refer to someone who equates God with the material universe, and said that Spinoza was a pantheist *par excellence*.

Prado was probably a pantheist in this sense. But Spinoza definitely was not. He explicitly denied that his God could be identified with any physical part of nature, or even with the physical universe as a whole. He wrote that those who identify God with "a kind of mass or corporeal matter . . . are quite mistaken." At first, this disclaimer seems puzzling. How can Spinoza hold that God is not the physical universe if he holds that He is nature? The answer is that Spinoza never stated that the terms "God" and "nature" always mean exactly the same thing. What he wrote was "I do not differentiate between God and Nature *in the way all those known to me have done*" (my emphasis). Although he rejected the traditional distinction between God and nature, he did distinguish between active and passive aspects of nature—by which he seems to have meant its creative power and the products of this power. And strictly speaking it was nature considered as an active force that he identified with God, not nature considered as the flowers, birds, mountains and so on which somehow embody this force. It is also worth noting that Spinoza was not inclined to treat any aspect of nature as deserving of worship, so his attitude towards it was not religious in any conventional sense.

SPINOZA maintained that the physical universe unfolds in an inexorable procession of causes and effects: "Things could have been produced . . . in no other way, and in no other order than they have been produced." It may not seem so at first, but the more we come to know about the laws of nature, the more we see how every step in the march of events has been choreographed in advance. Nature is fixed because its course reflects the nature or essence of God: to suppose that anything could have happened differently is to suppose that God Himself could have been different—and that, according to Spinoza, is an absurd idea. Characteristically, Spinoza compared the laws of nature to truths of geometry. The course of events, he said, proceeds "with the same necessity as from the essence of a triangle it follows that its three angles are equal to two right angles."

Did Spinoza then maintain that not even God is free to do whatever He wants? In one sense, yes. If freedom means being able to pick between alternative courses of action, then Spinoza would happily agree that God is not free. But this does not matter, because God cannot be said to have preferences or to want anything, so it is not as if He were somehow prevented from exercising his will. To suppose otherwise would be to make the old mistake of treating God as if He were a person. Besides, there is another sense of freedom, according to Spinoza, in which God is absolutely free. Indeed, God is the only being who has complete freedom in this sense.

At the beginning of his *Ethics*, Spinoza gave a definition of freedom in terms of autonomy: "That thing is called free which exists from the necessity of its own nature alone, and is determined to act by itself alone." In other words, something is free if it does not owe its existence to anything else and is unaffected by any external influence. It is easy to see that Spinoza's God has this sort of freedom. He is infinite and all-embracing, so there simply are no causes or influences that are external to Him. People, on the other hand, do not usually enjoy any such autonomy, because they are passive and at the mercy of countless forces that are in no sense part of themselves. Although they believe that they have a substantial degree of independence, this is an illusion that is easily accounted for: "men are deceived in that they think themselves free . . . an opinion which consists only in this, that they are conscious of their actions and ignorant of the causes by which they are determined." Spinoza joked that if a falling stone could think, it would believe that it was choosing to fall of its own free will, because it would not know the causes of its motion. The sobering truth, however, is that everything is determined by a cause "which is also determined by another, and this again by another, and so to infinity."

According to Spinoza, each thing in nature is driven by an urge to maintain itself in existence and to develop its potential. It faces fierce competition in this endeavour from everything else, which is of course trying to do exactly the same. Even the behaviour of falling stones may be explained in this way, because the laws of motion (e.g., the law that "a body in motion moves until it is determined by another body to rest") are instances of the universal drive towards self-preservation and self-assertion. Human desires and the human will are also manifestations of this striving. But there is a crucial difference between people and stones. One of the things that can affect the course of people's thoughts and feelings—though not the trajectories of falling objects— is the exercise of reason. It turns out that this makes it possible for man to enjoy a small taste of the autonomy enjoyed by God.

The clearest illustration of how this happens is provided by Spinoza's favourite school-subject, geometry. Consider what is going on in the mind of a man who is quietly working his way through a proof from Euclid's *Elements*. If we examine the causes of his mental states and ask why he believes, say, a certain theorem, we shall find that the explanation goes something like this. He believes it because he can see that it follows necessarily from another theorem, which follows from an earlier theorem, which in turn follows from an axiom that is self-evidently true. Thus each of the man's thoughts is determined not by any externally caused mood or image that happens to be passing through his mind, nor by anyone else's words or actions, but solely by the thought which preceded it in a rigorously logical sequence. In other words, the causes of his mental states lie entirely within the rational processes of his own mind. Spinoza maintained that such engrossing forms of mental activity show the intellect at its most self-contained and independent. It is fully engaged in the project of developing its own potential and is least subject to external influences. While it is doing geometry, therefore, it is as autonomous as it is possible for a person's mind to be.

As for less intellectual pastimes, man can obtain a satisfying degree of autonomy in everyday life by trying to understand the hidden causes of his feelings and actions. Spinoza offered an analysis of psychology according to which the most pleasurable emotional states are those that are the least affected by external factors. To let oneself be cast down by things that are outside one's control, or even to be elated by them, is to lead a most unrewarding sort of life. We can, however, take command of our thoughts, emotions and desires to some extent by bringing them under the sway of reason. The way to do this is to uncover their causes, for by becoming conscious of what determines us to act in the way that we do, we can transform our mental states into active expressions of ourselves rather than mere effects of our environment. For example, by discovering the ultimate causes of my anger towards someone who has injured me, I can, according to Spinoza, turn the anger into something less disruptive and painful. The more I know about the circumstances which led to my injury, and which determine my response to it, the less inclined I shall be to blame everything on my enemy. Rational understanding will replace passion, and thus my mental state will become more tranquil and more like the autonomous exercise of reason that is involved in working out geometrical demonstrations.

Some people have compared Spinoza to Freud, whose psychotherapy similarly promised liberation through self-knowledge. Freud, however, would not have regarded geometry as particularly liberating, and might well have found some unflattering explanation for Spinoza's obsession with it. Another difference between the two is that Spinoza's ideal of rational understanding has more of a spiritual dimension. For Spinoza, to attain the deepest level of understanding of oneself and the world is to share's God's perspective, and thus to enjoy a taste of divine bliss. To comprehend phenomena in the purest rational way—i.e., to deduce the how and why of things with mathematical certainty—is not only to see them "from the point of view of eternity," as God does, but in some sense to become part of the eternal. Our "salvation, or blessedness, or freedom" lies in "the mind's intellectual love of God." And because we are ourselves part of nature, or God, this love is "part of the infinite love by which God loves himself."

Spinoza's attempts in his *Ethics* to deduce the how and why of things are extremely hard to follow in detail. Hegel inexplicably remarked that "the philosophy of Spinoza . . . is very simple, and on the whole easy to comprehend," but most readers are likely to sympathise with the character in a tale by Isaac Bashevis Singer who was still struggling with it after more than three decades. Dr Nahum Fischelson, a former librarian of the Warsaw synagogue in Singer's story, spent several hours a day on the *Ethics*, but the more he studied, "the more puzzling sentences, unclear passages, and cryptic remarks he found. Each sentence contained hints unfathomed by any of the students of Spinoza."

∞

IN SOME WAYS, Spinoza's work had as much in common with the Hellenistic philosophers of life as it had with the scientifically oriented philosophy of Descartes and other moderns. Like the ancient Epicureans, Stoics and Sceptics, Spinoza thought that one of the principal aims of philosophy was to overcome "disturbances of the mind" and deliver tranquillity.* He began his first work with these words:

> After experience had taught me that all the things which regularly occur in ordinary life are empty and futile . . . I resolved at last to try to find out whether there was anything which would be the true good . . . something which, once found and acquired, would continuously give me the greatest joy, to eternity.

Some twenty years earlier, Descartes had begun his *Meditations* with the following:

> Some years ago I was struck by the large number of falsehoods that I had accepted as true in my childhood, and by the highly doubtful nature of the whole edifice that I had subsequently based on them. I realized that it was necessary, once in the course of my life, to demolish everything completely and start again right from the foundations if I wanted to establish anything at all in the sciences.

The verbal similarity is striking, but so are the emotional differences. Descartes was beset by doubt; Spinoza was troubled by futility. Descartes wanted certainty, but Spinoza sought bliss.

---

* See *The Dream of Reason*, chapter 13.

Spinoza saw no need to address the radical doubts that Descartes raised and then attempted to dispel. Why bother to answer worries that nobody actually has? Yet he was by no means wholly uninterested in the topic of knowledge. He shared Descartes's concern with the relation between ideas and the physical world, and his dismissive attitude to the senses. Like Descartes, Spinoza believed that sensory perception gives us only confused and erroneous ideas of things. In order to get the sort of "adequate" ideas that are required for a God-like perspective on the world, it is necessary to focus on mathematical-style proofs that give a complete explanation for each phenomenon. According to Spinoza, it is "inadequate" ideas that are responsible not only for ignorance but also for much emotional suffering. As we have seen, a rational understanding of nature, and of the inevitability of everything in it, will help to defuse our debilitating passions.

Spinoza's impassive attitude to fate echoes the ancient Stoics. Descartes's ethical remarks also owed something to Stoicism, but Spinoza's debt to it was much larger. Some passages of his *Ethics* could almost have been written by Epictetus or Marcus Aurelius. "Human power," wrote Spinoza,

> is very limited and infinitely surpassed by the power of external causes. . . . Nevertheless, we shall bear calmly those things which happen to us . . . if we are conscious that we have done our duty, that the power we have could not have extended itself to the point where we could have avoided those things, and that we are a part of the whole of nature, whose order we follow.

Spinoza's conception of nature also recalls that of the Stoics, whose unified universe lacked any absolute divide between God and the world or between mind and matter. A further parallel lies in the Stoics' idea of an impulse towards self-preservation and self-assertion which is present throughout nature. Like Hobbes before him, Spinoza made this the centrepiece of his account of human behaviour.

Hobbes saw people as naturally selfish creatures who can lead a civilised existence only when they yield to an authority that has the power to keep the peace between them. Spinoza agreed with Hobbes's egoistic approach to morals and politics: he wrote that "the first and only foundation of virtue is the seeking of our own advantage." But Spinoza had a more sophisticated idea of what a person's best interests consist in, and this made his ethics far from selfish in the ordinary sense of the word. Hobbes, for example, held that each person aims simply at satisfying the desires to which his physiology subjects him. For Spinoza, on the other hand, man's deepest satisfaction lies in the rational understanding of God or nature. It is therefore in the pursuit of such lofty goals—and not in the gratification of base appetites—that one's own true advantage is to be found.

The fact that Spinoza had something concrete to say about what is ultimately good for man sets him apart from some of the later thinkers who echoed the gospel of toleration and freedom of expression that he had defended in his *Tractatus*. This gospel is often identified with John Stuart Mill (1806–1873), whose *On Liberty* was published nearly two centuries later. However, Mill's defence of diversity and toleration is in one sense incomplete. The main reason why he argued that everyone should be permitted as much latitude as is consistent with the liberty of others is that he believed such flexible arrangements would allow everyone to find happiness in his own way. Perhaps wisely, Mill had little further to say about what that happiness would consist in: Mill regarded liberty as desirable because he believed it would encourage diversity and experimentation in styles of living, and that this would speed the discovery of the best sort of life—whatever that might turn out to be. Spinoza, by contrast, thought he already knew what the best sort of life consists in. It is one that gives our higher faculties the exercise they naturally crave, which Spinoza argued was possible only in conditions of political and religious freedom.

Spinoza's eloquent plea for liberty was not, on the whole, what later thinkers found valuable in his writings. When his reputation eventually recovered from the stigma of atheism, it was the picture of "God, or Nature" presented in his *Ethics* that attracted attention. This picture meant different things to different people. The poets Coleridge and Shelley saw in it a religion of nature. The novelist George Eliot, who translated some of it into English before she turned to fiction, liked Spinoza for his vehement attacks on superstition. Marx liked him for what he took to be his materialistic account of the universe. Goethe could not say exactly what it was that he liked, but he knew that he was deeply moved by something or other:

> after I had searched everywhere in vain for a means of cultivating my strange personality, I finally happened upon this man's *Ethics*. I could not possibly give an account of what I read out of this work, or into it. Let me just say, I found something in it to calm my emotions, and it seemed to open a broad, free view over the physical and moral world.

Some of Spinoza's admirers were enamoured of his views even though they did not actually share them. A friend of Coleridge's recalled the poet clutching a copy of a book by Spinoza: "he kissed Spinoza's face in the title-page, and said, 'This book is a gospel to me.' But in less than a minute he added, 'his philosophy is nevertheless false.'"

Perhaps the most famous self-proclaimed disciple of Spinoza in the twentieth century was Einstein, who, when asked by a rabbi whether or not he believed in God, replied, "I believe in Spinoza's God, who reveals himself in the harmony of all being, not in a God who concerns himself with the fate and actions of men." Einstein was probably just being diplomatic when he answered the rabbi. Spinoza's God is, after all, a convenient deity for those who might more accurately be described as non-religious. The "religion" of Spinozism is in fact rather close to modern secularism. It insists that morality has nothing to do with the commands of a supremely powerful being, and that it does not require a priesthood or the threat of an unpleasant afterlife to sustain it. It rejects the idea of a personal God who created, cares about and occasionally even tinkers with the world. It dismisses the notion of the supernatural, and regards religious ceremonies as merely comforting or inspiring, if you like that sort of thing. It advocates freedom of thought in religious matters (though not, as we have seen, a total separation between church and state). And it places its faith in knowledge and understanding—rather than in faith itself—both to improve the circumstances of human life and to make that life more satisfying. The poet Heine, writing in the 1830s, seems to have glimpsed how far ahead of his times Spinoza was in this respect: "There is in Spinoza's writings a certain inexplicable atmosphere, as though one could feel a breeze of the future. Perhaps the spirit of the Hebrew prophets still rested on their late descendant."

What would this "God-intoxicated" man have made of his own intellectual descendants? They include many people who openly profess atheism, and even though atheism now carries no stigma in economically developed countries except the United States, it is hard to imagine Spinoza being altogether happy to embrace it. What were for him the most important qualities among those traditionally attributed to God are, in his philosophy, qualities of the universe itself. God is not fictitious; He is all around us. Spinoza's God is admittedly so different from anyone else's that a case can be made for saying that he was an atheist without realising it; but it does appear that he believed that he believed in God.

It is sometimes said that the birth of Judaism constituted an intellectual advance over most earlier religions because it reduced a panoply of gods to the one God of monotheism. On this way of thinking, Spinoza may be considered to have continued the work of his distant Hebrew ancestors by performing a further subtraction of the same sort, and reducing the duo of God and world to one.

# 4

## PHILOSOPHY FOR THE BRITISH
# *Locke*

JOHN LOCKE WAS A LATE STARTER IN PHILOSOPHY. HE WAS BORN IN THE same year as Spinoza, but his career as an original thinker was only just beginning when Spinoza died in 1677. Locke's first forty-five years were far from idle, though. He did a little teaching at Oxford; worked as an assistant in the chemistry laboratory of Robert Boyle; practiced medicine; became secretary to the Council of Trade, and had other government jobs; travelled as a diplomat; wrote a constitution for the American colony of Carolina, and got caught up in the intrigues of his patron and employer, the Earl of Shaftesbury, who was a leading politician in the court of Charles II.

It was not until Locke was fifty-seven that he published his main works, the *Essay Concerning Human Understanding, Two Treatises of Government* and the *Letter Concerning Toleration*, all of which came out in 1689. He wrote on many subjects in the course of his long life—monetary policy, the interpretation of scripture, education, and herbal medicine, among other things—but it is for the productions of 1689 that he is mainly remembered. They are sometimes described as among the most influential of the modern world. The *Second Treatise of Government* has been called an inspiration not only for the French Revolution but for the American Constitution and Declaration of Independence as well. Thomas Jefferson, the main author of the Declaration, wrote that "as to the general principles of liberty, and the

rights of man . . . the doctrines of Locke . . . and of Sidney [a British politician and writer] . . . may be considered as those generally approved by our
fellow citizens." Jefferson rather exaggerated the influence of Locke on his
fellow revolutionaries. Nowadays, British scholars are mainly sceptical of
the notion that Locke's ideas had much of an effect on the American Revolution; American writers tend to be fonder of the claim. But the respect
accorded to Locke's political writings by intellectuals is attested by the fact
that Jefferson's Royalist opponents invoked them, too.

Locke's *Essay* was even more renowned in many places. It was her-
alded by modern-minded thinkers in the eighteenth century, particularly
in France, as the philosophical counterpart to Newton's *Principia*, which
had been published in 1687. Newton and Locke were often pronounced
to be the twin prophets of the Enlightenment, of which the bible was the
French *Encyclopédie* (1751–1772). Jean d'Alembert, one of the editors of the
*Encyclopédie*, expressed the confidence of the age when he announced that
"the true system of the world has been recognised, developed and per-
fected." This "true system" consisted above all of the physics of Newton
and the philosophy of Locke, particularly Locke's account of the workings
of the mind.

In later centuries, Locke's appeal became less international. He is now
sometimes seen as the founder of a movement whose ideas are peculiarly
appropriate for the British, perhaps for much of the English-speaking
world, but certainly not for the French or Germans, whose intellectual
interests have often diverged from those of their English-speaking col-
leagues. Voltaire's descendants today do not usually share their forefa-
ther's high opinion of Locke, nor the conviction he expressed, when
contrasting Locke and Descartes, of the general superiority of the British
way of doing things. Hegel noted disapprovingly that "there is no trace of
speculation" in Locke's works. Unlike the Germans, the British cannot
really tell the difference between elevated philosophy and mere science,
Hegel suggested. Following his example, many German thinkers since
the early nineteenth century have barely recognised Locke as a philosopher at all.

An essay by a twentieth-century scholar neatly summed up the intellectual tradition of which Locke was the first great exemplar:

It is marked by a tendency to stay close to the common sense shared by ordinary people, to avoid raising paradox into profound truth, to accept without much fuss the fact of an external world that our senses tell us something about, and to grant reason the role of supreme arbiter. . . . [I]t has generally been responsive to new events in science. [It] is also a mode of philosophy that thrives on communication and discussion, does not expect that truth will come in a flash (if it ever comes), and has a low estimate of the claims of isolated genius and of speculative brooding on deep matters. It treasures good style, a certain vivacity of mind, humor, and the gratifications of social life, combined with a sense of responsibility for the welfare of all.

Since the late nineteenth century, this philosophical cast of mind has been known as British empiricism. Early hints of it can be found in the works of William of Ockham (c. 1285–1349) and Hobbes; later examples include Hume in the eighteenth century, John Stuart Mill in the nineteenth, and Bertrand Russell and A. J. Ayer in the twentieth. But it is Locke who most typifies the down-to-earth and commonsensical virtues that are now seen as quintessentially British. He was even interested in gardening.

On the surface Locke's writings are plainer and simpler than those of many other philosophers, which is one main reason why they quickly won him a popular audience. There is, however, much dispute about what exactly his simple message was. Gilbert Ryle, an Oxford philosopher who died in 1976, recalled a flippant conversation he once had about Locke with Bertrand Russell. The two men agreed that "Locke made a bigger difference to the whole intellectual climate of mankind than anyone had done since Aristotle." But what precisely did he do? wondered Ryle.

Russell . . . suggested, on the spur of the moment, an answer which dissatisfied me. He said, "Locke was the spokesman of Common Sense." Almost without thinking I retorted impatiently, "I think Locke invented Common Sense." To which Russell rejoined, "By God, Ryle, I believe you are right. No one ever had Common Sense before John Locke—and no one but Englishmen have ever had it since."

Ryle's considered view was that the value of Locke's *Essay* lay in the way that it "teaches us how to be sensible or reasonable in our adoption, retention and rejection of opinions." The verdict of an American philosopher, C. S. Peirce, was terser and more telling: "Locke's grand work was substantially this: Men must think for themselves."

If Locke had one main message, then that is indeed what it was. As we shall see, his attack on the notion of "innate" knowledge in the first part of the *Essay*—perhaps the most famous part of the book—is in no small part an assault on the lazy acceptance of received opinions. In the rest of the *Essay*, Locke repeatedly argues that one should avoid pinning one's faith on the opinions of others: "there cannot be a more dangerous thing to rely on . . . since there is much more Falsehood and Errour amongst Men than Truth and Knowledge." Instead he counsels each person always to weigh up the evidence for himself and to apportion his degree of belief accordingly:

> the Mind, if it will proceed rationally, ought to examine all the grounds
> of Probability and see how they make more or less, for or against any
> probable Proposition, before it assents to or dissents from it, and, upon
> a due ballancing the whole, reject or receive it, with a more or less firm
> assent, proportionably to the preponderance of the greater grounds of
> Probability on one side or the other.

This now sounds like obvious advice, and rather wordily put, for Locke could be long-winded. But it appears that nobody before him took such pains to spell out how probability can be used as a guide to life, or why it ought to be.

In questions of religion, Locke's leading idea was that theological doctrines must be answerable to the court of reason: "*Reason* must be our last Judge and Guide in every Thing." He acknowledged that some truths, such as the resurrection of the dead, are "*Above Reason*," in the sense that they are revealed to us by God and so do not need to be proved. But he held that if any supposed revelation were to go so far as to contradict what reason plainly tells us, then it is reason which must be given the final word. For man's intellect is a gift from God, and God would want us to use it. In a tract entitled *The Reasonableness of Christianity*, which was published in 1695, Locke argued that nothing in the scriptures was contrary to reason, and that God had generously expressed himself in terms that can be understood even by "the poor of this World, and the bulk of Mankind."

Locke's rationalistic approach to religion did not go as far as that of some of his contemporaries, such as John Toland, whose *Christianity Not Mysterious*, was published the next year. This twenty-five-year-old author was condemned in parliament and threatened with arrest in Ireland for asserting that doctrines which were "above reason" were as suspicious as those which were contrary to reason, and that Christianity was better off without them. Although Locke did not arouse nearly so much ire as Toland, he was regularly accused by conservative churchmen of indirectly encouraging atheism in various ways, and of not having enough to say about the Trinity.

Still, Locke was a pillar of orthodoxy when compared with Spinoza. Locke espoused the traditional idea that God is a king-like ruler of the universe, that the promise of God's punishment or reward after death is the foundation of morality, that miracles occur and are the mark of a revelation from God, and that most of the stories in scripture are literally true—all of which Spinoza denied. On the question of religious toleration, however, Locke usually argued for much the same sort of freedom of belief that Spinoza had defended: "men cannot be forced to be saved," he wrote in his *Letter Concerning Toleration*, "they must be left to their own consciences." Locke was not prepared to grant full political rights to every sort of believer and non-believer, though. He was suspicious of Catholics, because, like Hobbes, he held that they owe their first allegiance to a foreign power, namely the pope. He was also not inclined to extend toleration to atheists (including polytheists, who counted as atheists for Locke), because he held that they cannot be trusted to keep their promises or stand by any solemn oaths. Indeed, atheism "ought to shut a Man out of all Sober and Civil society." Nevertheless, he maintained that on the whole people should have the liberty to make up their own minds on religious topics.

In matters of morality, too, Locke argued that men must think for themselves. They should not blindly accept the practices and standards of the day, because "moral Principles require Reasoning and Discourse, and some Exercise of the Mind, to discover the certainty of their Truth." Neither should they unthinkingly accept the authority of their rulers. Locke's *Second Treatise of Government* stressed the right of the people to use their own judgement in weighing up the legitimacy of a government. In extreme circumstances, the people should overthrow the state authorities: "the community perpetually retains a supreme power of saving themselves from the attempts and designs of any body, even of their legislators, whenever they shall be so foolish, or so wicked, as to lay and carry on designs against the liberties and properties of the subject."

This idea was particularly topical in Britain when it was published in 1689. It retrospectively justified the overthrow of the Catholic King James II in 1688 and his replacement by William of Orange. In the preface to the *Treatises*, Locke wrote that he hoped his arguments

> are sufficient to establish the throne of our great restorer, our present King William . . . and to justify to the world, the people of England, whose love of their just and natural rights, with their resolution to preserve them, saved the nation when it was on the very brink of slavery and ruin.

They were in fact sufficient to do more than that. After his death, the arguments of the *Second Treatise* established Locke as the pre-eminent intellectual defender of the right to rebel. A century later, his name was invoked in the struggles of the French people against their rulers and of the Americans against the imperial British.

Locke would have been aghast to discover that ideas from his book were later used against the British colonial regime, in which he himself played an enthusiastic part. He would have had more sympathy for the use that many colonist preachers had earlier made of that book's theory of property, namely to justify taking land away from the Native Americans. Cynics might say—though there would be no way to decide the issue, even if one could ask him—that it was partly in order to rationalise such appropriation that Locke, who profited from colonial enterprises, formulated the theory in the first place. According to his theory, "Whatsoever . . . [a man] . . . removes out of the state that nature has provided and left it in, he hath mixed his labour with, and joined to it something that is his own, and thereby makes it his property." Because the colonists did more to cultivate American land than the natives did, it followed, according to Locke, that the land really belonged to them. There is little reason to suppose that he would have enjoyed seeing this reasoning turned against the British.

Some of Locke's works, particularly his defence of religious tolerance, helped to inspire the development of liberalism; but it would be a mistake to think of him as some sort of contemporary liberal in seventeenth-century garb. The fact is that Locke was in some respects not even a liberal by the standards of his own times, let alone later ones. For example, the constitution which he wrote for Carolina in 1669 advocated an extreme form of feudalism that had long ago died out in England and which was not found in any other American colony. Serfdom was to be hereditary, according to Locke's plans. All the descendants of a serf were to be serfs forever, to be bought and sold with the land they worked on, and with no right of appeal to anyone beyond their owners.

A set of proposals on poverty that Locke wrote in 1697 for the Board of Trade (of which he was then a commissioner) makes equally unsettling reading. Locke regarded the poor as largely responsible for their own miserable state and the unemployed as either merely lazy or else parasites. In his proposals, he invented many Draconian regulations and new punishments for the jobless. He said that the first step in finding work for them should be "a restraint of their debauchery . . . by the suppression of superfluous brandy shops and unneccessary alehouses." Fortunately, his harsh plans were never implemented. Most other members of the Board of Trade believed that unemployment was caused not by debauchery but by a shortage of jobs.

As we have seen, Locke was something of a political Hobbist in his youth. In 1660–61, he had defended a conservative authoritarianism that sharply contrasts with the revolutionary sentiments of his later *Treatises*. "No one," he wrote, "can have a greater respect and veneration for authority than I. . . . [A] general freedom is but a general bondage. . . ." He added, "All the freedom I can wish my country or myself is to enjoy the protection of those laws which the prudence and providence of our ancestors established. . . ." Plainly something changed by the time the *Treatises* were written. But was it Locke's fundamental views that altered, or just the English political scene? With the monarchy only recently restored, Locke had seen instability as the greatest threat facing his country, and so had advocated obedience and a respect for existing institutions. Later, however, he came to regard Charles II as a worse threat, and began to see the point of rebellion. If the events of the 1680s somehow turned Locke into a man whom modern liberals can more easily admire, the effect was suspiciously short-lived. There is no trace of any such transformation in his writings thereafter. The Locke who wrote the Draconian proposals on poverty in 1697 is very much the same Locke who wrote the cruel Carolina constitution nearly thirty years earlier.

IT WAS NOT until some while after his death that people came to regard Locke as much of a political thinker at all. This is not just because the *Treatises* were published anonymously (it was only in a codicil to his will that Locke acknowledged having written them). His immediate fame, both at home and abroad, rested on the views of human knowledge and the nature of the mind expressed in his *Essay Concerning Human Understanding*. This easily outshone everything else that he did, and it is doubtful whether a wider knowledge of the authorship of the *Treatises* could have dimmed it.

The *Essay* was rightly seen as an ambitious elaboration and extension of the "new philosophy" of Galileo, Descartes, Newton and the Royal Society. One aspect of this world-picture which particularly captured the imagination of laymen and poets was Locke's version of the distinction between physical qualities such as size and shape and apparently subjective ones, such as colour. It is no exaggeration to say that Locke made many readers change their view of all the scenery around them. In 1712 the poet and essayist Joseph Addison wrote,

> our souls are at present delightfully lost and bewildered in a pleasing delusion and we walk about like the enchanted hero of a romance who sees beautiful castles, woods, and meadows, and at the same time hears the warbling of birds and the purling of streams; but upon the finishing of some secret spell the fantastic scene breaks up, and the disconsolate knight finds himself on a barren heath or in a solitary desert. . . . I

have here supposed that my reader is acquainted with that great modern discovery, which is at present universally acknowledged by all the inquirers into natural philosophy: namely, that light and colours, as apprehended by the imagination, are only ideas in the mind, and not qualities that have any existence in matter.

The *Essay* was at first notorious and exciting—there were attempts to ban the reading of it at Oxford—because it was part of the challenge to Aristotelian scholasticism that was being mounted by mechanistic science. Indeed, it was part of something even larger. With its focus on thinking for oneself, on questioning past wisdom, and in its outspoken distaste for the pseudo-logical quibbling that still lingered in European universities, the *Essay* played a role in helping to erase the medieval world-picture.

∞

LOCKE'S FATHER owned some land and a few houses in Pensford, near Bristol, where Locke grew up. He added to the income from this small estate (of which Locke inherited a part in 1661) by working as a lawyer. He had also served as a cavalry captain on the parliamentary side during the civil war, and it was through the influence of his father's former commander that the young Locke managed to get a place at Westminster, which was then the best school in England. The education at the school consisted largely of Latin and Greek, with some Hebrew for especially bright pupils such as Locke. Westminster led to Oxford, where Locke was subjected to the traditional scholastic curriculum of rhetoric, grammar, Greek, geometry and moral philosophy. He did not enjoy it.

Many of the remarks in Locke's *Essay* show his distaste for intellectual life at Oxford. People fill their talk with an "abundance of empty unintelligible noises and jargon, especially in moral Matters," he wrote. Scholastic learning is largely "*learned Gibberish*." Its practitioners "cover their Ignorance, with a curious and unexplicable Web of perplexed Words." Locke was not merely bored and annoyed by traditional learning. He thought that by modelling themselves on the medieval schoolmen and copying their narrow prejudices, the academic establishment of his day was wasting its chance to contribute to human progress.

The medieval scholastics were, he wrote, "no wiser, nor more useful than their Neighbours; and brought but small advantage to humane Life or the Societies, wherein they lived." It was instead to "the unscholastick Statesmen, that the Governments of the world owed their Peace, Defence and Liberties; and from the illiterate and contemned Mechanick (a Name of Disgrace) that they received the improvements of useful Arts." These were the sorts of people whom Locke wanted to emulate. So, when he graduated in 1658, he decided to devote himself as much as possible to practical affairs, especially to science in the form of the new "mechanical philosophy" and to medicine.

While officially teaching the traditional curriculum of Greek, rhetoric and moral philosophy at his Oxford college, Locke collaborated with Boyle, who had a laboratory in Oxford and became a close friend. Locke also privately studied and practised medicine. And in 1665 he accepted a job as secretary on a diplomatic mission to persuade the elector of Brandenburg not to side with the Dutch in England's war against them. Locke may have been personally chosen for this task by King Charles II, who had been staying in Oxford to shelter from the Great Plague of London. He seems to have done well, since he was offered two further diplomatic posts when he returned from his mission. But Locke declined them because he was resolved to become a teacher of medicine.

He had not reckoned with the Oxford medical faculty. It refused him a doctorate—as it did Thomas Sydenham, later renowned as "the English Hippocrates"—because he had not followed the prescribed course of study. This ruled out Locke's chosen career, but fortunately something even better came along. Locke had set up a pharmacy with an Oxford doctor, David Thomas, which by chance brought him into contact with Anthony Ashley Cooper, a member of the king's privy council who was later made Lord Chancellor. Ashley was impressed by Locke and invited him to join his London household as personal physician and secretary, which he did in 1667. This move propelled Locke into the company of livelier minds than he would have met as an Oxford lecturer.

Locke's occupations in London reflected the breadth of Ashley's interests and the range of his own abilities. In addition to his domestic duties, which included supervising an operation on Ashley's liver and taking charge of the education of his son, Locke wrote briefing papers for his employer on political and economic topics of the day. One of the first of these argued against the use of legislation to control interest rates. Another, which was apparently intended to be shown to the king, was about religious toleration. This troublesome subject occupied Locke throughout his life: the main issue at the time was how much freedom should be allowed to Protestant Nonconformists in their style of worship. Ashley was one of the most prominent defenders of such toleration, and Locke the most eloquent.

One of the first of Locke's new associates among London men of science was Sydenham, whom Locke sometimes accompanied on his rounds. Sydenham was posthumously recognised as one of the founders of modern clinical medicine; among his innovations were the use of laudanum and the identification of scarlet fever. He was also among the first to use iron in the treatment of anemia and to advocate quinine for malaria. Yet the medical establishment of his day hated him, and it is not hard to see why. Sydenham ridiculed most of his fellow doctors. He condemned their theories as unfounded and their treatments as ineffective. Like the followers of the ancient "empiricist" schools of medicine, he claimed to base his own practice on plain experience and direct observation, and never to let himself be "deceived by idle speculations":

> The function of a physician [is the] industrious investigation of the history of diseases, and of the effect of remedies, as shown by the only true teacher, experience. . . . True practice consists in the observations of nature. . . .

Sydenham liked to observe the properties of a disease, the circumstances in which it flourished and the treatments that were most effective against it. Nowadays this approach sounds like mere common sense, but it was unorthodox at the time. The more usual technique was to focus on the patient rather than the disease and to prescribe a treatment based on the peculiarities of the person rather than the nature of his illness. Sydenham's novel view that diseases are specific entities requiring specific remedies was supported by his studies of the relationship between environmental conditions and patterns of illness—the times of the year when malaria was most prevalent, for example. Locke sometimes helped him to gather the data for these studies.

Such epidemiological surveys were typical of the sort of "natural history" pursued by the Royal Society, which Locke joined in 1668. An ode to the society spoke of "the riches which do hoarded . . . lie / In Nature's endless treasury"—riches that its members sought to catalogue and investigate. What united the rather diverse membership of the society, which included not only men who would now be regarded as scientists but also Christopher Wren, Samuel Pepys and John Dryden, was a belief that fresh experience was a better guide to life than old volumes and the word of authority. The society's motto, *Nullius in verba*, may loosely be translated as "Look for yourself. Don't take anyone else's word for it." Locke played his part in the society's day-to-day business; he was on the committee that supervised new experiments. But his main contribution to the Royal Society was to articulate the philosophy that lay behind it.

That philosophy was laid out in his *Essay Concerning Human Understanding*, which had its origins in a discussion club that met in Locke's rooms at Ashley's London house in 1671. Ashley himself, Sydenham, John Mapletoft (another doctor), James Tyrrell (a political writer), Locke and maybe others attended the meetings, where the talk ranged over theology, morality and politics as well as science and philosophy. One day the club was discussing the principles of morality, when, according to Locke, they found themselves

> quickly at a stand, by the Difficulties that rose on every side. After we had a while puzzled our selves . . . it came into my Thoughts . . . that, before we set ourselves upon Enquiries of that Nature, it was necessary to examine our own Abilities and see what Objects our Understandings were, or were not, fitted to deal with.

Locke set about writing such an examination, which he worked at for many years before it was published in 1689 as the *Essay*. By explaining how the mind works, and thus what its limits are, it was intended to shed light on all types of enquiry, from the scientific investigations that most interested the Royal Society to the moral and political topics that then preoccupied Ashley and his household.

Ashley had held office under Charles II ever since the restoration of the monarchy in 1660. He had not, however, always been a supporter of the crown. After briefly favouring Charles I in the civil war, he went over to the side of parliament and later helped Cromwell to power. But he soon became dissatisfied with Cromwell and in 1660 played a part in installing Charles II. The grateful new king appointed him to his privy council and then to a succession of posts culminating in the Lord Chancellorship in 1672. Almost as soon as he had been appointed to this powerful job, however, the Earl of Shaftesbury (as Ashley had then become) grew suspicious of Charles II and started to turn against him as well.

His suspicions were well-founded. In 1670 Charles had made a secret agreement with his Catholic cousin, Louis XIV of France. Under the terms of the deal Charles received large sums of money in exchange for a promise to declare himself a Catholic at some convenient future moment. Charles was not in fact particularly pious—he never got round to keeping his promise—but he admired the absolutist style of Catholic monarchy in France, and he wanted the money. Shaftesbury and his circle rightly feared that Charles intended to copy the theocratic authoritarianism of Louis XIV, who vigorously persecuted religious minorities, and in effect ruled France by personal decree. When Charles's heir to the throne, his brother James, who had secretly become a Catholic, married another Catholic in 1673, Shaftesbury attacked the marriage and was dismissed from his government posts. He became the leader of the opposition to the king and his Catholic absolutist ambitions. Locke watched this political drama closely from the wings. How active a part he played in it is unknown, but the scope of royal power and of religious freedom became central topics in his political works.

In 1675 Locke decided to leave London, ostensibly for medical reasons. He had always suffered from the foulness of the London air, and the atmosphere was certainly becoming unhealthy for Shaftesbury's close associates. In 1676 Shaftesbury was imprisoned and spent a year confined to the Tower of London. Locke, meanwhile, was expanding his philosophical horizons in France. He stayed first in Montpellier, where he became friendly with several eminent doctors and learned French. Moving to Paris, he began a close study of the works of Descartes. The French government had at the time forbidden the teaching of Cartesian philosophy in schools and universities, but private discussions were allowed. Locke also got to know several followers of Gassendi, a pioneering advocate of the "mechanical philosophy" who sought to reconcile Christianity with elements of ancient Epicureanism. The views of the Gassendists influenced him as he continued to work on his *Essay*, particularly their emphasis on the role of sensory experience in the formation of knowledge.

When Locke returned to England in 1679, the country was full of talk of a "Popish plot." Catholic priests, it was said, planned to kill the king, install his Catholic brother on the throne and foment a massacre of Protestants. This groundless rumour stemmed from the allegations of Titus Oates, a twisted former parson with a grudge against the Jesuits. It was fanned by memories of the Gunpowder Plot and the unexplained murder of a magistrate before whom Oates had sworn his testimony. The resulting wave of anti-Catholic feeling was useful to Shaftesbury and his allies, who exploited it in a campaign to have James excluded from the royal succession. When this campaign failed, Shaftesbury became even more openly rebellious. Dryden, the poet laureate, depicted the struggle between the king's supporters and those of Shaftesbury in his *Absalom and Achitophel* (1681). Shaftesbury—barely disguised as Achitophel—did not come out of it well:

> *A name to all succeeding ages cursed:*
> *For close designs and crooked counsels fit.*

Shaftesbury's worst sin, in Royalist eyes, was to hold that it can be right in certain circumstances for subjects to oppose the will of their king. That would be disastrous, they argued, in a Hobbesian spirit, because once royal authority had been overturned, chaos would follow:

> *For who can be secure of private right,*
> *If sovereign sway may be dissolved by might?*

*Nor is the people's judgement always true:*
*The most may err as grossly as the few;*
. . . . . . . . . . . . . . . . . . . . . . . . . . . .
*If they may give and take whene'er they please,*
*Not kings alone (the Godhead's images)*
*But government itself at length must fall*
*To nature's state, where all have right to all.*

The case against rebellion was made at length in *Patriarcha: The Natural Power of Kings Defended Against the Unnatural Liberty of the People*, a tract published in 1680 by some of the king's supporters. Its author, Sir Robert Filmer, had been dead for over twenty-five years, but was now disinterred as a useful provider of propaganda. Filmer had written Royalist pamphlets during the civil war, including *The Necessity of the Absolute Power of All Kings: And in Particular, of the King of England*. His *Patriarcha* was never published in his lifetime, apparently because even the then-king, Charles I, thought it went too far.

Filmer argued that the authority of a father over his family, and the authority of a king over his people, are divinely ordained and come to much the same thing. Adam was the first king, appointed by God and granted absolute power over his descendants and all earthly goods. This power was passed on from eldest son to eldest son, or so Filmer—himself the eldest son of a landowner—maintained, and subsequent legitimate kings thus owe their status to their alleged descent from Adam. (As Locke later pointed out, the fact that everyone is supposedly a descendant of Adam is rather a problem for this theory.) Filmer denied that people are in any sense born free and equal, either as children or as subjects. To rebel against a legitimate king was as unthinkable as to rebel against one's father.

This defence of patriarchy, primogeniture and the divine right of kings was so extreme that it backfired against the Royalists. Instead of subduing their enemies, it inspired them: its indefensible arguments focussed the minds of the king's opponents and prompted several vigorous defences of political freedom. The most famous and influential of these reactions to Filmer is Locke's *Second Treatise of Government*, to which we shall turn in a moment. But it was not the first. Another tract in the same vein, which Locke read before writing his own, which is strikingly similar to his, and which has now been all but forgotten, was *Patriarcha non monarcha*, by Locke's close friend, James Tyrrell. Many of the political ideas that are commonly thought of as Lockean could just as well be described as Tyrrellesque, though Locke often developed Tyrrell's themes and took them to more radical conclusions.

Locke never admitted to Tyrrell that he was the author of the anonymous *Treatises*. Locke was often secretive, and with good reason, given the dangerousness of the times and the company he kept. In 1681, for example, Stephen College, a fellow supporter of Shaftesbury, was hanged for treason. Locke was watched for a time by the king's spies, and at one point the king himself demanded that he be expelled from his Oxford job. But the danger to Locke had passed by the time the two *Treatises* were published, and anyway he trusted Tyrrell. Embarrassment appears to have been the reason for Locke's silence. It seems that some of the main ideas in a book that is, among other things, one of the most influential works on the theory of property were themselves stolen property.

∞

IF RULERS do not owe their authority to divine right, where does political power come from? This is the question with which Locke began his *Second Treatise*. Unless we are prepared to admit the depressing conclusion that "all government in the world is the product only of force and violence, and . . . men live together by no other rules but that of beasts," we must find some other source of legitimate political authority, wrote Locke. The answer he proposed is a form of social contract. By making a pact to join together and form a community, men lay the foundations of political power, which is then exercised on their behalf by a ruler or government. The authority of a ruler thus derives from a type of contract freely entered into by his subjects, and is neither imposed by God nor based on brute force.

Traces of the notion of a social contract can be found scattered throughout the history of Western thought. Thus Antiphon, an Athenian teacher in the fifth century BC, said that "the laws of men are fixed by agreement," and the character of Glaucon in Plato's *Republic* explained that people "determine that it is for their profit to make a compact with one another neither to commit nor to suffer injustice, and . . . this is the beginning of legislation and of covenants between men. . . ." The Greeks seem to have thought that before such covenants were first made, life was brutal and solitary, and people banded together for protection against animals. According to a version of this tale from the first century BC,

> the first men to be born, they say, led an undisciplined and bestial life, setting out one by one to secure their sustenance and taking for their food both the tenderest herbs and the fruits of wild trees. Then, since they were attacked by the wild beasts, they came to each other's aid, being instructed by expediency, and when gathered together in this way by reason of their fear, they gradually came to recognize their mutual characteristics.

After this, so the story goes, they learned to communicate and started making the agreements that are the foundation of morality and political life.

In medieval times, the idea of a tacit contract between a ruler and those he governs arose in the eleventh century out of a dispute about the respective powers of popes and secular sovereigns. Pope Gregory VII decreed that if an emperor abused his position, a pope could depose him, which gave rise to the idea that although a pope's authority is absolute, that of a secular ruler depends on a kind of contract or trust. Thus one outspoken defender of papal power, Manegold of Lautenbach—whom even the sober *Catholic Encyclopedia* calls rude and fanatical—compared secular rulers to swineherds, who may summarily be dismissed if they fail to do their jobs. Nobody needs to obey a secular tyrant if he breaks the implicit trust to which he owes his authority, wrote Manegold: "is it not clear that he deservedly falls from the dignity entrusted to him and that the people stand free of his lordship and subjection, when he has been evidently the first to break the compact for whose sake he was appointed?" In the succeeding three centuries, this idea was endorsed by many philosophers who wrote about politics, including John of Salisbury (c. 1115–1180), St Thomas Aquinas (1224/5–1274) and William of Ockham.

The social contract was thus fairly familiar by the time Hobbes, Locke and Rousseau came to develop their theories on the subject. It is worth noting, though, that there are really two distinct elements in the broad idea of a social contract: an agreement between people to form a society; and an agreement or tacit trust between such a society on the one hand and its ruler or government on the other (let us call the latter a "ruler's contract"). The Greeks on the whole focussed on social contracts in the first sense, as did Hobbes and Rousseau. But medieval writers were mostly concerned with rulers' contracts, which neither Hobbes nor Rousseau believed in. For Hobbes, as we have seen, once a community had been formed, it transferred all its political powers to a ruler and did not retain any right to dismiss him. A Hobbesian ruler had unconditional power, just like Manegold's pope. Rousseau had no place for ruler's contracts for the quite different reason that in his utopian version of society, the people are somehow to govern themselves.

Locke mixed the two forms of contract. According to him, when people join together to form a political society, they make an explicit agreement (or "compact") with one another. The rulers or governments who are then chosen by the people hold their authority as trustees: although there is no explicit ruler's contract, they can, like Manegold's swineherd, be dismissed if they abuse this trust.

One problem with this tale is that it seems to be a fantasy. It is simply not true that governments are on the whole, let alone always, based on any sort of agreement. As David Hume later objected: "Almost all the governments which exist at present, or of which there remains any record in story, have been founded originally, either on usurpation or conquest, or both, without any pretence of a fair consent or voluntary subjection of the people." In 1887 Nietzsche put a similar point more colourfully:

some pack of blond beasts of prey, a conqueror and master race which, organized for war and with the ability to organize, unhesitatingly lays its terrible claws upon a populace perhaps tremendously superior in numbers but still formless and nomad. That is, after all, how the "state" began on earth: I think that sentimentalism which would have it begin with a "contract" has been disposed of. He who can command, he who is by nature "master," he who is violent in act and bearing— what has he to do with contracts!

Even if Nietzsche's pack of vicious blond beasts is as fanciful as Locke's gentler alternative, the fact remains that real social contracts are few and far between. Some defenders of Locke have tried to argue that this does not matter because he never intended his theory as an account of what actually happened. But this is not so. Locke considered and rejected the objection that "there are no instances to be found in story of a company of men . . . that met together, and in this way began and set up a government." He replied, unconvincingly, that this merely reflects the fact that the earliest stages of each society's history are so brief and inconsequential that few people thought them worth recording. Besides, he continued, government tends to come before the invention of writing, and by the time people get round to composing their histories, they have forgotten what happened.

Still, Locke added, there are in fact a few known episodes of the birth of government through explicit contract: he cites the founding of Rome and of Venice. But such cases, even if they are historical, just raise another problem. For even if the distant forefathers of a society did sign up to a social contract, why should this remain binding on their descendants? As Hume put it: "being so ancient, and being obliterated by a thousand changes of government and princes, it cannot now be supposed to retain any authority today." Locke should have been the first to notice this difficulty, because much of his own *First Treatise* is devoted to establishing that even if the biblical Adam had been awarded his authority by God, it would be impossible to tell who his heirs are now, and thus to verify the claims of any present ruler. The theory of political legitimacy espoused by Locke in his *Second Treatise* falls victim to arguments put forward in his *First*.

Still, it is possible to rescue the gist of Locke's idea by stripping it of its historical pretensions. The social contract can be cast in a hypothetical form and construed not as an account of what anybody actually did agree to, but of what they would agree to if they were fair and rational.

This was the approach taken by Kant in the eighteenth century and by more recent political thinkers such John Rawls (1921–2002). Thus Kant explained that

> we need by no means assume that this contract . . . actually exists as a *fact*. . . . It is . . . merely an *idea* of reason, which nonetheless has undoubted practical reality; for it can oblige every legislator to frame his laws in such a way that they could have been produced by the united will of a whole nation, and to regard each subject . . . as if he had consented within the general will. This is the test of the rightfulness of every public law.

Similarly, Rawls aimed to establish a set of principles of justice by asking us to imagine a group of people who come together to agree on the distribution of wealth, liberties, opportunities and other basic goods. We are to suppose that they are self-interested, rational and reasonably knowledgeable about the world, but are behind a "veil of ignorance" as to "how the various alternatives will affect their own particular case." The point of this stipulation may be seen by considering the example of a birthday cake. Suppose you are cutting it up to be divided among a group of people including yourself. If you do not know which slice you will receive, there is not much point in making one slice bigger than the others in the hope of eating it yourself. So the result of this "veil of ignorance" at the kitchen table is fair shares for all. Rawls called his imaginary convocation "the original position," and noted that it "is a purely hypothetical situation. Nothing resembling it need ever take place. . . ." On this version of a Lockean social contract, the rules and other arrangements of a society may be justified by reference to what could reasonably have been agreed to in such an imaginary "original position."

Locke began the main argument of his *Second Treatise* by describing what he calls the "state of nature," which plays a role similar to that of Rawls's "original position," except that it purports to be the situation in which people actually find themselves before they form a mature political society. Like Hobbes, Locke thought that the Native Americans of his own time largely still lived in such a state, and much of his account was inspired by contemporary books about them. Locke had nearly two hundred travel narratives in his library, most of them describing trips to America by European explorers, though (like Hobbes) he was selective in what he gleaned from them, and seems to have ignored any aspect of Native American life that did not fit his theories. He maintained, for example, that the Native Americans were lazy and ineffective in cultivating land, that they did not hold land privately but only for collective use, and that they developed no stable forms of government. All of this was contradicted by evidence available to him, but it sat more comfortably with his defence of colonial appropriation. If he had admitted that the Native Americans did sometimes make good use of their land, it would have been harder to justify taking it away from them.

As we have seen in the discussion of Hobbes, Locke explicitly held that moral rules have some sort of validity in the state of nature, even if its brutish inhabitants take no notice of them: "the state of nature has a law of nature to govern it, which obliges everyone." Locke added that

> reason, which is that law, teaches all mankind who will but consult it that, being all equal and independent, no one ought to harm another in his life, health, liberty or possessions: for men being all the workmanship of one omnipotent, and infinitely wise maker . . . they are his property . . . made to last during his, not one another's pleasure.

The main reason why people choose to leave the state of nature and unite into societies is the "enjoyment of their properties in peace and safety." In theory they already have rights to some property under the terms of the law of nature, according to Locke, but they are unlikely to be able to enforce these rights effectively by themselves. So they make a trade. In exchange for the protection of a government that is entrusted to make and enforce laws on their behalf, they give up their natural entitlement to take the law of nature into their own hands and privately punish those who steal from them. It may be wondered how Locke and Hobbes would explain the fact that the Native Americans allegedly never got around to making this trade. They would presumably say that the Americans weren't clever enough to see that it was in their own interests to form governments.

More enlightened people who are in the state of nature are not, how-

ever, free to set up just any form of government: the law of nature sets
limits to what they may do, according to Locke. For example, they cannot
choose to let the legislative body have absolute and arbitrary power over
their lives, because "nobody can transfer to another more power than he
has in himself, and nobody has an absolute arbitrary power over himself,
or over any other, to destroy his own life, or take away the life or property
of another." This explains why the people may resist overambitious rulers, such as, in the eyes of Locke and Shaftesbury, the dictatorial king of
France. A ruler's legitimate powers derive solely from those which God laid
down for man's benefit in the state of nature, and which the people pass
on to him in trust. He cannot be given any more, even if he is the king
of France, because the people do not have any more to give. (The code-
name Locke used for the manuscript of his *Second Treatise* was *de morbo
Gallico*—the "French disease," a medical term for syphilis. He regarded
authoritarian monarchy as a similarly noxious French malady.)

When God made the world, he gave it to all "mankind in common,"
Locke wrote, citing the Psalms. How, then, does man in the state of nature
come to have any right to private property? As we have seen, Rousseau
regarded the invention of private property as on the whole a regrettable
development that is to blame for many of the ills of life. Locke, by contrast,
thought it was a wonderful thing, which God invented so that the fruits of
the earth could be made useful to mankind.

Given that God provided deer and other creatures for people to eat,
there must be some way for a man who kills one to appropriate it for himself and his family. After all, if the carcass belonged to everyone equally,
it would feed nobody, because it would be torn to shreds by all the com-
peting claimants. According to Locke, when a deer runs free—or an apple
hangs unplucked on a tree, or a piece of land lies untilled—it belongs
to all in common, i.e., nobody. But as soon as anyone has expended his
labour on making it useful, and thereby "added something . . . more than
nature . . . had done," it thereby becomes his.

This theory has some consequences that may seem a little odd. It seems
to imply that if you take the trouble to pick an acorn from a tree, then the
acorn is yours, but if it just falls into your pocket, it isn't. A more serious
problem concerns how much your labour entitles you to. Locke answered

that you must not take such a greedy portion of the fruits of the earth that they will go bad before you can use them up. This is because "nothing was made by God for man to spoil or destroy."

That, at any rate, is how things worked in the state of nature. But as civilisations advanced and populations grew, matters became more complicated, especially with the introduction of money. When man decided to treat, say, pieces of gold as exchangeable for goods that were more immediately useful, such as food, he thereby invested value in something that did not spoil, and which could therefore safely be hoarded in great quantities. In this way, the invention of money not only made large economic inequalities possible, but according to Locke actually justified them.

This train of thought is not very clear, but on the whole Locke made a good case for entrepreneurial commerce. He pointed out, for example, that

> he who appropriates land to himself by his labour does not lessen but increase the common stock of mankind. For the provisions serving to the support of human life produced by one acre of enclosed and cultivated land, are . . . ten times more than those which are yielded by an acre of land of an equal richness lying waste in common. And therefore he that encloses land and has a greater plenty of the conveniences of life from ten acres than he could have from an hundred left to nature may truly be said to give ninety acres to mankind.

In other words wealth-creation is, as contemporary economists would put it, not a zero-sum game. If someone makes a piece of land more productive than it would be if left in common, then although he may become rich in the process, this is not necessarily at the expense of anyone else. It might well happen that everyone is better off as a result.

Locke's enthusiastic defence of private property has sometimes been seen as intellectual window-dressing for the business interests of the merchants and colonial proprietors of his day. But there is no reason to suppose that his views were not sincerely held, and it is worth noting that, considered in its historical context, his theory of property belongs on the left rather than the right of the political spectrum. Charles II, who was perpetually short of funds, wanted to be able to raise money without recourse to parliament—an attitude that harks back to the feudal system of property, according to which everything belongs ultimately to the king, who may therefore demand its return at any time. By arguing for a natural right to property for everyone, Locke was undermining such reactionary theories.

Locke did not, of course, advocate a full democracy as we understand it. It was much too early to expect that from anyone other than a fanatical extremist. He was content with a fairly powerful monarchy, a hereditary house of lords and a limited franchise that denied the vote to all women and many men. But what he did espouse was fairly radical for the times: political power, as he repeatedly stressed and Hobbes also maintained, was to be exercised strictly on behalf of and for the benefit of the people.

Locke may have rejected Filmer's account of the divine right of kings, yet time and again his political and moral arguments depend on an appeal to scripture or to what God has ordained. The "law of nature," which plays a large part in his political theory, is, he says, a declaration of "the will of God." The strength of Locke's Christian convictions is also evident, though in a different way, in his *Essay Concerning Human Understanding*, which we turn to next. He wrote that its aim was to investigate the nature and origin of human knowledge, and to mark its boundaries so that we may avoid fruitless attempts to transgress them. Although "the *Comprehension* of our Understandings, comes exceeding short of the vast Extent of Things," Locke wrote, this does not matter at all, because people have "Light enough to lead them to the Knowledge of their Maker and the sight of their own Duties." The *Essay* is permeated by a belief that the human mind is perfectly adequate for the purposes intended by God.

∞

In 1708, by which time the *Essay* was widely known from magazine and encyclopedia articles, Jonathan Swift took a telling satirical swipe at Locke's curious interest in the mind and its ideas. Discussing a writer who proposed to investigate "what is contained in the idea of Government," Swift noted in passing,

This refined way of speaking was introduced by Mr Locke. . . . All the former Philosophers in the World, from the age of Socrates to ours, would have ignorantly put the question, *Quid est imperium?* [What is government?] But now it seemeth we must vary our Phrase; and since our modern Improvement of Human Understanding, instead of desiring a Philosopher to describe or define a Mouse-trap, or tell me what it is; I must gravely ask, what is contained in the Idea of a Mouse-trap?

Locke had anticipated such criticisms, and apologised for his frequent use of the term "idea." But he explained that it is the word that "serves best to stand for whatsoever is the Object of the Understanding when a Man thinks," and pointed out that since he wanted to analyse the nature and limits of thinking, he could hardly avoid it. Besides, his discussions mainly concern ideas that are of special philosophical interest: God, infinity, matter and so on. If mousetraps had presented one of the great philosophical conundrums of his day, he would no doubt have dealt with the idea of them too.

Swift was correct, though, to suggest that under the influence of Locke—and, before him, Descartes—philosophy was turning in certain respects inwards. In Laurence Sterne's novel *Tristram Shandy* (1759), the *Essay* is described as a "history-book . . . of what passes in a man's own mind." Is it, then, intended as a work of psychology rather than philosophy? The question would have puzzled Locke, because it was not until the late nineteenth century, when some German philosophers set up experimental laboratories, that psychology became a distinct discipline. However, Locke did say that he was not concerned with the physiology of the brain or sense-organs, or with the relationship between mind and matter. One might well wonder how such things could fail to be relevant to the workings of the mind. Isn't everything he said now bound to be out of date? It seems not. Several eighteenth-century thinkers who saw themselves as following in the footsteps of Locke—David Hartley and Joseph Priestley, for example—did try to provide crude physiological explanations of mental activity, and their work has indeed been duly forgotten. Hartley attempted to explain the brain as a sort of xylophone of rattling tubes, in which one vibration sets off another in a sonorous chain of mental associations. But most of the main points Locke makes about the mind stand or fall regardless of what it is made of, and so are still worth considering today.

One of those points echoed Gassendi, the French Epicurean who influenced Descartes and Hobbes. Four decades before Locke's *Essay*, Gassendi wrote that

> a man who is born blind has no idea of colour, because he lacks the
> sense of vision which alone could give him one; and the man who
> is born deaf has no idea of sound, because he is without the sense of
> hearing by which he could acquire it. This is so to the extent that if
> there could be a person who lived deprived of every sense . . . then
> he would have no idea of a single thing and thus would imagine
> nothing.
>
> Here is the point of the well-known saying "there is nothing in
> the understanding which was not first in the senses," and the dictum that . . . the mind is a blank tablet on which nothing has been
> engraved or painted.

Locke famously made much of this notion that the human mind is at first rather like a blank sheet of paper, and that none of our knowledge is innate; we shall come to that often-misunderstood view shortly. But first it is worth taking a closer look at the way our ideas are supposedly formed from the raw material of experience. This hypothesis was a recurring theme in earlier philosophy: it is found not only in the Epicureans whom Gassendi followed but also in some of the ancient Stoics, St Thomas Aquinas and other medieval scholastics, Hobbes and many others. Locke's novelty was to explore the theory in greater depth than earlier thinkers had done, and to develop its implications.

Locke did not think that all our ideas are derived directly from observations of the external world. Many of them come, he said, from observing the activities of our own minds as they consider or react to the ideas they receive from outside—that is, from introspection, which he calls "reflection." The simple ideas that are generated by sensation or reflection are then compounded and manipulated by the mind to compose more complex ones. Thus the idea *snow* is assembled out of such ideas as *white, cold* and *wet* that we receive through our senses. Here, to take a more intricate concoction, is Locke's recipe for the idea of *God*:

> having . . . got the *Ideas* of Existence and Duration; of Knowledge and Power; of Pleasure and Happiness; and of several other Qualities and Powers, which it is better to have than to be without; when we would frame an *Idea* the most suitable we can to the supreme Being, we enlarge every one of these with our *Idea* of Infinity; and so, putting them together, make our complex *Idea of God*.

Although simple ideas of sensory qualities are passively imprinted on the mind's blank sheet of paper, the mind is far from passive when it builds up its more complex ideas. The idea of power, for example, is formed, Locke writes, when we notice changes taking place in the world, then reflect on these changes, and conclude that "like Changes will for the future be made, in the same things, by like Agents, and by the like ways." By noticing, reflecting and reasoning, we develop the idea that certain objects have certain powers to do things—for example, that fire has the power to melt gold. Thus the mind is active and rational in the acquisition of such complex concepts.

That is why it is misleading to depict Locke's account of mental activity as "associationist." Some historians and many textbooks of psychology today report that Locke "presented man's make-up as entirely a product of learning from experience, through the association of ideas." This is wide of the mark. In a short chapter added as an afterthought to later editions of the *Essay*, Locke discussed what he called "the association of ideas":

> *Ideas* that in themselves are not at all of kin, come to be so united in some Mens Minds, that 'tis very hard to separate them . . . and the one no sooner . . . comes into the Understanding but its Associate appears with it. . . . Custom settles habits of Thinking in the Understanding . . . which, once set a going continue in the same steps they have been used to, which by often treading are worn into a smooth path, and the Motion in it becomes easy and, as it were, Natural.

As an example of this process of "association," Locke mentioned children who, whenever they find themselves in the dark, think of goblins, because they have been told too many fairy tales. He also cites an example of a man who once gorged on honey and later felt sick whenever he thought of the stuff. Locke regarded such "wrong and unnatural Combinations of *Ideas*" as a mild but potentially dangerous form of madness that causes superstition, irrational fears and indeed many of the "greatest . . . errors in the world." This chapter had a large but odd influence. Although Locke saw the passive association of ideas as a lamentable aberration, and not at all typical of the way the mind normally works, a later school of thought, the "associationists"—of which Hartley and Hume were members—argued that it was the basis of most mental activity. Locke would have been bemused to discover that he himself would later be counted among them.

He would have objected to associationism for some of the same reasons that he was suspicious of the theory that knowledge is innately implanted in us: both make the mind sound lazier than it is. If we were born with a ready-made set of truths lodged in our heads, we would not try to work things out for ourselves. And if our ideas were formed by mere subjective associations, there would be little room left for rationality.

Locke began his attack on "innate notions" by considering two curiously empty maxims: " 'Tis impossible for the same thing to be, and not to be" and "Whatsoever is, is." This might seem an odd place to start, yet these propositions were regarded by scholastic philosophers as in some sense the best-known and most fundamental of truths. It was claimed that everybody accepts them, and that the best explanation for this universal agreement is that they are somehow "stamped upon the Mind of Man" before birth. But Locke pointed out that it is just not true that everyone endorses these maxims. Consider children and idiots: they never even think of them. And how could that be, if they were imprinted on their minds?

Perhaps it will be said, Locke continued, that everyone with the power of reason would assent to them. But, Locke asked, if you must develop your rational faculties before you possess these pieces of knowledge, in what sense were they in your mind all along? Surely it would not really be these truths themselves which were innate, but merely the capacity to know them. And in that case, what is so special about these maxims? Why not say that all the truths to which any rational person would agree—such as *"That White is not Black, That a Square is not a Circle, That Yellowness is not Sweetness"*—are innate in the same sense? Yet that would produce even more problems, says Locke. For how could the knowledge that, for example, "white is not black" be innate unless the ideas of whiteness and blackness were innate as well? And surely everyone accepts that our ideas of sensory qualities, such as colours, are acquired by experience and are therefore not inborn.

We may be tempted to say that an "implicit" knowledge of various truths is somehow imprinted on our minds, but Locke rightly insisted that it is unclear what could be meant by such a claim. If something were in any sense naturally present in the understanding from birth, surely it would make its plainest appearance in the minds of the simplest creatures:

> One would think . . . That all these native Beams of Light (were there any such) should in those, who have no Reserves, no Arts of Conceal-ment, shine out in their full Lustre, and leave us in no more doubt of their being there, than we are of their love of Pleasure, and abhorrence of Pain. But alas, amongst *Children, ideots, Savages,* and the grossly *Illiterate,* what general Maxims are to be found? . . . A Child knows his Nurse, and his Cradle, and by degrees the Play-things of a little more advanced Age: And a young Savage has, perhaps, his Head fill'd with Love and Hunting, according to the fashion of his Tribe. But he that from a Child untaught, or a wild Inhabitant of the Woods, will expect these abstract Maxims and reputed Principles of Sciences, will, I fear, find himself mistaken.

So much for the idea that fundamental abstract truths are lodged in our minds from birth. Locke's next target was the claim that moral principles are innate as well. Many of his contemporaries believed that God had implanted the rules of conduct in the minds of men, including, for example, "God is to be worshipped," "parents are to be honoured" and "a man's word is to be kept." It was said, in a sermon at St Paul's in 1662, that such innate principles are "the ground of all virtue, and civility, and the foundation of religion." But Locke quickly proved that this way of thinking is hopelessly parochial. If we consider the morals of other people long ago or far away, we soon find that there is not a single rule of conduct that has not been rejected by some society or other. Locke unearthed many tales of appalling foreigners to make his point: people in parts of Asia who carry their sick outside and leave them to die, a tribe in Peru that fattens and eats children, and a Saracen holy man whose way with goats can only be recounted in Latin. Even if some or all of these travellers' tales turn out to be unreliable, the fact remains that there is no universal agreement about morals, so morals cannot be innate in any straightforward sense.

One marked difference between moral principles and the abstract truths which are supposed to be innate, such as "Whatsoever is, is," is that the latter appear to be self-evident and unquestionable, whereas "*there cannot any one moral Rule be propos'd, whereof a Man may not justly demand a Reason.*" Locke did not mean by this that one can never be certain in one's ethical opinions, or that there are no absolute moral truths. He firmly believed that Christian teachings were the true teachings, and that God has provided us with adequate evidence of this fact. His point is rather that understanding our obligations and interpreting the will of God call for the exercise of the mind. Locke noted that even when different groups of people agree on some moral maxim, such as the importance of keeping promises, they will offer varying reasons in support of it. Thus a Christian will say that we should keep our promises because God requires it of us, and an ancient Greek might say that it would impede the flourishing of humanity to do otherwise. If moral principles were imprinted in our minds, why would people bother to reason about them, dispute them, or try and teach them to their children?

Many of the truths that were said by theologians and moralists to be innate concerned God's will and man's duties towards Him. Locke pointed out that if any such principles were indeed innate, then the notion of God must itself be innate too. It would, besides, be odd of God to have failed to imprint Himself when He had the chance. But then why, asked Locke, do the travel books tell of whole nations—in Brazil, the Caribbean, Siam,

PHILOSOPHY FOR THE BRITISH: LOCKE

China and other places—who do not seem to have any idea of God? How is it that even in a single country you will find people with very different ideas of God? And what about the vengeful, amorous, deceitful, impetuous and sometimes even embodied gods of the ancients, who resemble people more than they do the Christian or Jewish deity? Did the heathens have the same idea of God as us? Talk to country people, says Locke, or children

> and you shall find, that though the name of GOD be frequently in their mouths; yet the notions they apply this Name to, are so odd, low, and pitiful, that no body can imagine, they were taught by a rational Man; much less, that they were Characters written by the finger of God Himself.

With so little to recommend it, it might well be wondered why talk of innateness survives. One reason, Locke suggested, is that people cannot remember being taught or first acquiring their basic principles, and so conclude that they must have been present from birth. Also, it was convenient for the lazy-minded—and for those who want to control them—to regard some truths as innate:

> it eased the lazy from the pains of search, and stopp'd the enquiry of the doubtful. . . . And it was of no small advantage to those who affected to be Masters and Teachers, to make this the Principle of *Principles*, That Principles must not be questioned.

This encouraged an attitude of "blind credulity" in which people "might more easily be governed."

Some say that Locke's assault on "innate notions" is too simple to be effective because the points he makes seem almost obvious. Do they really disprove the views of any sophisticated thinker? But this objection misunderstands Locke's strategy. He is not refuting a precise doctrine but unravelling a vague one. His tactic is to show that literal versions of it are false, and to challenge its adherents to come up with something better, confident that they will fail to do so. The fact is that talk of "innate" knowledge or ideas has always traded on its own imprecision, and continues to do so.

Consider Descartes. As we have seen, when he was accused of holding that infants are born with a great deal of knowledge already in their heads, he crossly denied it.* But much of what Descartes wrote about learning, God and mathematics shows that he was strongly tempted by the notion of innateness without knowing quite what he meant by it. For example, he wrote that "eternal truths," such as the truths of mathematics, are "inborn in our minds," and that it is this fact which explains how we manage to grasp them. Of course, this is not a real explanation of mathematical knowledge at all, but rather an attempt to evade an awkward question. It is as if we were to ask a child where he got a suspiciously large amount of money, and the child replied, "Nowhere. I've always had it." Elsewhere, Descartes wrote that an infant in the womb "has . . . the ideas of God, of itself and of all such truths as are called self-evident, in the same way as adult human beings have these ideas when they are not attending to them." But what way is that? To say that an adult possesses various truths or concepts even when he is not attending to them is presumably to say that he would, if asked, be able to make use of them or explain them. This is clearly not true of an infant in the womb. So, once more, the talk of innateness seems like a meaningless dodge.

Still, Descartes did make one good point. He noted that what actually reaches us via the senses when we perceive an external object is always some form of physical motion—that is, an object touches us, or emits sound waves, gases or particles, or reflects certain wavelengths of light. But how, for example, do particular wavelengths of electromagnetic energy come to be perceived by us as colours? "The ideas of pain, colours, sounds and the like must be innate," wrote Descartes, "if, on the occasion of certain . . . motions, our mind is to be capable of representing them to itself, for there is no similarity between these ideas and the . . . motions." What Descartes meant is that we are naturally constituted so as to experience certain patterns of motion as colour and other sensory qualities. This is surely right: as a biologist might put it nowadays, our genes make our eyes

---

* See p. 31, above.

and brains turn wavelengths into colours. Although in the womb we have no understanding of colour, it is thanks to our biological inheritance that we can later acquire one. Thus while it is misleading of Descartes to claim that we possess an innate idea of colour, he is correct to suggest that we have an innate capacity to experience it.

Locke would have had no problem with this. He repeatedly declared that man has all sorts of innate capacities and inclinations. In an early work, he clearly stated that man is equipped with an "inborn constitution" comprising his faculties of sense-perception, reasoning and understanding. He noted that people have innate dispositions to act and feel in various ways ("I deny not, that there are natural tendencies imprinted on the Minds of men. . . . ") And the inherent limitations of men's minds was a recurring theme of the *Essay*: God has designed and given us a particular mental constitution to serve our everyday needs and spiritual welfare. In his writings on education, Locke also allowed that the characters and dispositions of children are partly inborn and cannot be altered by education. So it is wrong to cast him as an opponent of the view that the mind is shaped to a considerable extent by its inborn nature.

The distinction between innate capacities and dispositions (which Locke accepted) and ready-made knowledge of truths that are stamped on the mind before birth (which is what he attacked) is one that is still often blurred. In the 1960s, for instance, Noam Chomsky argued that all normal people have an innate "knowledge" of grammar—not the everyday rules that some people learn at a school and everybody breaks thereafter, but of basic ones that underlie all human language. He maintained that without some such assumption it was impossible to account for the ease with which people learn to speak, and that the science of linguistics therefore supported philosophers like Descartes against philosophers like Locke. Yet the most that Chomsky's evidence suggests is that children have a propensity to produce sentences which fit certain rules, which Locke would have no reason to deny.

Gottfried Leibniz, a German polymath who usually found something worthwhile in everyone's views, reached what amounts to a compromise on the issue of innateness. Like Descartes, he insisted that necessary truths, such as those of mathematics, are "proved by what lies within." Leibniz couldn't resist calling such propositions innate, but for him this did not preclude their being learned: "The truths about numbers are in us; but still we learn them." It emerges that what Leibniz means by "innate" is "inner": an internal faculty, rather than the perception of the outside world, is what we use to recognise and prove such truths. As Leibniz pointed out, Locke agreed with this. Still, Leibniz was more optimistic than Locke about the scope of this internal faculty. Leibniz was convinced that it provides us with plenty of "demonstrative knowledge"—that is, systematic and deductive proof—in all sorts of fields, whereas Locke, as we shall now see, thought we have rather little of it.

∞

SINCE LOCKE BELIEVED in the new "mechanical" view of the world, according to which nature is a machine, the behaviour of which is to be explained by the motions of its parts, he regarded a watchmaker's understanding of his own timepieces as the ideal example of natural knowledge. If only we were acquainted with natural substances in the same way that the designer of the very complicated clock in Strasbourg cathedral understood his creation, we could have a "perfect *Science* of natural Bodies." If we could discover the shape, size, texture and movements of the "minute Constituent parts" of any two physical objects, we would be able to predict their effects on one another with just as much as certainty "as we do know the properties of a square or triangle."

> Did we know the Mechanical affections of the Particles of *Rhubarb*, *Hemlock*, *Opium*, and a *Man*, as a Watchmaker does those of a Watch, whereby it performs its Operations, and of a File, which by rubbing on them will alter the Figure of any of the Wheels, we should be able to tell before Hand that *Rhubarb* will purge, *Hemlock* kill, and *Opium* make a Man sleep; as well as a Watch-maker can, that a little piece of Paper laid on the Balance, will keep the Watch from going, till it be removed. . . . The dissolving of Silver in *aqua fortis* [nitric acid], and Gold in *aqua regia* [a mixture of nitric and hydrochloric acids], and not

*vice versa*, would be then, perhaps, no more difficult to know, than it is to a Smith to understand, why the turning of one key will open a Lock, and not the turning of another.

Unfortunately it would be a lost labour to seek such "*scientifical*" knowledge, Locke wrote, as it will be forever out of our reach. This is largely because our senses are just not sharp enough to examine the tiny parts of things, and also because of the complicating effects of bodies that are too far away for us to detect, and a few other problems.

In one respect Locke's pessimism sounds gloomier than it is and merely reflects the different terminology of his day. "Science," at least in the philosophy textbooks of the time, meant a body of necessary truths that could be demonstrated in the way that the theorems of geometry are. Nowadays we do not demand such mathematical certainty of empirical science, so this lack is not much of a disappointment. Nor was it really for Locke, since he believed that great progress could be made, and was already being made, in "*experimental* philosophy," which reliably informs us about probabilities—though not certainties—and is quite adequate for practical purposes. Actually, he added, it is rather fortunate and a mark of God's wisdom that we do not have much more acute senses and the sort of "Microscopical Eyes" that would enable us to perceive the tiniest scale of things. If we did, we would be distracted by the quietest sounds and unable to go about our business. For instance, if what we saw when we looked at a clock was its minuscule workings, we would be unable to make out its hands, and so would be incapable of telling the time. This does not seem to have been a joke.

Today we know a great deal about the "minute constituent parts" of matter. This is thanks in part to improved apparatus, but mainly to a facet of science that Locke apparently underestimated, namely the formulating and testing of theories; the difference between Newton and contemporary scientists is, after all, not just that the latter have more impressive microscopes. Yet this improved knowledge of the very small does not enable us to deduce the interactions of bodies in quite the way that a mathematician can demonstrate "the properties of a square or triangle." Applied physics is not a body of necessary truths like pure mathematics—nor, indeed, is the knowledge that a watchmaker has of his own handiwork. So Locke was mistaken in two respects: he was wrong that we would never be able to investigate the microscopic world, and wrong about the sort of knowledge that we would get if we could. The trouble is that he was pulled in two directions. On one hand, he was sure that the microstructure of matter was the key to its behavior; on the other, he was influenced by the old Greek idea that geometry is the paradigm of knowledge. This is what made it hard for him to see what a real science of physics would be like.

While such a science would always remain beyond us, according to Locke, a science of morals is perfectly possible. Morality, he believed, could be reduced to a matter of demonstration, though when a friend invited him to produce such ethical demonstrations, Locke replied that he didn't have time. He did, however, give a taste of roughly what he had in mind:

> *Where there is no property, there is no injustice*, is a Proposition as certain as any Demonstration in *Euclid*: For the *Idea* of *Property*, being a right to any thing; and the *Idea* to which the Name *Injustice* is given, being the Invasion or Violation of that right; it is evident, that these *Ideas*, being thus established, and these Names annexed to them, I can as certainly know this Proposition to be true, as that a Triangle has three Angles equal to two right ones.

But Locke had surely been misled once more by his admiration for geometry, since this train of thought would enable us to deduce the answers to ethical problems only by turning them into merely verbal disputes. As the young George Berkeley remarked in a notebook, on Locke's view "to demonstrate morality it seems one need only make a dictionary of words and see which included which." It is difficult to imagine how this could help to answer the weighty questions about conduct which Locke says partly prompted him to write his *Essay*.

Locke's definition of knowledge in general is, once again, unfortunately better suited to mathematical and other necessary truths than to many other topics:

> *Knowledge* then seems to me to be nothing but *the perception of the connexion and agreement, or disagreement and repugnancy of any of our*

*Ideas. . . .* Where this Perception is, there is Knowledge; and where it is not, there, though we may fancy, guess, or believe, yet we always come short of Knowledge. For when we know that *White is not Black*, what do we else but perceive that these two *Ideas* do not agree? When we possess ourselves with the utmost security of the Demonstration, that *the three angles of a triangle are equal to two right ones*, What do we more but perceive, that Equality to two right ones, does necessarily agree to, and is inseparable from the three Angles of a Triangle?

Given his assumptions, it is not hard to see how he arrived at this account of knowledge. Look into your mind, says Locke, and what you will find are ideas. He seemed to presume that knowledge is some sort of internal perception, so it must consist in seeing relationships between those ideas. Thus we can see by inspection that our idea of white is not the same as our idea of black, so we know that *white is not black*. But this is an unusual illustration of knowledge: most everyday examples of what we think we know do not seem to fit Locke's definition at all. Consider "The boiling point of water at sea-level is 212° F," "Socrates was condemned to death" or "The dog next door has been sick again." None of these things can be known merely by looking into our own minds; they call for some form of external observation, experiment or study. At a pinch, Locke could claim that we come to know mathematical truths by perceiving relationships between our own ideas (for example, by working through proofs in our heads). But he was forced to conclude that wherever there is "a want of *a discoverable Connection* between those *Ideas* which we have . . . we are utterly incapable of universal and certain Knowledge; and are . . . left only to Observation and Experiment. . . ."

Later in the *Essay*, however, Locke found room for an inferior form of knowledge that is derived from the observation of the external world:

*The notice we have by our Senses, of the existing of things without* us, though it be not altogether so certain, as our intuitive Knowledge, or the Deductions of our Reason, employ'd about the clear abstract *Ideas* of our own Minds; yet it is an assurance that *deserves the name of Knowledge* . . . For I think no body can, in earnest, be so sceptical,

as to be uncertain of the Existence of those Things which he sees and
feels.

This "sensitive" knowledge, as he called it, cannot be squared with his
official definition of knowledge, but Locke preferred common sense to consistency and could not stomach the conclusion that we do not know about
what we see and feel.

He was well aware that all his talk of ideas raised the spectre of scepticism: "How shall the mind, when it perceives nothing but its own ideas,
know that they agree with things themselves?" He poked and prodded at
the question a little, but was too imbued with common sense to engage
seriously with the sorts of doubts raised by Descartes. If anyone claims
that "all we see and hear, feel and taste, think and do, during our whole
Being, is but the series and deluding appearances of a long Dream," Locke
wrote, "I must desire him to consider that, if all be a Dream, then he doth
but dream, that he makes the Question; and so it is not much matter, that
a waking Man should answer him." And even if this life is but a dream,
Locke adds, the pain and pleasure we experience in it make it quite real
enough for us.

Still, although Locke discounted such radical forms of scepticism, he
insisted that the scope of our knowledge of the physical world is much
more limited than many have thought. It "*extends as far as the present Testimony of our Senses*, employed about particular objects that do then affect
them, and no farther." For example,

> though it be highly probable, that Millions of Men do now exist, yet,
> whilst I am alone writing this, I have not that Certainty of it which
> we strictly call Knowledge; though the great likelihood of it puts me
> past doubt, and it be reasonable for me to do several things upon the
> confidence, that there are Men now in the world: But this is but prob-
> ability, not Knowledge.

Descartes himself would not have been so cautious. Although it was he
and not Locke who thought that an earnest answer must be given to the

question "How do I know I am not dreaming?," in the end it was Locke who trimmed back his ambitions for knowledge.

Locke fearlessly applied his moderate form of scepticism to some of the philosophical controversies of the day. While Descartes, and indeed most other thinkers, maintained—at least in public—that it was impossible for mere matter to think, Locke could see no reason why God could not create purely physical beings who had the power of thought. We simply don't know enough to decide whether or not such a thing is possible. This was regarded as close to heresy, and was one of the topics disputed in a correspondence with the bishop of Worcester, who claimed that many of Locke's views undermined religion. In his treatment of this subject, Locke made an astute point that is still relevant to today's arguments about mind and matter. It is often said that it is impossible to conceive of how brute material substance could be conscious, and that this disproves any physical account of the mind. But Locke pointed out that it is equally mysterious how an immaterial soul could be conscious either, so the fact that consciousness is baffling cannot settle the question either way.

Locke's musings on the soul led him to the issue of "personal identity"—that is, the question of what makes me the same person at various stages of my life. This was a lively topic in the pulpits at the time, since it was generally believed, or at least hoped, that our bodies would be resurrected on the day of judgement, and that we would thereby live again. This presented several conundrums. Was it necessary that the same particles of matter that composed our earthly bodies be reassembled? If so, what would happen if I had been eaten by a cannibal? And if Descartes was right that the soul is separate from the body, why should it matter what happens to my body anyway? Related puzzles are raised today, but usually by writers of science fiction rather than theology. In *Star Trek*, for example, people regularly travel by a transporter beam which "dematerializes" them in one place for reassembly at another. But would such a beam need to carry the atoms of the original person or just information about those atoms? In several episodes of the series, the transporter goes wrong, and produces two persons (or perhaps we should say two bodies) at the destination. This implies that it transports only information, not atoms, and that the travellers' bodies are destroyed at departure, then created afresh on arrival from new materials according to a transmitted blueprint.

Locke would have wanted to know what happens to the travellers' consciousness in such cases. He defined a "person" as a self-conscious being that "can consider it self as it self," and argued that it is having the same consciousness at different times and in different places that determines personal identity. Locke did not say much about what having the same consciousness amounts to, but it seemed to be primarily a matter of memory: "as far as any intelligent Being can repeat the *Idea* of any past Action with the same consciousness it had of it at first, and with the same consciousness it has of any present Action; so far it is the same *personal self*." The novelty of this suggestion is that it renders irrelevant all questions of what people are made of. It does not matter if a resurrected or transported body consists of the same physical stuff as the original, or indeed if it bears any physical relationship to the original at all. Nor does it matter whether or not any immaterial souls are involved. All that counts when deciding cases of putative personal identity is consciousness and memory.

This idea had some odd consequences, which Locke calmly accepted. A person could, for example, change bodies: "should the Soul of a Prince, carrying with it the consciousness of the Prince's past Life, enter and inform the Body of a Cobler as soon as deserted by his own Soul . . . he would be the same Person with the Prince, accountable only for the Prince's Actions." And if a sober man has no memory at all of what he did when he was drunk, then the drunk and sober men are literally different persons. Locke noted that it was, though, perfectly reasonable for the law to punish a sober man even if he claimed not to recall what he did when drunk, because it is impossible to prove that he is not lying. One may leave it to God, Locke adds, to ensure that only just punishments and rewards are handed out on the day of judgement.

Locke's discussion of personal identity was the first sustained philosophical treatment of the subject. In the eighteenth century, several thinkers made powerful criticisms of it. Bishop Butler, a theologian and philosopher, and others argued that memory presupposes personal identity and therefore cannot be used to define it: I may think I remember doing something, but I only really remember it in the relevant sense if it really was me who did it. And what are we to say if a young man remembers his childhood, and, when he is an old man, remembers being a young one, but no longer remembers his childhood once he is old? According to Locke's theory, it seems to follow that the young man is the same person as the child, and the old man is the same person as the young man, but the child is not the same person as the old man. In 1741, the poet Alexander Pope and some friends made great fun of such discussions in their satirical *Memoirs of the Extraordinary Life, Works and Discoveries of Martinus Scriblerus.* Scriblerus falls in love with one of a pair of Siamese twins who are joined at "the organs of generation," and marries her, but the other twin marries a different person, leading to a frightful and hilarious series of lawsuits that revolve around the question of how many persons are involved, and who is married to whom. In the end, both marriages are dissolved.

Locke himself never married, but he ended his days in the company of a woman to whom he was particularly close, Damaris Masham, whose father, Ralph Cudworth, was the leader of a group of philosophers who came to be known as the Cambridge Platonists. Although Damaris was, like all women, barred from any formal higher education, she developed a strong interest in philosophy and published two philosophical books. She met Locke in 1681, when she was in her early twenties and he was almost fifty. They soon began to write letters and poems to each other, in which Locke signed himself Philander—a typical name in Renaissance literature for a flirtatious male character—and she signed herself Philoclea, the daughter of the Duke of Arcadia in Sir Philip Sidney's poem, who had been told by the Delphic oracle that his daughters would be stolen by unsuitable lovers. It seems from the letters that Locke and Damaris were in love with each other, though never quite at the same time.

Four years after she met Locke, Damaris married Sir Francis Masham, a widower thirteen years her senior, and moved to his house at Oates, in Essex. She was not close to her husband and complained to Locke of her boredom. Six months after her marriage, she was particularly keen for Locke's company, and he became a regular visitor. Both Locke and Newton were guests at the house at Christmas in 1690, and shortly afterwards Locke moved in permanently. Damaris and Locke gardened and discussed philosophy together. One exceptionally obnoxious critic of Locke wrote that he was "governor of the seraglio at Oates," but there is no reason to doubt that Locke's union with Damaris was purely Platonic.

Locke died at Oates on 28 October 1704, and at present there does not seem to be anyone who plausibly remembers having been him. If there were, or if Locke had lived on another three hundred years—which, according to his theory of personal identity, comes to much the same thing—he might well have abandoned that theory. For at the end of his treatment of the topic he added an important caveat and a radical suggestion. In our present state of ignorance about "that thinking thing, that is in us," he wrote, it is pardonable to suppose that the same person may occupy different bodies at different times. But if we knew more, and were perhaps to discover that there is a material basis for consciousness, then we might need to adopt a different opinion.

∞

IN THE PREFACE to his *Essay*, Locke made what has been taken, especially by English-speaking philosophers, to be a statement of the proper aims of their subject:

> The Commonwealth of Learning, is not at this time without Master-Builders, whose mighty Designs, in advancing the Sciences, will leave lasting Monuments to the Admiration of Posterity; But every one must not hope to be a Boyle, or a Sydenham; and in an age that produces such Masters, as the great . . . Huygenius, and the incomparable Mr. Newton, with some other of that Strain; 'tis Ambition enough to be employed as an Under-Labourer in clearing Ground a little, and removing some of the Rubbish that lies in the way to Knowledge. . . .

A. J. Ayer quoted Locke's remark about under-labourers in support of the view that it is the business of science to discover truths about the world, and of philosophy merely to analyse the statements made by scientists.

This reads too much into the passage, though. There is no reason to think that Locke's expression of the modesty that was fitting in the presence of giants such as Newton was meant as any sort of manifesto for thinkers of all future ages. Be that as it may, the work of Leibniz, to which we shall turn in the chapter after next, was much more ambitious than that of Locke. While Locke was content to tinker with the edifice of knowledge piece by piece, Leibniz aimed to build a complete system of the world that would explain pretty much everything.

# 5

## AN INTERLUDE ON A COMET
# *Bayle*

THE YEAR 1680 IS A NOTABLE ONE IN PHILOSOPHY BECAUSE OF AN occurrence that did not amount to anything much and a book about this non-event by a philosopher of whom few have now heard. The occurrence was an unusually bright comet. It was widely feared to be a warning from God, yet the expected disasters did not come. The book, *Various Thoughts on the Occasion of a Comet*, caused a scandal because it made the unprecedented claim that an atheist society might not be an immoral one. *Various Thoughts* launched the literary career of Pierre Bayle (1647–1706), who lived most of his adult life in the Netherlands after growing up in rural France, where his father was a Huguenot (i.e., French Calvinist) pastor. Bayle was no atheist himself, but he knew a bad argument when he saw one, and he realised that some common fears about atheism were groundless. He also had a gift for concocting good arguments: in Voltaire's opinion, Bayle was "the greatest dialectician who has ever written." Bayle's many other keen admirers in the eighteenth century included Thomas Jefferson and Frederick the Great of Prussia. Plenty of eighteenth-century philosophers, especially David Hume, lifted arguments and ideas from Bayle's *Historical and Critical Dictionary*, an eccentrically constructed work of over six million words that has aptly been described as the "arsenal of all Enlightenment philosophy."

Comets seemed to have presaged many unfortunate events in history, from the invasion of Greece by the Persian king Xerxes in 480 BC to the death of the queen of Spain two thousand years later. The fall of Carthage, the death of Caesar, the tyranny of Nero, the Norman invasion of Britain and countless other disasters were suspiciously preceded by comets, or by other sights that were taken to be comets. One pope in the fifteenth century, Calixtus III, is commonly said to have exorcised or excommunicated one of these celestial harbingers of doom. That story is a myth, but there is no doubt that the comet of 1680 was widely regarded by preachers as a clear sign from God that now would be a good time to repent. Hundreds of pamphlets about it were published in Europe and North America. It was first spotted from Germany, where writers on the subject were particularly gullible and gloomy.

At the time, Bayle was a professor of philosophy at a Calvinist academy in north-eastern France. He was, he said, constantly questioned about the comet by the curious and the alarmed, and he decided to explain why it would not be in God's nature to use comets to send messages. The book that grew out of Bayle's writings on this subject, which was published in 1682 when he had moved to Rotterdam, presented dozens of reasons to doubt the significance of comets and various other superstitions. It loosed an avalanche of sceptical arguments on its readers' heads: one analysis of the book's structure finds, for example, seven proofs of the seventh reason for the fourth response to the first objection to the seventh reason why comets do not presage evil.

Bayle's most original argument against the idea that comets are divine warnings is that the use of awe-inspiring phenomena to deliver religious messages would be likely to backfire and encourage the worship of false gods. Since the Bible makes it plain that God is a jealous God who hates idolatory, it follows that He would not use comets in this way. What could He possibly have meant to achieve by the comets that appeared before the birth of Jesus? They could only serve to make pagans more zealous in their paganism. A comet, after all, does not spell out its warning in an unambiguous way. It does not come with the signature of any particular deity. Ancient Romans, for example, might think that a comet was warning them to make more sacrifices to Jupiter. And even in Christian times, Christians are a minority: "most men remain idolators or have become Mohammed-

ans." So why would God send comets that were likely to "reanimate false
and sacrilegious devotion almost everywhere on earth" and "increase the
number of pilgrims to Mecca"?

Perhaps, Bayle suggested, some people will say that God hates atheism
even more than He hates idolatory. If God thought it was better for people
to believe in the wrong gods than to believe in no gods at all, it might
make sense for Him to send comets to frighten them out of atheism. It was
in this context that Bayle made his shocking suggestion about morality
and religion. The main reason why people regarded atheism as a terrible
thing, which God would be bound to abhor even more than He abhors the
worship of false gods, is that atheism would lead to such wickedness that
society would disintegrate. Yet Bayle argued at great length that atheism
would not necessarily have any such effect. In his own day, the question
could not be settled definitively because there were no known atheists to
observe, but he has subsequently been proved right. In Scandinavia, for
example, atheism is widespread yet wickedness and chaos are not.

Bayle's main reason for doubting that a society of atheists would be
terminally immoral is that people mostly act according to their inclinations and characters, not in accordance with the principles that they officially profess. How else could one explain the existence of wickedness in
Christian countries? Also, atheists would naturally want the respect and
approval of others, and this would help to keep them as well-behaved as
anyone else. An atheist's morality would in one sense be defective, according to Bayle, because it would not be motivated by the love of God. But his
actual behaviour would probably not be as bad as people feared. Thus, as
one of Bayle's admirers put it in the early eighteenth century, "it ought not
to appear more strange to us, that an Atheist should be a quiet moral Man,
than that a Christian should lead a very wicked Life."

If atheism is not bound to lead to moral collapse, then there is no reason to think that God—who was, of course, assumed to be the Christian
God—would prefer pagans or Muslims to atheists, in which case He would
have no motive to send comets. These things in the sky, Bayle suggested,
are probably just natural phenomena that can be explained by natural laws.

Five years after Bayle's book appeared, the relevant laws were found.
Drawing on observations by an astronomer, Edmund Halley, Newton

showed that comets travel through the solar system according to a time-table set by the laws of motion and gravity rather than by any apparent religious agenda. After a comet duly turned up in 1759, close enough to a date predicted by Halley, supernatural accounts of comets more or less went extinct, at least among the educated. But the fear of them did not. Thanks to mankind's enduring appetite for predictions of global disaster, comets were transformed from supernatural warnings into unguided missiles that might damage the planet. Newton's successor at Cambridge University calculated that a comet had triggered Noah's flood in 2349 BC and would return in 2255 with equally dire consequences. In 1773, and again in 1832, there were panics in parts of Europe when misleading reports of astronomical calculations led people to believe that a comet was about to collide with the earth.

Bayle's second major philosophical work addressed a genuine disaster that befell his own family in France. The French Protestant minority had been granted some freedom of religion by a royal edict in 1598, the Edict of Nantes, as part of a settlement that ended the French wars of religion. But severe repression of Protestants began to return in the 1670s, and in 1685 the edict was revoked. Bayle's eldest brother died in prison that year; he would have been released if he had agreed to convert to Catholicism. The next year, Bayle published a defence of religious toleration that was as unwieldy as its title—*A Philosophical Commentary on These Words of the Gospel, Luke 14:23, "Compel Them to Come In, That My House May Be Full."* The book made at least as powerful a case for religious freedom as Locke's better-known *Letter Concerning Toleration*, which had been written at around the same time but not published until three years later. Like the latter half of Hobbes's *Leviathan*, and much of Spinoza's *Tractatus*, Bayle's *Philosophical Commentary* contained a great deal of scriptural analysis, which is one reason why it is not much read today.

According to an influential discussion by St Augustine in some of his letters, the passage from Luke's gospel was an endorsement of religious coercion that had come straight from the mouth of Jesus himself. It was cited for centuries as a justification for persecuting heretics and then killing them if they refused to mend their ways. Bayle had little difficulty showing that this was a questionable reading of the biblical story, which ostensibly concerns a dinner-party. But his main point was about the nature of conscience. Bayle argued that God would want people to act according to their own deepest convictions, provided that these convictions were the result of an earnest and careful search for truth. Why else would He have given them a conscience? Thus, coercing them to practice one faith when they believed another could not be the right thing to do. An honest mistake is no sin, and so should not be punished. To illustrate this point, Bayle used the example of Martin Guerre, a French peasant who had disappeared from his village in 1548 and apparently returned in 1556. Guerre's wife was sure that a man who turned up in 1556 claiming to be Martin was indeed her husband, and she had two children with him. But three years later, the real Martin Guerre came back and the impostor was executed for fraud and adultery. Because the woman sincerely believed that the impostor was her husband, she was not judged guilty of any crime. Similarly, Bayle argued, "a sincere heretic, even an infidel" should not suffer for his honest beliefs.

Furthermore, Bayle pointed out, every heretic is convinced that he is a true believer and that it is others who are heretics. So if the persecution of heresy were encouraged, the result would be endless bloodshed. This, Bayle reasoned, was surely not what Jesus had in mind. Besides, coercion is an ineffective way to make people embrace the true faith, since belief arises from inner conviction and cannot be changed at will. Bayle concluded that religious coercion was pointless, irrational and unchristian. Even non-Christian religions should be tolerated, if their adherents are sincere, and so too should highly unorthodox Christian sects such as the Socinians, who accepted that Jesus spoke for God but not that he was himself divine.

Bayle had reservations about Catholics, though. They presented a special problem because they apparently could not stop persecuting others. He acknowledged that if Catholics obsessively punished heretics and infidels because that is what their consciences told them to do, they were in one sense not sinning. Neverthless, it had to stop.

Religious toleration was one of two theological controversies that Bayle addressed repeatedly. The other was the so-called problem of evil. The travails endured by the victims of persecution were just droplets in a sea of troubles: if God is good and all-powerful, why does He allow His creatures to suffer quite so much? "Man is wicked and miserable," Bayle noted in his *Dictionary*. "It suffices to have been alive for five or six years to be completely convinced of these two truths." Travel anywhere and you will see the same thing: "Monuments to human misery and wickedness are found everywhere—prisons, hospitals, gallows, and beggars. Here you see the ruins of a flourishing city; in other places you cannot even find the ruins." Bayle was not satisfied with any of the usual explanations for the existence of evil. It was, for example, often said that the harm that people do to one another is a consequence of the free will that God gave them, and is therefore man's fault. But Bayle objected that since God must have foreseen that man would use his freedom to do evil, His gift of free will was like giving a man a knife when you know it will be used for murder. There is, Bayle added, "no good mother who, having given her daughters permission to go to a dance, would not revoke that permission if she were assured that they would succumb to temptations and lose their virginity there." And if it is said that God allowed man to rebel so that He could redeem him through Jesus, this makes God like "a father who allows his children to break their legs so that he can show everyone his great skill in mending their broken bones."

Bayle concluded that "the way in which evil was introduced under the government of a supreme, infinitely good, infinitely holy, and infinitely powerful being is not only inexplicable, but also incomprehensible." He was not, however, trying to show that God was either bad, weak or non-existent—at least, he did not claim to be doing so. Bayle's professed aim was to convince his readers that belief in God's goodness and omnipotence had to rest solely on faith, because human reason was too weak to clear up such ultimate mysteries. As he put it, sceptical reasoning "may have its value in making men conscious of the darkness they are in, so that they will implore help from on high and submit to the authority of the faith."

Some of Bayle's readers thought that this stance was a diplomatic ruse. Many believers who were suspicious of him, and some later admirers who were unbelievers, took it that Bayle's goal was to undermine Christianity whilst pretending to be its champion. Why else would he so often have undermined theological arguments and positions, such as the wickedness of atheists, the conventional explanations of evil, and everyday superstitions that usefully bolstered the faith? As we shall see, David Hume did later use the gambit of which Bayle was suspected,* but there is no solid reason to suspect that Bayle was a thoroughgoing infidel of Hume's stamp. Unlike Hume, Bayle was an active member of his church, and there is no record of him making any private admissions of unbelief.

Perhaps Bayle's faith was strong at some times and less so at others. This would accord with his intellectual disposition, which was one of constant questioning and dissatisfaction with settled dogmas. Bayle was strongly attracted to Pyrrhonism, which he characterised as "the art of disputing about all things and always suspending one's judgment." It was his use of the arguments of ancient Sceptics that later philosophers borrowed most often from his *Dictionary*, and it would have been natural for Bayle to feel the force of such arguments more keenly at some times than at others. He wrote that Pyrrhonism could be dangerous in religion—one should not go so far as to suspend judgement about the existence of God—but a cautious attitude of moderate scepticism was the right one to take in matters of science and politics, as well as in some of the finer points of theology. Bayle's deepest conviction seems to have been that human reason is fragile and limited. The impossibility of rationally comprehending the goodness of God was a case in point. So one must, in the spirit of Socrates and the Pyrrhonists, keep probing and questioning, and never be intellectually complacent.

There is a story that a French cardinal once asked Bayle about his religious beliefs. Bayle is reported to have answered, "I am a good Protestant . . . for . . . I protest against everything that is said, and everything that is done." Whether or not he ever uttered these words, they encapsulate his spirit. It was Bayle's critical attitude to more or less everything which made him something of a Socrates to those thinkers in the eighteenth century and beyond who thought of themselves as enlightened.

---

* See chapter 7, below.

# 6

## THE BEST OF ALL
## POSSIBLE COMPROMISES
# *Leibniz*

"W HEN ONE COMPARES ONE'S OWN TALENTS WITH THOSE OF LEIBNIZ," wrote Denis Diderot, "it is tempting to throw away one's books and go off to die in some quiet corner." Diderot was the author of many of the articles in the 35-volume Paris *Encyclopédie*, as well as its guiding spirit, and was a powerful thinker himself. He did not often agree with Leibniz, and knew only a fraction of his works. But he was familiar enough with his writings and activities to see that stupefied awe is the only fitting first reaction to them. Gottfried Leibniz, who was born in Leipzig in 1646 and died in 1716, was the greatest polymath since Aristotle; there has not yet been a third person who can stand alongside them.

Leibniz chose to publish only a small part of his work, plenty of which still languishes in archives. Aside from philosophy, it is mainly for his achievements in mathematics, logic and physics that he is remembered, but even in those fields only about a tenth of his writings has been printed. Leibniz was one of the two independent discoverers of the infinitesimal calculus—the key tool for analysing continuous change. Newton developed it first, but published later, and it is Leibniz's notation, terminology and methods that are used by mathematicians today. Leibniz also invented a pioneering form of mechanical calculator; he developed the binary arithmetic of 1s and 0s on which digital computers were later based; and, if his work on mathematical logic had come to light earlier than it did, he would have been regarded as the father of that subject, which is a sort of algebra for thoughts. Most of Leibniz's writings on logic were not published until the nineteenth century, just after other mathematicians had begun to explore similar ideas. In physics, he made significant contributions to dynamics and came close to the modern concept of kinetic energy.

It is unlikely that there are any mathematical or scientific treasures of comparable value yet to be unearthed from Leibniz's papers. But some surprises are still emerging, such as his proposed cipher machine. In 2001, some memoranda that he had prepared in 1688 for the Holy Roman Emperor Leopold I were belatedly published, and in 2012 a working model was made of the device specified in the memos. The machine turned out to be more effective than all the cryptographic equipment used until the beginning of the twentieth century. Leibniz's secret machine was an adaptation of his mechanical calculator, designed to make it as quick and easy to encode or decode a letter as it would be to write it, but Leopold was apparently not interested.

Leibniz's secretary estimated that his master's literary remains amounted to over a million pages. There are more than 50,000 items by him in the State Library of Lower Saxony, including about 15,000 letters, and at the present rate of progress, it will take two more centuries before his complete works are published. As for the range of this material, Diderot mentioned Leibniz's contributions to history, mathematics, theology, logic, ethics, physics, law and metaphysics, to which should be added chemistry, medicine, botany, natural history, philology, etymology, geology, architecture, politics and technology. A eulogy of Leibniz delivered to the French Academy of Sciences the year after his death also praised his Latin verse. Others mentioned his fine collection of minerals and fossils.

One of the few things that he did not do was write music. If Leibniz had been a composer, most of his symphonies would have been unfinished. He habitually flitted from one project to the next, leaving work undone because something else caught his eye. A striking example is his incomplete history of the origins of the ducal Brunswick-Lüneburg family, who were his main employers for most of his life. This history was originally supposed to start with the eighth century and end with the seventeenth, but despite working on it sporadically for neary three decades, Leibniz had only reached the year 1005 when he died. This end-point fell just short of the rise of the Guelf dynasty, which was the period of greatest interest to his exasperated employers. What doomed this project—at least from the perspective of the long-suffering Brunswick-Lüneburgs—was Leibniz's uncontrollable curiosity, and his desire to fold many of his own pet projects into the enterprise. Instead of beginning with medieval Europe, Leibniz could not stop himself from going all the way back to the formation of the earth and its minerals, and tracing the earliest human migrations, as well as scouring monastic libraries across Europe for possibly pertinent documents, and diverting himself into irrelevant byways, such as exposing the myth of Pope Joan.

In addition to his restless intellectual appetite, another reason for what has been called his "almost perpetual jumble" of activities was his duties to the courts and potentates who paid him, and the range of projects for the public good that he urged upon them. Leibniz may, as his secretary claimed, have "studied incessantly" and sometimes not risen from his chair for several weeks, but he was also—unlike Aristotle—a man with many practical jobs and enthusiasms. One of the most time-consuming of the tasks which got him out of his chair was his attempt to solve drainage problems at his employers' silver mines in the Harz mountains in northern Germany. Leibniz visited these mines more than thirty times in the 1680s and worked on many designs for windmills and suction pumps, all of which failed. He claimed that obstructive workers undermined his schemes because they feared for their jobs. Historians of mining say the problem was rather that he was out of his depth, distracted by academic disquisitions on the concepts of force and friction while his machines repeatedly broke down around him.

Little is known about the success or otherwise of Leibniz's myriad inventions and proposals in other fields, many of which probably never progressed beyond the vast drawing-board of his mind. They included an improved design for watches, various navigational devices, a compressed air-engine, a fishing machine, better nails, recipes for brandy, more efficient cooking-pots, a submarine, novel techniques for the manufacture of steel, steam-powered fountains, a desalination process, and spring-loaded shoes with which to escape from pursuers. No doubt it is not only Leibniz's bouncing boots that belong with the schemes of Sir Nicholas Gimcrack, the prototypical hare-brained scientist in an English comedy of the time. It is a common fate for energetic inventors that some of their conceptions seem laughable to posterity.

When Leibniz tried to convince Emperor Leopold of the merits of his cipher machine, he also presented plans for an insurance scheme, a factory to produce mineral dyes and a reform of the coinage. Philosophers and mathematicians may understandably wish that he had stayed at his desk to focus on the work he was really good at. But such an attitude ignores Leibniz's deepest motivations and the circumstances of his time and place. As he explained in a briefing paper for Leopold, he had since early life directed his "mind toward the common good." Other plans which he urged on various authorities in the 1680s included a system of vocational training, public health-care and a pension scheme. He later wrote that poverty, unemployment and bad education were among the chief causes of unhappiness, so the fight against such evils was a key part of improving public welfare. This battle required getting one's hands dirty in the world of business, because

> one must furnish the poor with the means of earning their livelihood, not only by using charity . . . but also by taking an interest in agriculture, by furnishing to artisans materials and a market, by educating them to make their productions better, and . . . by putting an end to abusive practices in manufactures and commerce.

Investigations into science, philosophy and theology also played a role in the welfare of mankind, since they revealed the workings of the world in which man found himself, and what he must do to attain happiness. Thus Leibniz's activities outside his study and within it were all of a piece, at least to his way of thinking. All of them were means to the common good, whether he was trying to explore the laws of motion, set theology on a firm foundation, reform health-care or build a better mousetrap.

Bertrand Russell passed a damning judgement on Leibniz's decision to work for aristocrats instead of pursuing a purely academic life. Leibniz chose a "courtly" existence, Russell wrote, which led to an "undue deference to princes, and a lamentable waste of time in the endeavour to please them." Russell did not need the patronage of aristocrats—he was one himself—and seems not to have appreciated that a courtier of Leibniz's stripe was more of a civil servant or government adviser than a sycophant, cup bearer or provider of entertainment. Leibniz's employers were the local rulers: they were the people to lobby and to work for if you wanted to get anything done. As Leibniz himself put it: "The . . . most efficacious means of augmenting the general welfare of men . . . would be to persuade great princes and their ministers. . . . "

SOME OF Leibniz's noble patrons and acquaintances, such as Queen Sophie-Charlotte of Prussia, a daughter of one of the Brunswick dukes, shared his interest in philosophy. Others no doubt did not, including presumably a duchess of Orléans who revealed her attitude to things of the mind when she remarked that Leibniz was one of the few intellectuals who did not stink. In his *History of Western Philosophy*, Russell pronounced that although Leibniz was "one of the supreme intellects of all time," he shamefully chose to publish only shallow ideas that would not upset the nobility or theologians, and kept his best philosophical ideas to himself. This charge was unfair. Leibniz did not have a public philosophy and a private one, but a single metaphysical system, albeit one that underwent changes, was sketchy in parts and was always a work in progress. Its main pieces mostly fitted together neatly: "My principles are such that they can hardly be torn apart from each other. He who knows one well, knows them all. . . ." These principles are to be found in some articles for learned journals, in letters, in a few summaries that he passed around and in two book-length works of philosophy, both of which were prompted by discussions with Sophie-Charlotte. One of these books was a critical commentary on Locke's *Essay*, written in the hope that Locke would respond to it, which Leibniz put aside when Locke died. The other, published when Leibniz was in his sixties, openly defends the ideas that were most important to him, and contains an extended defence of his famous doctrine that ours is the best of all possible worlds, of which more later.

Leibniz's system is strikingly peculiar even for a metaphysical theory—that is, an account of the reality supposedly underlying daily experience and scientific findings. Kant called it "a sort of enchanted world." Hegel found it to be "like a metaphysical romance." For Russell, it was a kind of "fairy tale." I shall summarise the version of this romance that Leibniz expounded from around the age of fifty.

Each of the basic elements of reality, which Leibniz called a "monad"— from the Greek for "unit"—is "a world of its own, having no connections of dependency except with God." These "true atoms of nature" are self-contained and cannot affect one another: they have "no windows through which something can enter or leave." Their destinies unfold independently, each from its own blueprint. Thus in their case, as the pop Buddhist saying has it, all change comes from within.

When Leibniz referred to his monads as "atoms," he did not mean that they are the smallest units of matter. In fact they are not in themselves material at all, though each created monad is somehow united with a parcel of matter. He intended "atom" in the sense of its Greek derivation, which is "uncuttable" or "unsplittable," and, in his view, matter is infinitely splittable, so there are no such things as the smallest pieces of it. Thus any genuinely "atomic" units would have to be non-material. According to Leibniz, some such ultimate building-blocks must exist. He seems to have felt that without a bedrock of things that are indivisible and thus have no parts, there would be no universe at all.

Since monads have no parts, Leibniz argued that they can neither disintegrate nor grow. Every monad, except one, came into existence when the world was made and will expire only when the whole world ends. The exception is God, who is the mightiest monad, though he is different from all the others in several respects. Leibniz's God has all the usual attributes of a monotheist's deity: He is the eternal, perfect, all-knowing, all-powerful and beneficent creator of all, and is never united with anything so lowly as matter.

Monads are co-ordinated by a "pre-established harmony" that was arranged by God when He created each monad and implanted the seeds of all its future activities within it. The situation, Leibniz explained, is like

> several different bands of musicians or choirs separately playing their
> parts, and placed in such a way that they do not see and do not even

hear each other, though they nevertheless can agree perfectly, each following his own notes, so that someone hearing all of them would find a marvellous harmony there.

This recalls the analogy of two synchronised but unconnected clocks which some philosophers in the previous generation had used to describe the relation between mind and body.* When one clock shows twelve, the other chimes noon, and when I will one of my arms to rise, up the limb goes—but in neither case, according to this theory, does one event cause the other. Leibniz used this two-clocks idea to explain the co-ordination of mind and body as well as to account for the harmonious behaviour of monads.

Although each monad is cut off from all the others, except from God, it does in some sense reflect the states of every other monad. Each monad is thus a "mirror of the universe." It contains not only "traces of everything that happens to it," but also traces of "everything that happens in the universe, even though God alone could recognize them all." Leibniz called these traces "perceptions," despite the fact that many of them are said to be unconscious. It is only dimly that each created monad registers all the others. Leibniz likened the situation to a person hearing the roar of the sea: "I hear the particular noises of each wave, of which the whole noise is composed, but without distinguishing them."

Each monad's "perceptions" are different, because they reflect the universe from a unique perspective, and these perceptions change as the future unfolds. The changes come, as always, from within. All monads have an inbuilt tendency—or "appetition," as Leibniz called it—to progress from one state to another. Only higher monads have conscious desires and explicit goals that prompt them to act, but all monads have a sort of drive towards self-realisation as they strive to fulfill their implanted destinies. For Leibniz, all activity requires life of some kind, so every monad may be said to be alive.

How DO WE, and the rest of the furniture of the visible universe, fit into this enchanted world? Leibniz struggled with this question, but he was

---

* See p. 28, above.

sure of two things. First, the only objects that have "absolute reality" are monads. Secondly, monads are minds, or are mind-like, because they have perceptions and appetites.

Nowadays, philosophers do not have much use for talk of what is absolutely real. Something either exists or it doesn't, and there are no halfway houses. But in Leibniz's time, reality came in degrees, partly because philosophers had inherited a concept of "substance" according to which some things exist in their own right while others exist only in a second-class sort of way.* Leibniz defined a substance as "a complete being" or "a being which subsists in itself." Monads are the sole true substances, according to him, because only they are complete in themselves. All physical objects and physical forces somehow "result from" them. But in what sense do physical things result from monads?

Leibniz tried to explain himself by comparing matter to rainbows and parhelia (i.e., halos that are sometimes seen around the sun). The idea is that just as rainbows are observed by everyone and have a basis in nature, and yet are not really where they appear to be, so physical bodies are also not quite what they seem, but are only appearances somehow thrown up by monads. Yet this analogy is too strained to be of much help. Rainbows and parhelia result from the behaviour of light when it hits water droplets or ice crystals in the earth's atmosphere. But monads—unlike light, water and ice—are not physical, so it is unclear how tables, chairs or mountains could be said to result from them in anything like the same way.

In some places Leibniz wrote as if the physical world were a sort of co-ordinated dream shared by all monads: it is to be explained "solely through the perceptions of monads functioning in harmony with each other." He seems to have meant that the reality of everyday things somehow lies in the consistency of the private films that monads watch in their windowless solitude. Each film portrays a world from one monad's point of view; put the films together, and you have the universe. This is an intriguing idea, but nobody is quite sure what to make of it, or how to square it with other things that he wrote.

Leibniz refused to go as far as "the one in Ireland who attacks the

---

* See pp. 102–3, above.

reality of bodies." He was referring to George Berkeley, the great eccentric of Anglophone philosophy, who infamously argued in his *Principles of Human Knowledge* (1710) that the notion of matter is nonsensical, and that nothing exists except God and some other minds and their perceptions. Bishop Berkeley, as he later became, made many penetrating criticisms of Locke and of other proponents of the "mechanical philosophy." Some of Berkeley's reasoning is so ingenious that he is still avidly studied by philosophers, even though almost all of them regard his main conclusions as doubly absurd. Not only did Berkeley maintain that minds and their perceptions are the sole contents of the universe, he also claimed that this thesis is plain common sense, and would be accepted by any ordinary person who had not been corrupted by bad philosophy. Leibniz noted in his copy of Berkeley's *Principles* that "much here . . . is correct and close to my own view. But it is expressed paradoxically. For it is not necessary to say that matter is nothing, but it is sufficient to say that it is a phenomenon, like the rainbow."

Leibniz usually made it sound as if monads were somehow inside physical things: "there is no part of matter in which monads do not exist." They are not inside matter in the way that a yolk is inside an egg—you would never be able to extract them, for instance—but monads play a role in the constitution of every piece of matter. Consider Leibniz's account of living creatures. According to him, each of the objects that we ordinarily recognise as a living thing, such as a tree, a spider, a giraffe or a person, has a dominant monad that somehow organises the matter of which the creature is composed. This dominant monad turns the creature's parts into a functioning whole. What sort of a creature it is depends on the sophistication of its dominant monad, which Leibniz calls the "soul" of the body concerned. If this monad has relatively distinct perceptions and a memory, then the creature is an animal. If not, it is a mere plant. And if the dominant monad has a rational understanding of things, then the creature is either a person or an angel. It turns out that there are vastly more living things than one might think. The physical world is teeming with them, even where the naked eye cannot detect them: "there is a world of creatures, of living beings, of animals . . . of souls in the least part of matter." Indeed, "every particle of the universe contains a world of an infinity of creatures," so "there is nothing fallow, sterile or dead in the universe."

Leibniz was mightily impressed by microscopes. When he was in his early twenties, he visited Antoni van Leeuwenhoek, a Dutch cloth-merchant who more or less invented microbiology. Leeuwenhoek had just discovered spermatozoa, which he called "little animals in the seed of males." What Leibniz saw when he looked through Leeuwenhoek's lenses supported the idea that living things are like nested Russian dolls: there are creatures within creatures. The microscope also revealed chalk to be made of the shells of tiny sea animals, so even apparently non-living matter could be made of creatures, too. If only more people worked on microscopy—"a hundred thousand wouldn't be too many," wrote Leibniz—much light could be shed on the nature of matter, "for the use of medicine, food, and mechanical ends."

Yet it was not just because of sperm and chalk that Leibniz believed there was an infinity of living things in every speck of dust. Although microscopes provided some welcome confirmation of the idea, philosophical considerations played a larger role. Matter in itself is "merely passive," according to Leibniz, so something alive must be added to it in order to account for activity in the universe. And because matter must, for various reasons, be "actually subdivided without end, each part divided into parts having some motion of their own," there have to be infinitely many tiny creatures associated with it, each of which has an active monad for a soul.

LEIBNIZ's philosophical convictions were shaped above all by a desire to reconcile and combine the great systems of the past. "Truth," he once wrote, "is more widespread than people think." Almost everyone manages to get hold of some of it, and thus most schools of thought are "right in a good part of what they propose." His aim was to mine the wisdom of the ages and extract a core of doctrine that dovetailed with recent scientific work. The resulting synthesis, he claimed, united "Plato with Democritus, Aristotle with Descartes, the Scholastics with the moderns, theology and morality with reason." His eclectic philosophy found room for many others, too. The Stoics were right to say that all things are connected. The

Pythagoreans were on to something with their "reduction of everything to harmonies and numbers." The ancient Sceptics were correct about the "lack of substantial reality in . . . sensible [i.e., perceptible] things." Even devotees of the Cabala, who mix medieval Jewish mysticism with a late version of Platonism, have a glimpse of the truth when they "put a kind of feeling into everything."

Leibniz's biggest diplomatic challenge was to arrange a marriage between the Aristotelian scholasticism of university theologians and the new-fangled explorations of matter and motion. Such a match would reconcile "the mechanical philosophy of the moderns with the caution of some intelligent and well-intentioned persons who fear . . . we are withdrawing too far from immaterial beings, to the disadvantage of piety." There is room for both modern and more traditional views of nature, once one realises that they amount to different perspectives on the same thing:

> In general, we must hold that everything in the world can be explained in two ways: through . . . efficient causes [i.e., prior events or circumstances which push things along], and through . . . final causes [i.e., purposes or aims, which pull things towards their goals]. . . .

Leibniz called the realm of efficient (or mechanical) causes the "kingdom of power," and the realm of final causes the "kingdom of wisdom." God governed both kingdoms "for his glory" and they "everywhere interpenetrate each other without confusing or disturbing their laws."

MONADS, which are minds or mind-like, enabled Leibniz to reinstate the goal-directed "final" causes that the mechanical philosophy liked to ignore but which the pious found to be appropriate for a God-governed universe. According to Leibniz, final causes were indeed superfluous in everyday physics, but they were essential for metaphysics—that is, for a deeper view of things. He wrote that all physical phenomena can be "derived from . . . mechanical causes, but . . . these very mechanical laws as a whole are derived from higher reasons." So, once again, everyone was right.

Leibniz's project of universal reconciliation was not limited to philosophy. It also extended to religion. He was brought up a Lutheran, and declined an offer to become librarian of the Vatican because that would have meant converting to Catholicism. But, he claimed, if he had been born a Catholic, he would happily have remained one. The main versions of Christianity did not differ on any really important point, so you might as well stay wherever you are. He was fond of telling a story he'd heard about two English brothers in Elizabethan times, one of them a Protestant and the other a Catholic. Each man debated tirelessly to convert his brother to his own faith. It worked in both cases and so they changed places.

Leibniz toiled for decades to formulate a set of doctrines that would be acceptable to all the major denominations, thus continuing the work of Hugo Grotius, a Dutch lawyer and diplomat, whose manual for a proposed common form of Christianity was published two decades before Leibniz was born. Grotius's book was translated into many languages for use by missionaries, but Leibniz's was never finished. Also like Grotius, Leibniz played a part in various diplomatic negotiations aimed at unifying the churches, none of which had much success. Leibniz's strategy for securing peace between religious factions was more ambitious and less practical than the policy of toleration advocated by Locke, Bayle and (later) Voltaire. In place of their emphasis on putting up with others even if you disagree with them, Leibniz wanted to convince people that they didn't really disagree in the first place.

He even maintained that Chinese religion was closer to Christianity than it appeared to be, so the Chinese could be brought into the fold as well. He did not go so far as Joachim Bouvet, a Jesuit missionary who thought that Fu Xi, the supposed author of the *I Ching*, may have been the same person as the prophet Enoch. But when Father Bouvet told Leibniz that the diagrams of the *I Ching* seemed to encode the biblical story of creation, he seized on this excellent news. Prompted by Bouvet, Leibniz concluded that the *I Ching*'s hexagrams, which are sets of six broken and unbroken lines, represent a version of the binary arithmetic that Leibniz himself had recently invented—or, as it now emerged, reinvented. The religious significance of this fact was that, according to Leibniz, a knowledge of binary arithmetic, which generates all numbers from 1s and 0s, reveals a tacit understanding of "the origin of things from unity and nothing."

And because it was generally held to be almost impossible to get pagans to accept the biblical idea of creation out of nothing, this suggested that it would not be as hard as people thought to convert the Chinese. Leibniz bent over backwards to interpret Chinese texts and folklore in ways that made them sound more Christian. For example, although he had to acknowledge that "the Chinese scholars speak neither of Hell nor of purgatory," still "it is possible that some among them believe or have believed at other times that the wandering souls which prowl here and there in the mountains and the forests are in a sort of purgatory." On the whole, Leibniz wrote, "the substance of the ancient theology of the Chinese is intact and, purged of additional errors, can be harnessed to the great truths of the Christian religion."

∞

LEIBNIZ'S ECLECTIC TASTES and intellectual ambition were evident early in life. By the time he was eight years old, he had shown himself to be a prodigious little scholar and was allowed to devour anything he wanted in the library of his late father, a professor of moral philosophy at Leipzig University who had died when Leibniz was six. The boy ingested ancient authors, Church Fathers, medieval philosophers, Renaissance scholars, and some modern thinkers, including Hobbes. Poetry, history and logic were among his favourite subjects. At the age of thirteen, he was trying to improve on Aristotle's logic, an endeavour which his schoolteachers discouraged.

At fourteen, he enrolled at his father's former university to study ancient languages, rhetoric, mathematics and philosophy. Leibniz later claimed that at this stage he was already looking for a way to fuse scholastic and modern thought. Be that as it may, the germs of some of his distinctive philosophical ideas and schemes were already evident in his late teens. A dissertation that he completed before he was twenty was his first stab at what he later called an "alphabet of human thoughts." This was to be the basis of a logical language by means of which "a fundamental knowledge of all things" could eventually be obtained. Leibniz worked on this project sporadically for many years, but did not publish his results, which fell short of his early hopes.

Two years before his death, he mused that if only he had been less distracted by other tasks, or had some talented young people to help him, he "should still hope to create a kind of universal symbolistic in which all truths of reason would be reduced to a sort of calculus." Such an invention would, he wrote, prove to be the "key to all sciences." Readers of George Eliot's *Middlemarch* may recall the novel's obsessive scholar, Edward Casaubon, whose life's work was an unfinishable "Key to All Mythologies"—and who, like Leibniz, had "a mind weighted with unpublished matter." Unlike Casaubon's project, though, something did eventually come of Leibniz's efforts to find a universal key. His pioneering development of mathematical logic was a direct result of it.

The idea of an artificial language that could improve one's reasoning and advance the sciences had been in the air for quite a while. Some four decades before Leibniz's student days, Descartes had mused that if one could "explain correctly what are the simple ideas in the human imagination out of which all human thoughts are compounded," one could in theory construct a language in which "it would be almost impossible to go wrong . . . thus enabling peasants to be better judges of the truth of things than philosophers are now." Descartes does not seem to have spent any time trying to develop such a language, though others did. What was novel about Leibniz's approach was its emphasis on numbers and the notion of applying mathematical techniques to the art of reasoning. In his youthful dissertation, he praised Hobbes, who "rightly stated that everything done by our mind is a *computation*, by which is to be understood either the addition of a sum or the subtraction of a difference." By assigning numbers to concepts, and manipulating them mathematically, Leibniz believed that his proposed language could reduce all intellectual disputes to simple matters of calculation. Even the truths of religion could thus be made manifest, and so missionaries would find it easier to convert heathens. One of Leibniz's techniques was to let prime numbers stand for primitive concepts and let composite numbers denote combinations of these primitives, a device that was exploited by Kurt Gödel (1906–1978) to produce the two most important theorems in twentieth-century mathematical logic. However, juggling with concepts in such ways has not proved to be of much use outside mathematics.

Armed with degrees in philosophy and law from Leipzig, Leibniz enrolled in the law faculty at the University of Altdorf, near Nuremberg, in 1666 and submitted a doctoral thesis within six weeks. Its topic was the resolution of hard cases in civil law: Leibniz argued that an answer to them could always be derived from the principles of international or natural law. The faculty was impressed and offered him a professorship a few months later. But the twenty-year-old Leibniz wanted to make his way in the wider world, and turned the job down. Within a year, his life settled into the pattern it followed until his death: a constant shuttling between the realm of science and philosophy and the world of politics and diplomacy.

His first two patrons were Archbishop von Schönborn of Mainz, one of the eight prince-electors of the agglomeration of states that Voltaire memorably described as neither holy nor Roman nor an empire, and Schönborn's former prime minister, Baron Boineburg. The archbishop set Leibniz to work assisting with a reorganisation of the legal code, and later appointed him a judge in one of Mainz's highest courts. Boineburg employed Leibniz as an adviser, assistant and librarian; the two became friends, and Boineburg soon involved him in some secret work, to which Leibniz gave a logician's twist. One of the candidates for election to the throne of Poland, which fell vacant in 1668, asked Boineburg for help, and Boineburg had Leibniz write campaign literature that was to be published under the name of a fictitious Polish aristocrat. Leibniz produced a booklet that used the scientific methods of Galileo, Bacon, Hobbes and Descartes—or so its preface claimed—to deduce from some sixty propositions and their corollaries the conclusion that their man ought to win. Because of printing delays, the booklet did not in fact appear until after he had lost.

At the same time, Leibniz was writing about physics, philosophy and theology. These subjects were closely connected in his mind, because he felt that the new science of matter and motion threatened his "life's greatest good, the certainty of an eternity after death and the hope that divine benevolence would some time be made manifest." It was the job of philoso-

phy to remove this apparent threat. As a first step towards reconciling religion and the new science, the young Leibniz presented various arguments
to show that matter "is not self-sufficient and cannot subsist without an
incorporeal [i.e., non-physical] principle." Thus Leibniz went one step further than Descartes and maintained not only that matter cannot account
for mind but that mind is needed to account for matter.


WHILE HE WAS at Mainz, Leibniz mused about an encyclopedia that
would organise all branches of knowledge. This was perhaps prompted
by the experience of arranging Boineburg's chaotic collection of books.
He also drew up a plan for a magnum opus that would start with the
principles of science and logic, proceed to prove the existence of God
and the immortality of the soul, and then defend Christianity's distinctive beliefs. Although the threefold nature of God and the presence of
Jesus's body in consecrated bread could not be demonstrated beyond
doubt, they could, according to Leibniz, at least be shown by philosophy to be coherent and plausible. The work would finish by dealing
with scripture and the authority of the Church. The result would be a
theology for everyone.

Schönborn's court was a good place to hatch such ecumenical schemes.
Both he and Boineburg had negotiated for peace among the churches. But
Mainz was hardly the epicentre of science and philosophy in Europe. In his
early twenties, Leibniz began to seek contact with innovators and scientific
societies elsewhere.

He wrote a letter of fulsome praise to the eighty-three-year-old
Hobbes, applauding his writings on motion and asking him to say more
about the nature of mind. Although Leibniz liked Hobbes's idea that
reasoning is computation, he rejected his materialism and urged Hobbes
to "undertake that task which Descartes started but did not finish, of
strengthening our hopes of immortality"—that is, he wanted an account
of the mind which made it clear that it was independent of the body. In
later life, Leibniz came up with a striking image to suggest that something
inside us is not physical. Suppose, for the sake of argument, that there
could be a machine "whose structure makes it think, sense, and have per-

ceptions." Now imagine it greatly enlarged, "so that we could enter into it, as one enters into a mill." What would we see as we walked around inside this clanking machinery? Only "parts that push one another." We would surely "never find anything to explain a perception." This little thought-experiment does not settle anything, but it neatly expresses a common intuition.

In his letter to Hobbes, Leibniz also praised the old man's political philosophy, and mentioned that he himself was constructing a theory of jurisprudence along Hobbesian lines. People were quite wrong to call Hobbes's works impious and licentious, the twenty-four-year-old reassured him. Yet just a few months later, Leibniz—ever the diplomat—was congratulating one of his former teachers for an attack on Spinoza's "intolerably licentious" *Tractatus theologico-politicus*, which, Leibniz wrote, was all based on Hobbes. The letter to Hobbes apparently never reached him; certainly there was no reply. Leibniz had more luck with Spinoza himself, to whom he sent an essay on optics, together with extravagant praise, and asked for the great man's comments, which were forthcoming. Leibniz also wrote rather boastfully to the now-eminent Arnauld, listing his own achievements. Leibniz had at this stage begun work on his calculating machine, and was in touch with French mathematicians and members of London's Royal Society, some of whom were impressed with him. It was time to try and meet some of these people. Luckily, Boineburg had some diplomatic and business errands for Leibniz to do in Paris.

Leibniz managed to stretch his stay in Paris to four and a half years. His diplomatic mission got nowhere, through no fault of his own, and the business was a small matter, so there was plenty of time for study and discussion. He immersed himself in the latest mathematics, physics and technology, spent time with leading thinkers such as Arnauld and Malebranche, and deepened his knowledge of Descartes's work. Most of Leibniz's important results in mathematics, including the differential and integral calculus, were arrived at in Paris, where he was more or less tutored by Christiaan Huygens. On a visit to London, he demonstrated a working model of his calculating machine to the Royal Society, which elected him a fellow. The machine was the first to perform multiplication and division directly — though it could not, as Leibniz had claimed, extract square and cube roots.

Leibniz would rather not have been extracted from Paris, but no suitable job could be found there, so he accepted an offer from the Duke of Hanover to be his counsellor and intellectual factotum. Hanover remained Leibniz's base for the rest of his life. Although he took every opportunity to travel, sometimes to the annoyance of the three successive dukes who employed him over the years, he was relatively isolated in northern Germany, so it is perhaps not surprising that he wrote so many letters. From his mid-forties onwards, Leibniz was usually corresponding with over a hundred people at any given time. He had no family life to divert him from work. According to his secretary, he considered marriage at the age of fifty, "but the person he had in mind asked for time to reflect. This gave Leibniz time to reflect, too, and so he never married."

ON HIS WAY from Paris to start work in Hanover, Leibniz stopped off in The Hague in November 1676 and spent several days with Spinoza, who died three months later. They talked about the political situation in the Netherlands, Descartes's theory of motion and Leibniz's plan for a universal language; but it was the theological implications of Spinoza's thought that most interested Leibniz. Two years later, he obtained a copy of Spinoza's posthumous *Ethics* and listed the points that made it a dangerous book. One of them was what Leibniz called Spinoza's "fatal necessity." Everything happens because it must, which seems to leave no room for free will. Spinoza's determinism was particularly troubling for Leibniz because he himself was committed to something similar. Leibniz was keen to explain that his own version of fate, unlike Spinoza's, was consistent with Christian ideas of human choice and moral responsibility.

Leibniz maintained, as we have seen, that the "true atoms of nature" follow patterns that are implanted in advance by God: "everything happens to each substance as a consequence of the first state God gave to it." The same is true of people, according to Leibniz—everything that they will think or do is fixed before they are even born—but this does not mean that they cannot exercise free will, because the ability to make decisions is one of the things that God has implanted in them. As far as Leibniz was concerned, if a person acts on the basis of a considered choice, and not as the result of pressure from other people, then that is enough to count as free will. It does not matter that the outcome of this choice was determined in advance.

What does matter, according to Leibniz, is whether or not our choices are "necessitated." Leibniz was fond of glossing his account of freedom by asserting that the causes of events and actions "incline without necessitating." The remark is rather obscure, because he was never inclined to explain what he meant by "incline." But he did explain what he meant by "necessitate." Leibniz distinguished two kinds of necessity, which he called "absolute" and "hypothetical." Something is absolutely necessary if it is necessary in itself, as truths of mathematics are said to be. Under no circumstances could two plus two have equalled anything other than four: the equation is true come what may, so it is absolutely necessary. But a hypothetical necessity is necessary only in relation to some other fact or assumption. For example, given the fact that Leibniz never married, it follows necessarily that he was a bachelor, even though he could have got married if circumstances had been different. It is thus hypothetically, but not absolutely, necessary that he was a bachelor. Similarly, according to Leibniz, our actions, and indeed all events, are only hypothetically necessary. They are necessary, given that God arranged the world in the way that He did, but they are not necessary in themselves, because He could have arranged it differently. Rather implausibly, Leibniz seems to have thought that this distinction between two kinds of necessity was enough on its own to rescue the notion of free will. Not many philosophers have agreed with him about this. Even if—to take one of Leibniz's own examples—God could have chosen not to create the Judas that He did create, it is hard to see how the actual Judas's decision to betray Jesus can really have been his own "free" choice, if, as Leibniz held, the poor man could not have done otherwise. It hardly seems relevant, or much of a consolation to Judas, that his betrayal was not "absolutely" necessary since the world might have been created differently.

Why was Leibniz convinced that events unfold according to a fixed pattern, once God has decided what He is going to create? There seem to be several strands to the story. One is Leibniz's doctrine that there is in God's mind a comprehensive "notion" of every object which incorporates all of its states and activities. Suppose that God had decided to make as His first man someone who did not eat Eve's apple. According to Leibniz, this hypothetical man would not be "our Adam," because the actual Adam's "notion" incorporates the fact that he gave in to temptation, but this man's does not. It follows that the biblical Adam could not have failed to eat the apple, because otherwise he would have been, as Leibniz put it, "another Adam."

Another strand in Leibniz's thinking about the fixity of all events and circumstances is what he called "the principle of sufficient reason," which states that "nothing happens without a reason why it should be so, rather than otherwise." Sometimes he expressed this vague principle as "there is no effect without a cause," and sometimes in terms of the intelligibility of all things: "a reason can be given for every truth." At the end of his life, Leibniz debated the principle of sufficient reason in an exchange of letters with Samuel Clarke, an English theologian and scientist who was a close friend of Newton's. Clarke agreed that the principle was true, but objected that the reason why things are as they are "is oft-times no other than the mere will of God." Leibniz begged to differ: it would be contrary to God's wisdom and perfection if He ever decided anything on no more than a whim. God's choices, which have "rendered every event certain and determined once for all," are always motivated by "His supreme reason."

Much of the debate between Leibniz and Clarke focussed on space, time and matter. Why did God create the world when He did, rather than one year earlier or later? Similarly, why did He not transpose the regions of space so that east was west, and vice versa? Surely, Clarke argued, God's choices in such matters were arbitrary and do not have any rational explanation. No, Leibniz answered, God did not make any such arbitrary decisions, because time and space are purely relative. They are not entities in their own right, but consist merely in the relations between objects, so it does not make sense to suppose that God could have done as Clarke imagined. For example, to envisage an earlier start to the universe is in effect to envisage a time before time, which is incoherent. (Einstein generously saw Leibniz's relational theory of time and space as a precursor to his own.

He wrote that Leibniz's rejection of space and time as absolutes, although "supported by inadequate arguments, was actually justified.")

Leibniz regarded his principle of sufficient reason as a tool that could be used to prove all sorts of important truths. For instance, it could be used to show that there can never be two exactly identical objects, because if there really were no intrinsic difference between them, there could be no explanation for the fact that there were two of them in different places. What possible reason could God have for putting one of them over here and the other over there, rather than vice versa? Since there must be a reason for everything, it follows that you will never find "two eggs or two leaves or two blades of grass in a garden that are perfectly similar." Clarke objected that Leibniz was presuming to know far too much about God's methods: how could Leibniz be certain that God did not in fact "have wise reasons for creating many parts of matter exactly alike in different parts of the universe?" Clarke's complaint was telling. Leibniz did, in effect, tend to confuse his own mind with that of God. If he couldn't think of a good reason why God would do something, he assumed that God would not be able to think of one, either. It was Leibniz's conviction that he could get inside the mind of God which made him so sure that this is the best of all possible worlds. For why would God make any other?

∞

"If this is the best of all possible worlds, what on earth are the others like?" So asks the bewildered and bloody hero of Voltaire's best-known story, *Candide, or Optimism* (1759), in which the young man suffers many misfortunes and sees plenty of examples of the barbarity of mankind. Candide had just escaped a disastrous earthquake at Lisbon. Like many of the calamities in Voltaire's tale, this episode is based on fact: an earthquake struck Lisbon, which was then the fourth-largest city in Europe, while the faithful were at Mass on All Saints' Day in 1755. Around thirty thousand people were killed by the quake and by the floods and fires that followed it. Having survived this natural disaster, Candide is seized by a mob who have been urged by the local academic authorities to avert any further damage to the city by burning several people who are suspected of various crimes, such as marrying one's godmother or reverting to Judaism after having converted to Christianity. Candide is, as usual, in the wrong place at the wrong time, and so is his companion, a philosopher named Dr Pangloss. It is Pangloss who had taught him that this is the best of all possible worlds, which Candide is now beginning to doubt.

Towards the end of the story, even Pangloss is driven to admit that he no longer really believes that all is well with the world, though he says he will continue to profess his sunny doctrine in public, "for, after all, I'm a philosopher and it would be inappropriate for me to change my mind."

Pangloss is Leibniz as Voltaire saw him. In 1710, Leibniz had published a long book entitled *Essays in Theodicy on the Goodness of God, the Freedom of Man and the Origin of Evil*, which sought to answer the arguments of Pierre Bayle, who maintained, as we have seen, that it is impossible for human reason to grasp why God's world contains so much suffering. Leibniz thought that Bayle had given up too easily. It was perfectly possible to explain rationally what God was up to. Leibniz invented the term "theodicy" (in its French and Latin forms) to mean the justification of God's ways to man—or, as an unbeliever might put it, the art of making excuses on behalf of God. Among other things, Leibniz tried to show that God had created what is, all things considered, "the best [*optimum*] among all possible worlds." It is only our imperfect understanding of the universe, Leibniz argued, which prevents us from appreciating this fact, and from seeing that God is therefore innocent of the charge of making a world that is worse than it needs to be. A review of Leibniz's *Theodicy* in a French Jesuit journal coined the term *optimisme* to describe its striking doctrine that this world is the best that could have been created. Voltaire's tale then popularised the term.

This philosophical "optimism" is more extreme than what is now ordinarily meant by the word. Nowadays an optimist is merely one who believes that the world is on balance more good than bad, or that it is in the process of improving—not, as Leibniz argued, that it could not possibly be any better. There is also a weaker form of optimism which is more of an attitude or temperament than a belief, and is exemplified in *Pollyanna*, an American children's book from the early twentieth century. Pollyanna liked to play the "just being glad" game, the aim of which was to "find something about everything to be glad about." In theory, someone might be rather pessimistic yet also be a Pollyanna. One might believe that the world is mostly bad, or that things are getting steadily worse, but still be inclined to play the "just being glad" game, in order to make life more bearable. Jewish humour can have a strain of pessimistic Pollyannaism.

Voltaire's Dr Pangloss was something of a Pollyanna as well as a Leibnizian optimist. Until his misfortunes eventually wore him down, he was inclined to look only on the bright side of things. One talent that helped him do so was his gift for concocting proofs of the hidden benefits of apparent disasters. For example, when he contracted syphilis, Pangloss reasoned that if Christopher Columbus had not brought the disease back to Europe from the New World, Europeans would not have had chocolate, either. Pangloss also tended to mangle Leibniz's doctrine that the world as a whole is the best possible one, and turned it into the absurd idea that each particular thing one happens to come across is the best possible exemplar of its kind. Thus Pangloss said of his former employer, the Baron Thunder-ten-tronckh, that he had "the most beautiful of all castles, and his wife was the best of all possible baronesses."

*Candide* is, of course, a lampoon rather than a philosophical treatise. Voltaire did sometimes try his hand at abstract argument, but he wasn't especially good at it, and the usual verdict among philosophers is that *Candide* is no more than a parody. It undermines some crude versions of philosophical optimism, but does not refute Leibniz's own careful statements of it. As we shall see, a closer look suggests that Voltaire did in effect succeed in highlighting fatal flaws in Leibniz's position, even if he made jokes while he was about it.

AT THE BEGINNING of his *Theodicy*, Leibniz summarised the Christian story of man's fall and its consequences:

Man is exposed to a temptation to which it is known that he will succumb, thereby causing an infinitude of frightful evils. . . . [B]y this means death and diseases being introduced, with a thousand other misfortunes and miseries . . . wickedness will . . . hold sway and virtue will be oppressed on earth. . . .

Moreover, "it is much worse when one considers the life to come, since but a small number of men will be saved and . . . all the rest will perish eternally." Among those who will suffer eternal torment are the countless unfortunates who have never heard of Jesus. Such, Leibniz notes, are among the "difficulties" facing Christian belief. Yet he is confident that he can "banish . . . the false ideas that represent God . . . as an absolute prince employing a despotic power, unfitted to be loved and unworthy of being loved."

Leibniz's first step is to establish the being and nature of God, which he does in a single dense paragraph. All the things we experience are contingent—that is, they might not have existed. So how did they come to be? According to Leibniz, the only satisfactory answer must involve another entity, separate from the world, which "carries with it the reason for its existence." This thing must be intelligent, because creation might have unfolded in all sorts of different ways, yet something seems to have picked out just one of them. And in order to have chosen and created everything, this intelligence "ought to be . . . absolutely perfect in *power*, in *wisdom* and in *goodness*," though Leibniz's reasoning on this last point is obscure.

Having proved to his own satisfaction that there must be a perfectly good and powerful God, Leibniz then argues that He "cannot but have chosen the best" when deciding which world to make. For if God had chosen the second-best, or any other world, it would follow that He could have done better, which clashes with the idea that He is perfect. Now, the world which is best overall may well have a great deal of evil in it, according to Leibniz, for "[w]e know . . . that often an evil brings forth a good whereto one would not have attained without that evil." Thus a world that is as miserable as ours could, in theory, be better than any other. And this, for Leibniz, is in fact the case:

> It is true that one may imagine possible worlds without sin and without unhappiness . . . but these same worlds again would be very inferior to ours in goodness. I cannot show you this in detail. For [how] can I know and can I present infinities to you and compare them together?

We have, Leibniz wrote, "gained Jesus Christ himself by reason of sin." If our minds were capacious enough to grasp all the interconnections in the universe—which is "all of one piece, like an ocean"—we would see that all the bad things that happen are required in order to secure some greater good, just as the existence of sin was required for the arrival of Jesus. (Leibniz assumed it was obvious that a world with both sin and Jesus is better than a world without either of them.) Thus although we can't ourselves explain why each disaster and every last bit of misery is necessary for the overall good, we do know that there must be such explanations, since otherwise God would have done things differently. So God is lovable after all, because He did the best that can be done. It is worth noting that this argument of Leibniz's would apply even if life were much more unpleasant than it is. Even if, for example, every being in the universe were tortured to death at the end of a short and unremittingly miserable existence, Leibniz would still be obliged to maintain that there is some godly reason for it.

NONE OF THIS was altogether new. Although Leibniz is nowadays singled out for ridicule because of his doctrine that this is the best of all possible worlds, the idea long predates him and even Christianity. It was expressed in Plato's dialogues, and elaborated with Panglossian enthusiasm by Stoic philosophers nineteen centuries before Leibniz. It was only Leibniz, however, who had the bad luck to attract the contemptuous wit of Voltaire.

Plato wrote that the works of the master-craftsman who fashioned the world must have been "the fairest," because this craftsman "desired that all things should be good and nothing bad, so far as this was attainable." Chrysippus and Cleanthes, two heads of the Stoic school in Athens, added that "providence has omitted nothing that could contribute to a more . . . useful organisation. If the world's business could have been better disposed, it would have been arranged accordingly." Like Voltaire's Pangloss, Chrysippus was not lost for explanations of providence's apparent lapses. The horrors of war help to solve the problems of overpopulation, he noted, and thus are ultimately beneficial. And fierce beasts serve the useful purpose of eliciting brave acts from hunters. Some Stoics went even further than Leibniz and embraced a sort of super-optimism. According to them, the world is so excellent just as it is that generous providence will ensure that the course of history is endlessly repeated down to the last detail.

Like the pre-Christian Stoics, St Augustine held that bad things exist only insofar as they "bring forth good out of evil" and that if it ever seems to you that God should have arranged things better, you may be sure that you are mistaken, and that there is a hidden reason why things are as they are. It was not, however, an altogether straightforward matter for medieval theologians to determine whether God could have made a better world. On the one hand, God is absolutely free, so He could have made any world He wanted—including, presumably, one that was better than what He actually chose. On the other hand, He is perfect, so He would not have made a flawed world. In the thirteenth century, St Thomas Aquinas reasoned that there can be no such thing as the best possible world, just as there can be no such thing as the largest possible number. Because God alone is infinitely good, there is a gap of infinitely many degrees of goodness between Himself and any other creature. So, for any given being whom God creates, there is a better creature whom He could have created. Any possible world is thus subject to improvement by the addition of a new creature who is better than any of the old ones. Still, there was for Aquinas one important sense in which God could not have made the actual world any better than it is. Although He could have made a different world consisting of better creatures, the arrangements in the actual world, given the creatures it contains, cannot be improved. For Aquinas, our world is like a jigsaw puzzle with all its pieces in the right place: God could have made another jigsaw out of better pieces, but He has put this one together perfectly.

Yet what exactly makes one set of arrangements better than another? A partial answer that impressed Leibniz was proposed in the 1670s by Malebranche. According to this philosopher-priest, one sparkling feature of our world is the fact that it is governed by principles which are "so simple and so natural that it is perfectly worthy of the infinite wisdom of its author." It would be undignified for God to keep tinkering with affairs on earth, so

He has instituted physical laws that keep things running smoothly on their own. Moreover, these laws help to explain some apparent defects in His workmanship. Take, for instance, the birth of deformed children. God has wisely arranged that the imagination of a mother will affect her unborn child, which has the beneficial effect of helping it to avoid some dangers. If the mother was afraid of lions, the child will inherit her fear and automatically steer clear of them. But one by-product of this ingenious mechanism, Malebranche suggested, is that a baby will occasionally take on the shape of a fruit that its mother craved during pregnancy.

The birth of a few pear-shaped children was the acceptable price to be paid for the boon of a generally efficient mechanism of inheritance. Similarly, the fact that rain falls pointlessly on the oceans and not just on cultivated land is a result of the admirable uniformity of the laws of motion. It would have been possible to make a world in which the rain fell only when and where it would do the most good, and in this sense Malebranche was prepared to concede that God could have made a world that is "more perfect than the one in which we live." But the physics of such a world would have been too convoluted, according to Malebranche. So when God chose from among the "infinity of possible worlds," He picked the one that was best "with respect to the simplicity of the ways necessary to its production or to its conservation."

Leibniz, who met Malebranche in Paris, liked this notion of a vast panoply of "possible worlds," and adopted Malebranche's account with one emendation. Leibniz thought it was misleading to say that God could in any sense have made a more perfect world. Since our world has the best possible balance between simple laws and desirable effects, it should be regarded as, all things considered, the best of all possible worlds.

WHEN NEWS of the Lisbon earthquake reached Voltaire, nearly forty years after Leibniz's death, he wrote to a friend:

Well, sir, physics can be a cruel science. It would really be quite difficult to work out how the laws of physics create such horrendous disasters in the best of all possible worlds. One hundred thousand ants, our neighbors, crushed all of a sudden in our ant heap. . . .

Voltaire had already been making fun of Leibniz for a while. A decade earlier, he had inquired ironically in another letter "why so many men slit each other's throats in the best of all possible worlds." Voltaire was no pessimist: he attacked Pascal for maintaining that the human condition was thoroughly miserable. But even though things aren't all bad, according to Voltaire, they could most certainly be better, and it is perverse to pretend otherwise. Within a few weeks of the earthquake, he had finished his *Poem on the Lisbon Disaster*, which berated the "deceived philosophers, who cry 'All is well,'" and confronted them with the devastation of Lisbon. The only fitting and humane response to such evils is to mourn, to hope for better things to come, and to acknowledge the incapacity of reason to make sense of disasters, just as Bayle had argued in his writings about evil. What Voltaire loathed was the idea that a bloodless philosophical system could demonstrate why human suffering is necessary and therefore not something about which one should get too upset.

Rousseau wrote to Voltaire to complain about the poem. In Rousseau's opinion, "most of the physical evils we experience are . . . of our own making," and the death-toll in Lisbon was just another result of our misguided modern ways. If only the city's inhabitants "had lived in less massive buildings, the destruction would have been a lot less, and perhaps insignificant." Moreover, the materialistic citizens had only themselves to blame for not running to safety after the first tremors: "How many poor creatures died . . . because one wanted to go back for his clothes, another for his papers, a third for his money?"

According to Rousseau, Voltaire generally exaggerated the amount of unhappiness in the world, because he had been talking to the wrong people. The rich aren't worth listening to, since they are satiated with illusory pleasures and are therefore bored. Intellectuals are too sedentary, which makes them unhealthy; and they think too much, which makes them miserable. If only Voltaire had paid more attention to peasants—though not French ones, admittedly, since they are oppressed by rich landowners—he would have found more people who are satisfied with God's creation. Rousseau was also inclined, like Leibniz, to find hidden benefits in apparently unpleasant aspects of life. His body would ultimately be eaten by worms, but that body "manures the earth," whose produce feeds children. And, again echoing Leibniz, Rousseau insisted that everything in the universe is connected, and that although we cannot show exactly how all sufferings are "inevitable aspects of its existence," we can infer from the perfection of God that somehow they must be. Rousseau concluded that although it would be inaccurate to say "all is well," it was indeed true that "all is well from the point of view of the whole."

ANY ATTEMPT to show how evils are counterbalanced by greater goods is sadly laughable: that is what the sophistries of *Candide*'s Dr Pangloss are supposed to illustrate. Does Voltaire's stab at Leibniz and Rousseau hit its mark? Since Leibniz stated that it is impossible for finite minds to grasp the details of God's plan, it may seem unfair to cast him as Pangloss, who happily spelled them out to anyone who would listen. But the fact is that Leibniz could not resist the temptation to talk like Dr Pangloss. For example, Leibniz explained that although most humans will suffer eternal damnation, modern astronomy tells us that there is an "infinite number of globes" in the universe, and these globes might well be peopled by countless aliens who will all end up in heaven. So we should not assume that the majority of rational creatures will suffer a terrible fate just because the majority of humans undoubtedly will. Pangloss would surely have been proud of this bid to conjure a happy ending out of a dire situation.

The climax of Leibniz's *Theodicy* is a fable that conveys his answer to the problem of evil "in a way most likely to be generally understood." The goddess Athena appears in a dream to Theodorus, the high priest of Jupiter, and shows him a palace with an infinite number of halls, each of which represents a possible universe. The structure is a pyramid with an infinitely large base, and the single hall at its apex is the actual— and therefore the best possible—world. By inspecting these halls, one can see what would have happened if history had unfolded in different ways. As an example, Athena takes an event from the early history of Rome at the end of the sixth century BC, when Sextus Tarquinius, the youngest son of Rome's last king, raped Lucretia, the wife of a friend, who then killed herself. The rape and death of Lucretia sparked a revolt that led to the overthrow of the monarchy, and thus to the founding of the Roman Republic, and thereby eventually to the Roman Empire. The rape thereby "serves for great things," as the goddess puts it. Athena shows Theodorus a hall (i.e., a possible world) in which Sextus, or rather someone very similar to the actual Sextus, does not commit his crime, but instead leads a quiet and happy life, buying a little garden and cultivating it. Such a world, we and Theodorus are supposed to agree, may be a pleasant one for this man, but ultimately it is not as good as the actual world, because it lacks the Roman Empire. (This inferior world seems to be echoed in the last line of Voltaire's tale, when Candide tells Pangloss that they must stop philosophising and cultivate their garden instead. The parallel may be a coincidence, but it looks like a wink at Leibniz.)

Is the suggestion that there would have been no Roman Empire without the rape of Lucretia, and that this empire was preferable to alternative political arrangements, any better than Pangloss's claim that without syphilis we would have lacked the blessing of chocolate? The only difference between Leibniz and Pangloss here is that Leibniz hides behind the goddess Athena, and puts his Panglossian speculations in her mouth instead of owning up to them himself. He does so because he is stuck in a dilemma. On the one hand, it is impossible, according to his official position, for a finite mind to explain away particular evils, because it cannot see all the interconnections which make them unavoidable. On the other hand, it would be most unsatisfactory for Leibniz to have to forgo all concrete examples of how the bad things in this world are outweighed by the good ones, since this would leave him in a position which is much too close to that of Bayle. For Bayle, only faith—not reason—can reconcile the evils of the world with the goodness of God. And if the only thing that Leibniz can establish by reason is that a perfect God must somehow have arranged things for the best, without being able to demonstrate a single supporting instance of this, then he has not done much more than Bayle to explain the mystery of it all. So it is hardly surprising that Leibniz was tempted to be more specific, and thereby laid himself open to the mockery of Voltaire.

∞

LEIBNIZ DIED in Hanover in November 1716, six years after the publication of the *Theodicy*, which was the only book-length work of philosophy to be issued in his lifetime. His final years were characteristically full of hopes and plans and copious work. There were also disappointments. It was disappointing that his main employer, Georg Ludwig, elector of Hanover, who had succeeded to the British throne as George I, would not let him move to England. It was also dispiriting that he failed to secure the jobs for which he had been angling in Vienna and Paris. On the other hand, Leibniz had the ear of the Russian tsar, Peter the Great, who made him his adviser on scientific matters; and he was appointed by Emperor Charles VI to one of the two highest courts in the Holy Roman Empire.

King George told Leibniz that he had to stay in Hanover until he finished the interminable family history that had hung around his neck for decades. The king probably also felt that it would be undiplomatic to favour Leibniz just when the supporters of Newton, who was one of the most distinguished of his new subjects, were accusing Leibniz of having plagiarised the great Englishman's work on the calculus. (Leibniz was innocent of the charge, but this was not generally known at the time.) Leibniz was also at this point engaged in attacking many of Newton's views in the course of his correspondence with Clarke. In addition to criticising Newton's treatment of space and time, Leibniz rejected his idea that motion in the universe would grind to a halt without regular interventions by God. According to Leibniz, this Newtonian thesis was in effect an insult to God. It implied that He was an inferior craftsman who could not fashion a mechanism that was capable of functioning on its own. To Clarke, on the other hand, it was Leibniz's physics that was impious, because it left too little for God to do. Leibniz was also suspicious of Newton's concept of gravitation, which involved an apparently mysterious force that acts over great distances. Like many other thinkers of the time, Leibniz was sceptical of such a force because it was incompatible with the "mechanical philosophy," according to which "nothing is moved naturally except through contact and motion." What Leibniz did not realise was that the mechanical philosophy, having served its purpose of displacing Aristotelian and occultist accounts of nature, was now itself in need of large modifications.

Leibniz never got round to compiling the comprehensive treatise on theology and philosophy that he continued to advertise to friends. The *Theodicy* was just the "forerunner" to such a magnum opus, he told one correspondent in 1710. As it turned out, the only philosophical works to emerge subsequently from his pen were brief, popularising summaries of his views. Perhaps the lack of any magnum opus was in the end no great loss. Leibniz seems anyway to have been at his best when remarking on the work of others or throwing out ideas for consideration. The commentary on Locke's *Essay* which Leibniz wrote during 1703–5, although it takes the form of an awkward and rambling dialogue, is in many places dazzlingly incisive. For instance, Locke had argued that to have property is to have a right to something, and injustice is the violation of a right, so if there were no property, there could be no injustice. But Leibniz pointed out that to own something usually means to have the exclusive right to it, so if everything were held in common, there would be no property in the ordinary sense and yet there could still be injustice (for example, if someone were to be denied access to common goods). Leibniz's commentary frequently includes inventive examples, such as a tale about a princess who becomes a parrot, and a blind man who thinks that the colour scarlet is like the sound of a trumpet. These lively thought-experiments often make telling points against Locke.

Leibniz's work in his last two or three years included his longest treatment of Chinese thought, improvements to his calculating machine and yet more of his history of the Guelfs. He also found time to edit and improve a friend's 15,000-verse Latin poem about cosmology. And still he tirelessly lobbied his patrons about his pet projects, such as church reunification and the establishment of scientific academies, and drew up proposals for piecemeal reforms, such as a training scheme for doctors and pharmacists.

Why strive to improve the world if it is already perfect? That seems to have been the gist of one criticism that Voltaire sometimes levelled at Leibniz. According to Voltaire, Leibniz "did the human species the kindness of making us see that we ought to be entirely satisfied, and that there was nothing more that God could do for us." Leibniz did indeed believe that God could not have done more for us; but it does not follow from this that there is no point in trying to do more for ourselves. Leibniz once addressed this very point:

> As for the future, we must not . . . stand ridiculously with arms folded, awaiting that which God will do . . . [rather], we must act in accordance with what we presume to be the *will of God*, insofar as we can judge it, trying with all our might to contribute to the general good. . . .

Voltaire claimed that the doctrine that ours is the best of all possible worlds "leads to despair," but it certainly did not do so in Leibniz's case. He was an optimist in all of the senses that the term now bears. Progress "never comes to an end," and the means are now at hand for people to become "incomparably happier." In one of the last things he wrote, Leibniz pronounced that

> things are bound to progress for the better, whether gradually or sometimes even by leaps and bounds. Although at times things do seem to change for the worse, this should be regarded as similar to the way in which we sometimes retrace our footsteps in order to leap forward with greater vigour.

# 7

# A TREATISE OF ANIMAL NATURE
## *Hume*

THERE ARE FEW AVOWED LEIBNIZIANS, LOCKEANS OR HOBBISTS TODAY.
Self-styled Spinozists and Cartesians are also rare. But there seem to be
plenty of Humeans. In 2009, David Hume, who was born in Edinburgh in
1711 and died there in 1776, won first place in a large poll of philosophers
who were asked to pick the dead thinker with whom they most identified.
Aristotle, Kant and Wittgenstein were the runners-up in this peculiar
race.

Three things help to explain why Hume is a role-model for philosophers. First there is his gift for disturbing the peace. Ever since the publication of his *Treatise of Human Nature*, which he wrote in his mid-twenties,
Hume has been recognised as brilliantly unsettling. Kant wrote that
Hume's writings stirred him from his "dogmatic slumber" and started him
on the road to his own philosophy. Thomas Reid, a prominent Scottish
contemporary of Hume's, reported a similar experience. Some writers in
the eighteenth and nineteenth centuries regarded Hume's work as primarily mischievous and destructive; but from the early twentieth century
onwards, it has generally been viewed in a warmer light. Instead of being
seen as perplexing in a bad way, his arguments are now usually seen as
challenging in a good way.

A second reason for Hume's appeal is the rise of "naturalism." Naturalism in philosophy has several components, all of which were promi-

nent in Hume's writings. In marked contrast to Leibniz, he did not rely on the notion of God to explain anything. Hume never sincerely invoked the supernatural, and did not consider religion to be a source of illumination. Religion was itself a natural phenomenon to be explained in psychological and historical terms. Hume also stressed the similarities between humans and animals. This zoological approach to mankind was, as we shall see, a distinguishing feature of his account of knowledge. More than a century before Darwin's *Descent of Man*, which proposed that "there is no fundamental difference between man and the higher mammals in their mental faculties," Hume had arrived at a similar conclusion. In general, Hume maintained that humanity should be studied by the same methods that cast light on the rest of nature—a view that is more common in our day than it was in his.

Lastly, Hume's genial good humour and benign disposition should be taken into account. He had a gift for inspiring affection, even among some of his intellectual opponents. In Paris, where Hume lived for just over two years when he was in his fifties, he was known as *le bon David*. Some of his friends in Edinburgh called him St David. One night, a high-spirited young Englishwoman chalked "St David's Street" outside his house; the name caught on and is now the street's official name. This St David was scathing about the "monkish virtues" of some better-known saints. Fasting, penance, mortification and the rest, Hume argued, should really be counted as vices, because they serve no useful purpose to society, but instead "stupefy the understanding and harden the heart, obscure the fancy and sour the temper." A "gloomy, hair-brained enthusiast" of this type may posthumously "have a place in the calendar," but he "will scarcely ever be admitted, when alive, into intimacy and society, except by those who are as delirious and dismal as himself."

A year after Hume's death, his close friend Adam Smith, who was a former professor of moral philosophy, published an account of his visit to Hume's deathbed:

> Thus died our most excellent, and never-to-be-forgotten friend, concerning whose philosophical opinions men will no doubt judge variously . . . but concerning whose character and conduct there can

scarce be a difference of opinion. His temper, indeed, seemed to be more happily balanced . . . than that perhaps of any other man I have ever known. Even in the lowest state of his fortune, his great and necessary frugality never hindered him from exercising . . . acts both of charity and generosity. . . . Upon the whole, I have always considered him, both in his lifetime, and since his death, as approaching as nearly to the idea of a perfectly wise and virtuous man, as perhaps the nature of human frailty will admit.

Educated readers of the day would have heard in these words an echo of Plato's account of the death of Socrates: "Such . . . was the end of our comrade, who was, we may fairly say, of all those whom we knew in our time, the bravest and also the wisest and most upright man."

Smith's effusive eulogy caused a scandal. Just before Hume's death, Smith had published a revolutionary book, *The Wealth of Nations*, which became the founding text of modern economics. But it was his encomium to Hume that made an immediate stir: Smith told a friend that it "brought upon me ten times more abuse than the very violent attack I had made upon the whole commercial system of Great Britain." The trouble was that Hume was widely known to be no friend to religion. Not only did it outrage some people to see an infidel painted as a good man, it was also shocking to hear that he had faced his death calmly and cheerfully.

In his eulogy, Smith recounted that when he visited the dying philosopher, Hume had just been reading an ancient satire about Charon, the ferryman in Greek myth who carries the dead across the river Styx to the underworld. In the satire, various souls pleaded with Charon in an attempt to delay their journeys, and Hume "diverted himself with inventing several jocular excuses, which he supposed he might make to Charon, and with imagining the very surly answers which it might suit . . . Charon to return to them." First Hume suggested that he would ask for more time to prepare a new edition of his works; but Charon would object that this would be a prelude to yet more editions and yet more delays. So, according to Smith, Hume then imagined another tactic:

"Have a little patience, good Charon, I have been endeavouring to open the eyes of the public. If I live a few years longer, I may have the satisfaction of seeing the downfall of some of the prevailing systems of superstition." But Charon would then lose all temper and decency. ". . . [T]hat will not happen these many hundred years. Do you fancy I will grant you a lease for so long a term? Get into the boat this instant, you lazy loitering rogue."

Smith had toned down Hume's joke for public consumption. In a private letter, he mentioned that Hume had envisaged asking Charon to wait "till I have the pleasure of seeing the churches shut up, and the Clergy sent about their business." Another witness to the scene privately reported that Hume had referred not to "prevailing systems of superstition" but to "the Christian superstition." This was an important difference. It was acceptable in those days to criticise superstition or fanaticism in general terms, but the rules of decorum discouraged any explicit attack on Christianity itself. If Hume's actual words had been quoted, the scandal would have been even worse. Smith will have been aware, as Hume keenly was, of the fine line that separated authors whose writings were disapproved of but tolerated, and those whose books could not be permitted in one's house.

Another visitor to the dying St David was James Boswell, Dr Johnson's acolyte and biographer, who had a morbid fascination with the demise of the wicked. Boswell recorded in his journal,

> I had a strong curiosity to be satisfied if he persisted in disbelieving a future state even when he had death before his eyes. I was persuaded from what he now said, and from his manner of saying it, that he did persist. I asked him if it was not possible that there might be a future state. He answered it was possible that a piece of coal put upon the fire would not burn; and he added that it was a most unreasonable fancy that we should exist for ever.

This unnerved Boswell: "I could not but be assailed by momentary doubts while I had actually before me a man of such strong abilities . . . dying in the persuasion of being annihilated." Boswell often discussed the disturbing case of Hume with Dr Johnson, who reassured him that Hume was probably lying when he claimed not to fear death. When Boswell reported that Hume was "no more uneasy to think that he should *not be* after this life, than that he *had not been* before he began to exist," Johnson retorted that in that case, "he is mad." Johnson himself lived in constant terror of death. He told Boswell that "the whole of life is but keeping away the thoughts of it." This was only fitting for a Christian, according to a sermon later preached in Oxford, which contrasted the deaths of the righteous Johnson and the wicked Hume. A Christian ought to be anxious about death, because he might, after all, turn out to be damned. Thus, this preacher reasoned, "the confidence or the tranquility of the infidel are no arguments in his favour."

Hume seemed to enjoy gently baiting the shockable Boswell. He told him that he did not entertain "any belief in religion"—an admission he would never have made in public—and "he then said flatly that the morality of every religion was bad, and, I really thought, was not jocular when he said that when he heard a man was religious, he concluded he was a rascal. . . ." According to Johnson, Hume may have seemed to be a good man, but this was only because his virtue had never been put to any proper test. Infidels may appear harmless when they are in comfortable circumstances, he told Boswell, but matters will be quite different if they run out of money, because such people have no principles to guard them against yielding to temptation. Johnson added that he would certainly not trust such a man "with young ladies, for *there* there is always temptation. Hume, and other sceptical innovators, are vain men, and will gratify themselves at any expence."

One flaw in such reasoning ought to have been especially evident to Boswell, but apparently it was not. Despite the defences provided by his religious principles, Boswell was an insatiable libertine who recorded more sexual conquests than his contemporary, Casanova. Boswell's habit was to confess his infidelities to his wife in a state of anguish and remorse, and then to go out and repeat them. Nevertheless, it was Hume, the "sceptical innovator," who ought really to be shunned. "I always lived on good terms with Mr Hume," Boswell prissily informed Johnson, but

"I have frankly told him, I was not clear that it was right in me to keep company with him."

∞

Hume's father was an Edinburgh lawyer and gentleman-farmer whose country place, in Berwickshire, had been in the family for a dozen generations. The family traced itself to a warrior-knight of the early fifteenth century, and boasted a string of earls. But Hume's branch of it was no longer rich, and his older brother inherited the small estate when their father died in David's infancy. At first, Hume studied law when he left college at the age of fourteen, but this nauseated him. So instead he indulged his passion for literature in various forms. By the age of eighteen, he was immersed in the private study of philosophy, which brought on both a mysterious illness and also some sort of major discovery—or so it seemed to the excited youth. Five years after the onset of his malady, Hume wrote a letter to a London doctor, asking for advice. He described both his symptoms and his line of thinking:

> Every one, who is acquainted either with the Philosophers or Critics, knows that there is nothing yet establisht in either of these two Sciences, & that they contain little more than endless Disputes. . . . Upon Examination of these, I found a certain Boldness of Temper, growing in me, which was not enclin'd to submit to any Authority in these Subjects, but led me to seek out some new Medium, by which Truth might be establisht. After much Study, & Reflection on this, at last, when I was about 18 Years of Age, there seem'd to be open'd up to me a new Scene of Thought, which transported me beyond Measure. . . .

It is not clear what exactly this initial revelation amounted to. But by the time he was twenty-one, Hume had concluded that the trouble with conventional "moral philosophy" was that it was not based on the careful observation of human nature. By "moral philosophy," Hume meant not just ethics but all of the human sciences, including politics, artistic criticism and the study of thought and feeling. All these branches of learning, he com-

plained, depend at present "more upon Invention than Experience," and
need reforming in the way that Bacon and other innovators had begun to
reform the study of nature. Just as the physical sciences need to be based on
examining the external world, so the human sciences should be based on
examining our mental activities. Hume filled many pages trying to expand
on this theme. But his ailment—which a local medic had laughed off as
"the Disease of the Learned"—made it hard for him to concentrate or to
express himself clearly. He needed a break from literary efforts for a while,
so he proposed to take a job in England as clerk to a merchant in Bristol.

Hume's career in business lasted only a few months. Then he moved to
France for three years, living mostly in La Flèche, in the Loire valley, where
Descartes had attended the Jesuit college a century earlier. It was a cheap
place to live and Hume had access to the college's large library. He also
sometimes got into discussions with the Jesuits. Once, as he explained in a
letter, one of them told him about "some nonsensical miracle performed in
their convent." An argument immediately occurred to Hume which purported to show that one should always be sceptical of such reports. The
Jesuit apparently could not find a flaw in it, but concluded that it must be
wrong, since otherwise it would cast doubt on the scriptures.

The change of scene in France seems to have cured Hume's malady,
because while he was at La Flèche he finished the first two parts of his *Treatise
of Human Nature*. The book was billed as *An Attempt to introduce the experimental Method of Reasoning into Moral Subjects*. In its introduction, Hume dan-
gled the prospect of "a compleat system of the sciences, built on a foundation
almost entirely new, and the only one upon which they can stand with any
security." He announced that there would eventually be five parts to the *Treatise*: one dealing with the understanding, one on the "passions" (i.e., feelings
and desires), one on ethics, one on politics and one on the arts. Only the first
three of these ever appeared, though Hume subsequently wrote about politics (including economics) and the arts in various short essays. These essays,
especially the ones on economics, and a six-volume *History of England* which
Hume wrote in his forties, sold much better than his other books. Hume's *History* remained the standard work on its topic until the late nineteenth century.

\*    \*    \*

THE FIRST INSTALLMENT of the *Treatise* was published when Hume was twenty-seven and it soon became clear that many of its readers were confused. So Hume issued a sort of executive summary, or *Abstract*, to underline its main points. A large part of the *Abstract* was devoted to an ingenious piece of reasoning that has come to be known as "the problem of induction"—though Hume himself did not regard it as presenting much of a problem. His argument was intended to show the extent to which our knowledge is based on limited experience, and thereby to encourage intellectual modesty.

Induction may loosely be defined as extrapolation from experience. Newton wrote that the best way to proceed in "natural philosophy" (i.e., science) begins with "making experiments and observations, and . . . drawing general conclusions from them by induction." This is also, as Hume pointed out, how we proceed in ordinary life. We find that bread has frequently nourished us, so we expect it to do so in the future. That is, from past experience we infer the general conclusion that bread is nourishing. According to Hume, this type of inference had been neglected by philosophers. The usual accounts of reasoning, he wrote,

> are very copious when they explain the operations of the understanding in the forming of demonstrations [e.g., mathematical proofs], but are too concise when they treat of probabilities, and those other measures of evidence on which life and action intirely depend. . . .

To remedy this neglect, Hume began by considering a simple example involving billiard balls:

> Suppose I see a ball moving in a streight line towards another, I immediately conclude, that they will shock, and that the second will be in motion. This is the inference from cause to effect, and of this nature are all our reasonings in the conduct of life: on this is founded all our belief in history: and from hence is derived all philosophy [i.e., science], excepting only geometry and arithmetic. If we can explain the

inference from the shock of two balls, we shall be able to account for this operation of the mind in all instances.

Why exactly do we conclude that the second ball will move if the first one hits it? Hume pointed out that the thinking involved cannot be anything like a mathematical proof. We cannot prove that the second ball must move, because there is no "must" about it. It may fail to budge. We confidently expect it to glide across the table when it is hit, but we also acknowledge that it is in theory possible that it won't. Recall Hume's answer when Boswell asked him if it was possible that there is life after death. Yes, Hume had implied, it is *possible*—just as it is *possible* that a lump of coal will not burn in the fire. He was, of course, confident that the coal would in fact burn in the hearth, just as he was confident that he himself would not be around to burn in hell. But he would not have claimed to be able to demonstrate either of these things. Similarly, any purported demonstration that the second billiard ball must move would be out of place here. It would prove too much. It would rule out something that should not be ruled out.

If there can be no proof that a billiard ball will move, just as there can be no proof that a piece of coal will ignite, where does our confidence come from? Hume argued that there is nothing we can detect in any individual ball which would tell us that it will move another. Our expectation comes instead from the fact that we have observed many balls, or similar objects, all of which behave in the same way:

> Every object like the cause, produces always some object like the effect . . . and when I try the experiment with the same or like balls, in the same or like circumstances, I find, that upon the motion and touch of the one ball, motion always follows in the other.

Thus our confidence in such inferences about causes and effects derives from the regularity we have observed in nature. In general, "all reasonings from experience are founded on the supposition, that the course of nature will continue uniformly the same"—or, as Hume also put it, that there is a "conformity betwixt the future and the past."

And what is that supposition itself founded on? According to Hume, it cannot be established by any sort of demonstration, just as there can be no demonstration that a particular ball must move or a piece of coal must burn. Such a proof would, once again, prove too much. It is, after all, possible that one day the course of nature will fail to "continue uniformly the same."

If we cannot demonstrate that the future will conform to the past, can we at least offer some evidence that it will probably do so? In one sense, no—not really, Hume argued, because that could only involve going round in a circle. If I am asked why I expect certain events to be followed by certain other events, and I answer that they have generally been found to do so, then that sounds perfectly acceptable. But if I am now asked to go much further than this and to provide some separate evidence for the principle that the future will resemble the past, what could I offer but evidence that it had done so in the past? This is not much of an answer, according to Hume, because it does not really add anything to what I had already said, namely that the past is a guide to the future. I would simply be repeating myself.

The upshot of all this, for Hume, is that our expectations and predictions are at bottom a matter of habit or "custom." Extrapolating from what has been observed is just something that we are prone to do. This habit, as he put it in a later work, "is nothing but a species of instinct or mechanical power, that acts in us unknown to ourselves." He also noted that we share it with animals.

Does this imply that the causal inferences on which we rely are in fact not rational? Hume occasionally made it sound so: "'Tis not, therefore, reason, which is the guide of life, but custom. That alone determines the mind, in all instances, to suppose the future conformable to the past." But here Hume was using the term "reason" in a narrow sense, and meant only to deny that causal inference is based on that particular kind of "reason." He called this special kind "demonstrative reasoning, or that concerning relations of ideas." This is what is involved when we construct mathematical proofs or draw out the consequences of definitions or concepts. Ever since the ancient Greeks, it had been usual to regard the sort of knowledge obtained by such reasoning as superior, purer and perhaps the only genuine kind. Hume went along with this old way of speaking to some extent: he referred to mathematics as "this more perfect species of knowledge," and to relations of ideas as "the proper objects of our intellectual faculties." But he spent more time discussing the other, less exalted form of thought, which we share with animals. This mundane form deals not with "relations of ideas" but with what he called "matters of fact." Matters of fact are circumstances that could have been otherwise: they cannot be discovered by inspecting relations between ideas or by constructing mathematical proofs. Observation and causal inference are required in order to find out about them. And far from branding such inference as irrational, Hume called it "just," and often referred to it as "experimental reasoning." It is produced by an instinct or habit, but it still counts as a form of reason.

Hume tended to play up the role in our lives of inferences about matters of fact and to play down talk of more elevated forms of knowing. In an essay that he published just after his *Treatise*, he wrote, "Man falls much more short of perfect wisdom, and even of his own ideas of perfect wisdom, than animals do of man. . . . " In other words, man is closer to the animals than he is to God. Perfect wisdom is, of course, what God has. God does not have to resort to extrapolating from limited experience, because He has a shortcut to all truths. Opinions differed among philosophers about the exact nature of this shortcut. For Leibniz, as we have seen, God had in His mind a "comprehensive notion" of each object, from which every truth about it could be deduced in mathematical fashion. According to Leibniz, human science could aspire to an incomplete version of such divine insight. Hume nurtured no such aspirations. If there was any such divine shortcut, Hume was sure that we, like other animals, have little access to it.

It was a mark of most philosophers' accounts of reason, Hume noted in his *Treatise*, that they set its bar too high: "they suppose such a subtilty and refinement of thought, as not only exceeds the capacity of mere animals, but even of children and the common people in our own species." It seemed plain to Hume that beasts, like all normal people, are to some extent "endow'd with thought and reason." Just as people adapt means to ends, and take care in the tactics by which they seek pleasure and avoid pain, so too do animals. Hume distinguished two types of apparent intelligence in beasts. First, there is everyday behaviour, such as the way in which a dog learns to associate a certain tone of voice in his master with the risk of a beating. Secondly, there are cases of instinctive "sagacity" which enhance "the propagation of their species," such as the fact that birds seem to know exactly how to tend their eggs. The first sort of intelligence seems very similar in man and beast. Common sense therefore suggests that we should look for similar causes in both cases, just as anatomists look for parallels in the physiology of different species. It seems clear that beasts "can never by any arguments form a general conclusion, that those objects of which they have had no experience, resemble those of which they have." That is, they observe, and they act on what they have observed, but they surely do not do so because they have formulated a principle of the uniformity of nature. Thus, Hume claimed, animals provide "strong confirmation" for his account of causal inference, because in their case it is seems undeniable that it is "by means of custom alone that experience operates upon them."

Debates about reason in animals had a long history, most of it not very complimentary to animals. Aristotle denied that any species lower than man had reason, intellect or even beliefs. On the whole, Plato seems to have been inclined to attribute reason to animals only when they were reincarnated humans, which was apparently quite often. One of the few ancient authors to allow a share of reason to beasts in their own right was Plutarch (c. 46–c. 120), whose generous attitude was revived in the sixteenth century by Montaigne. How is it, Montaigne pointedly asked, that dogs can be taught such intricate skills as guiding the blind if animals have no form of thought or reason?

Most early modern thinkers, however, were unwilling to grant more than a bare minimum to beasts. In the seventeenth century, Hobbes and Leibniz argued that although animals can learn from experience, it was precisely because they depended solely on experience that they did not have the sort of rational knowledge that is the mark of man. The type of know-how that is obtained merely from observation is markedly inferior, Hobbes wrote. It "is not attained by Reasoning, but [is] found as well in Brute Beasts, as in Man; and is but a Memory of successions of events in times past . . . whereas nothing is produced by Reasoning aright, but generall, eternall, and immutable Truth." Similarly, Leibniz noted that "beasts are . . . guided entirely by instances" and "never manage to form necessary propositions."

Thus Hume's train of thought ran in exactly the opposite direction to that of Hobbes and Leibniz. While they felt that extrapolating from experience cannot amount to much, because even animals do that sort of thing, Hume contended that reason must be simpler than it is made out to be, since even animals use a form of it. Leibniz made large claims for reason. He wrote that it "is capable of establishing reliable rules . . . and . . . of finding unbreakable links in the cogency of necessary inferences." But such "necessary inferences," "unbreakable links," and Hobbes's "eternall, and immutable Truth" are just what Hume refused to grant either man or beast, at least when it came to "matters of fact."

Did Hume go too far? If our everyday reasoning is at bottom similar to that of animals, why are we so much better at it than they are? And surely we, unlike animals, can evaluate and explain the principles of our reasoning. Doesn't that count for something? Hume addressed the question of why "men so much surpass animals in reasoning, and one man so much surpasses another." There are many factors, he explained, which can give one creature an edge over another, and these same factors account for some differences between species. One creature may have better powers of "attention and memory and observation" than another, which means that its beliefs will be based on better data. Being able to spot relevant circumstances will help, and that takes "attention, accuracy and subtility," which are unevenly distributed. Also, some creatures have a wider range of experience than others; in the case of people, their experience can be broadened by more reading and conversation. Some people jump too fast to conclusions, and some are more subject to bias from their education or party affiliation. In other words, some creatures are more like sheep than others—indeed, some of them actually are sheep. All these sorts of things help to explain why one creature can be better than another at making accurate inferences from experience.

Hume also offered some general rules by which "we ought to regulate our judgement concerning causes and effects." These will help us "learn to distinguish the accidental circumstances from the efficacious causes."

One should, for instance, be especially wary of drawing conclusions from too small a set of examples when several factors contribute to an effect. All such pieces of advice, Hume noted, are easy to formulate, "but extremely difficult in their application," because much care is needed in order to sift evidence properly. In general, the safest strategy is to focus on "enlarging the sphere" of one's observations and experiments.

Why should one believe that broader experience will lead to more reliable extrapolations? Hume would presumably answer in his usual way: because past experience suggests that it does, and we must rest content with that, since any attempt to provide further justification would just go round in a circle. But philosophers since Hume have generally not been content to leave it quite at that. The practice of extrapolating from experience is a "skeleton in the cupboard . . . which . . . Hume first exposed to view," as one twentieth-century philosopher put it. Extrapolation is "the glory of science," but "the scandal of philosophy," because we cannot spell out exactly why it should count as rational. In 1927, Bertrand Russell wrote that "Induction raises perhaps the most difficult problem in the whole theory of knowledge. Every scientific law is established by its means, and yet it is difficult to see why we should believe it to be a valid logical process." This puzzle is still much discussed: a recent encyclopedia of philosophy distinguishes nine rival approaches to it. Yet far from regarding the situation as a "scandal," Hume celebrated the fact that it is more a matter of instinct than of logic that we use the past as a guide to the future. It is fortunate for us that we are naturally inclined to extrapolate from experience, wrote Hume, because our lives depend on our ability to do so:

this operation of the mind, by which we infer like effects from like causes, and *vice versa*, is so essential to the subsistence of all human creatures, it is not probable, that it could be trusted to the fallacious deductions of our reason, which is slow in its operations; appears not, in any degree, during the first years of infancy; and at best is, in every age and period of human life, extremely liable to error and mistake. It is more conformable to the ordinary wisdom of nature to secure so necessary an act of the mind, by some instinct or mechanical tendency. . . .

According to Hume, our tendency to expect one sort of event to follow another, if the two have regularly been observed in tandem, is a natural phenomenon that is analogous to Newton's force of gravity. It is "a kind of attraction" between things in the mind, rather like the gravitational attraction between things in space. Hume divided the contents of the mind into two types, both of which are subject to principles of attraction or "association." The livelier, more vivid mental items are "impressions"—a term he stretched to cover emotions and desires, as well as sensations. The fainter ones, "*Thoughts* or *Ideas*," are what we have in our heads when we reflect on our "impressions." Various factors cause the mind to move easily from certain thoughts and feelings to others. For example, when we think of Paris, the memory of a familiar street may spring to mind. When we see one billiard ball rolling towards another, we anticipate their collision. And when we feel envy, a rush of malice often follows in its wake.

While Locke saw the mind's tendency to jump from one idea to another in this way as merely a source of irrationality and muddle, Hume maintained that the "association of ideas" is involved in both good and bad thinking. Since the forces of mental attraction are "the only ties of our thoughts, they are really *to us* the cement of the universe, and all the operations of the mind must, in a great measure, depend on them." Hume's emphasis on this point was, he claimed, his main contribution to the science of mind. Another novel element in Hume's science of the mind was his emphasis on tracing faint ideas back to lively impressions. He held that all our ideas are somehow produced by the impressions we have felt or sensed, and that if we can identify the particular impressions from which an idea results, we should get a clearer picture of what that idea amounts to. Sometimes the hunt for impressions will come home empty-handed, in which case we ought to become suspicious. Suppose, for instance, we are puzzled by some concept used by a writer. If we can find no suitable impressions from which such an idea could have been derived, we ought to conclude that anyone who uses the concept is talking nonsense.

HUME THOUGHT that his philosophy paralleled Newton's physics in several respects. As well as invoking a gravity-like force that affects the contents of the mind, Hume also took heart from the way Newton seemed to renounce speculations about the underlying nature of things. Hume was sceptical about the scope of human understanding. We can, if we are careful enough to learn from experience, spot patterns in events, which enables us to anticipate and exploit the flux of cause and effect. But there is some sense in which we cannot see into the heart of things. Similarly, the "Newtonian philosophy," Hume wrote, calls for a "fair confession of ignorance in subjects that exceed all human capacity." As good Newtonians, we should "confine our speculations to the *appearances* of objects to our senses, without entering into disquisitions concerning their real nature. . . ."

It was the way Newton dealt with gravity that made Hume take him for a fellow spirit. At the end of his *Principia*, Newton claimed to have explained "the phenomena of the heavens and of our sea" by showing that there is a force of attraction between bodies that "acts . . . in proportion to the quantity of *solid* matter, and whose action is extended everywhere to immense distances, always decreasing as the squares of the distances." But, Newton continued,

> I have not as yet been able to deduce from phenomena the reason for these properties of gravity, and I do not feign hypotheses. For whatever is not deduced from the phenomena must be called a hypothesis; and hypotheses, whether metaphysical or physical, or based on occult qualities, or mechanical, have no place in experimental philosophy.

It was by the methods of experimental philosophy, Newton explained, that the laws of motion and of gravity had been found, and "it is enough that gravity really exists and acts according to the laws that we have set forth and is sufficient to explain all the motions. . . ."

Just as Newton seemed content to describe and quantify the observable consequences of gravity, without offering any deeper explanation of how it exerts its long-distance effects, so Hume maintained that there is no point in trying to "go beyond experience" and "discover the ultimate . . . qualities" of either mind or matter. Among Newton's notable achievements, Hume wrote in his *History of England*, was the fact that although he "seemed to draw off the veil from some of the mysteries of nature," he also "restored her ultimate secrets to that obscurity, in which they ever did and ever will remain."

But Hume may have read too much into what Newton said about hypotheses. Newton never implied that he expected gravity to remain forever beyond us. He just did not yet have a full explanation of it that was solid enough to count as more than speculation. What he had established so far was enough to be going on with; but gravity, he told a friend, was something he wanted to "take more time to consider." He later made some conjectures about it. The story wasn't over yet.

Einstein's account of gravity as an effect of the curvature of space-time is now regarded as sufficiently well-confirmed to be no mere "hypothesis." It is thus a bona fide part of what Newton and Hume would have called "experimental philosophy," and it helps to make the workings of gravity less mysterious. If Hume had been around to learn of general relativity, he would no doubt still have wished to stress the fragility of human knowledge, and the need for caution. But he might have admitted that caution is also required in predicting the limit of our intellectual capacities.

∞

NEVER WAS a literary project "more unfortunate than my Treatise of Human Nature," according to Hume. "It fell *dead-born from the press*, without reaching such distinction as even to excite a murmur among the zealots." This was rather an exaggeration. The *Treatise* had been reviewed in British, French and German journals and caused a fair amount of murmuring among philosophers. It did not, however, spark quite the intellectual revolution Hume had been hoping for. He blamed himself. He came to think that the "Heat of Youth & Invention" had made him rush too early into print with the *Treatise*. Although Hume never repudiated its central ideas, he begged readers to ignore that "juvenile" work, and asked to be judged only by his later ones. This request has on the whole not been granted.

The gratifying popularity of some literary, moral and political essays that Hume published within two years of the *Treatise* helped him to get over its disappointing reception. But then came another disappointment. When he was in his early thirties, Hume was invited to apply for a professorship in moral philosophy at Edinburgh University. There was some opposition to his candidacy on account of the *Treatise*: a pamphlet from the enemy camp charged him with "sapping the Foundations of Morality, by denying the natural and essential Difference betwixt Right and Wrong," and with defending "Principles leading to downright Atheism." While he was waiting to hear about the Edinburgh job, Hume took a lucrative post as tutor and companion to a young aristocrat in England, the Marquess of Annandale, who was an admirer of his essays. The marquess was mentally unstable, which did not at first seem to be too much of a problem. Hume found time for writing and produced a pamphlet rebutting the allegations against him. He did not dispute the difference between right and wrong, he protested; he merely denied that "the propositions of morality were of the same nature with the truths of mathematicks and the abstract sciences," as some theologians had argued. Morality appeals to our feelings—it is not a matter of calculations and deductions. To the charge that he was a sceptic, Hume replied that his sort of scepticism aimed merely to encourage modesty and humility in reasoning. A month later, in June 1745, he learned that he did not get the Edinburgh job.

The professorship would probably not have suited him anyway, since one of its duties was to lecture each Monday on "the Truth of the Christian Religion." He stayed a year in England with the mad marquess until the latter's tantrums became more violent and Hume was fired. Next he joined Lieutenant-General St Clair, a distant relation, on what was at first supposed to be an expedition to Quebec but ended up as an attack on a town in Brittany. Hume enjoyed this posting and had some time for his own studies, though the mission was almost farcical from a military point of view. Voltaire singled it out for ridicule in one of his historical works.

Ever since he joined the mad marquess, Hume had been trying to recast the ideas of the *Treatise* in a clearer and more digestible form. The failure of his first book, he was sure, had been due more to "the manner than the matter." The first new version of his philosophy, a set of linked essays now known as *An Enquiry Concerning Human Understanding*, was published around his thirty-seventh birthday, while he was in Turin on a diplomatic mission with St Clair. These essays were not only more streamlined than the corresponding parts of the *Treatise* but also bolder. Their implications for religion were more evident, though still diplomatically expressed, and Hume included the argument about miracles that had struck him in La Flèche but which he had omitted from the *Treatise* for fear of causing too much offence.

The *Treatise* was indecisive in places: the juvenile Hume seems sometimes to have doubted his doubts. But the climax of the new *Enquiry* was blunt:

> When we run over libraries . . . what havoc must we make? If we take in our hand any volume—of divinity or school metaphysics, for instance—let us ask, *Does it contain any abstract reasoning concerning quantity or number?* No. *Does it contain any experimental reasoning concerning matter of fact and existence?* No. Commit it then to the flames, for it can contain nothing but sophistry and illusion.

This challenge is known as Hume's Fork, because it draws on his two-pronged distinction between "relations of ideas" and "matters of fact." Reasoning about ideas can produce conclusive demonstrations, but it yields knowledge only about mathematics and trivial matters of definition. Reasoning about matters of fact yields more substantial information, but such knowledge is "founded entirely on experience" and is "evidently incapable of demonstration." History, astronomy, politics and medicine, among other subjects, fall into this latter camp. Geometry and algebra fall into the former. But where do theology and scholastic metaphysics belong? Do they deal with relations of ideas or with matters of fact? According to Hume, the trouble is that they are often neither fish nor fowl, and therefore belong on the bonfire. Sometimes they masquerade as a sort of pseudo-mathematics, and advance purely abstract demonstrations of the existence of God, or of life after death. But such demonstrations cannot work, because only "experimental reasoning" can tell us what actually exists, by allowing us to infer the existence of something from its causes or its effects. When theology tries to persuade us of the being of God or of immortality, it will only have a "foundation in *reason*" insofar as it is "supported by experience." And if theology is going to use the methods of experimental reasoning, it must be judged by the standards of experimental reasoning. That means paying attention to the limited nature of our experience, and treating any ambitious inferences that are based on it with the appropriate caution.

It is in this light that Hume examined two religious topics in his *Enquiry*: the so-called "argument from design," and the credibility of reports about miracles. The argument from design is an inductive argument for the existence of God. We see in nature what we take to be signs of intricate workmanship, and—extrapolating from our experience of the fact that artefacts such as watches are made by watchmakers or other craftsmen—we infer a divine Craftsman who made the world. In one of his versions of this widely accepted argument, Newton took the example of animal physiology:

Atheism is so senseless & odious to mankind that it never had many professors. Can it be by accident that all birds beasts & men have their right side & left side alike shaped (except in their bowells). . . . Whence is it that the eyes of all sorts of living creatures are . . . so truly shaped & fitted for vision, that no Artist can mend them? Did blind chance know that there was light & what was its refraction & fit the eys of all creatures after the most curious manner to make use of it? These & such like considerations always have & ever will prevail with man kind to beleive that there is a being who made all things & has all things in his power & who is therfore to be feared.

Hume placed several layers of insulation between himself and his critique of this argument. There would be little point in launching a frontal attack, since all the best scientific minds of the day endorsed it. Also, casting doubt on what was generally seen as obvious evidence for God would have been perceived as a denial of God Himself. So Hume put his ideas into the mouth of "a friend who loves sceptical paradoxes," whom he pretended to report. This friend, whose opinions "I can by no means approve," purported to be making a speech on behalf of Epicurus (who, as an ancient Greek, usually spoke of "the gods" rather than of God).

The main point made by Hume's Epicurean spokesman is that the argument from design makes a large leap when it treats evidence for a Craftsman as if it were the same thing as evidence for a God. Even if the world does show signs of having been designed, its designer or designers might, for all we can tell from the available evidence, be very unlike the traditional idea of God:

> If the cause be known only by the effect, we never ought to ascribe to it any qualities beyond what are precisely requisite to produce the effect: Nor can we, by any rules of just reasoning, return back from the cause, and infer other effects from it, beyond those by which alone it is known to us. . . . Allowing, therefore, the gods to be the authors of the existence or order of the universe, it follows that they possess that precise degree of power, intelligence, and benevolence which appears in their workmanship; but nothing farther can ever be proved, except we call in the assistance of exaggeration and flattery to supply the defects of argument and reasoning.

Consider Newton's version of the argument again. How did he get from the nature of the eye, or any number of apparent signs of design, to "a being who . . . has all things in his power & who is therfore to be feared"—let alone to the other attributes of God, such as supreme wisdom, justice and goodness, which Newton mentioned later in the same essay? For all we can tell from his handiwork, the Craftsman may have had only limited powers over his materials. Perhaps he no longer has even those powers, or has ceased to exist altogether, in which case there is little to fear from him. And any evidence of design certainly does not itself license the inference that the designer is or was supremely just or good.

When we are familiar with many examples of a given kind of thing, it is reasonable to make certain extrapolations. We have, for instance, observed many people, and they have generally been found to have two feet; so if we see what looks like a human footprint in the sand, it seems sensible to infer that "there was probably another foot, which also left its impression, though effaced by time or other accidents." Similarly, we are familiar with many human craftsmen and with how they work, so if we see some intricate and plainly human artefact, such as a watch, this familiarity allows us to infer certain things about its maker, such as that he or she was probably not blind. But we cannot infer anything from the work of a solitary divine Craftsman in this way, because there is no available general information about divine Craftsmen on which we can draw:

> The Deity is known to us only by his productions, and is a single being in the universe, not comprehended under any species or genus, from whose experienced attributes or qualities, we can, by analogy, infer any attribute or quality in him.

Hume's Epicurean therefore declares,

> Let your gods . . . O philosophers, be suited to the present appearances of nature: And presume not to alter these appearances by arbitrary suppositions, in order to suit them to the attributes, which you so fondly ascribe to your deities.

One way in which people have sought to supplement the meagre information about their deities that may legitimately be gleaned from signs of design in nature is via miracles. Miraculous events function as certificates of authenticity for the utterances of prophets and other holy figures. If someone can turn water into wine, walk on water or raise the dead—feats which, it is assumed, require the assistance or cooperation of a deity— then perhaps what such miracle-workers have to say about the nature and desires of their gods should be given some credence. But what credence should be given to reports of miracles?

Hume was proud of the idea about this which had struck him in La Flèche: "I flatter myself, that I have discovered an argument . . . which, if just, will . . . be an everlasting check to all kinds of superstitious delusion." To Hume's readers in Protestant England and Scotland, "superstitious" was a coded way of saying "Catholic." Catholics accepted more stories about miracles than Protestants did, and it was no hanging offence to poke fun at their gullibility. Hume did not claim that miracles could never happen. He argued that the balance of probabilities would always weigh against reports of religious miracles, so that accepting any such report would have to be a matter of faith rather than of reason.

In everyday life, if a story seems somewhat unlikely, we might question the trustworthiness of its source. Is this witness usually reliable? Does that publication have a record of making things up? Evaluating testimony in such cases involves considering two sorts of factors, according to *Logic, or the Art of Thinking*, a seventeenth-century book that was still a standard work on its subject.* There are "external" factors, which relate to the witness or the report, and "internal" ones, which "belong to the fact itself"—i.e., the intrinsic likelihood of the event reported. However, having distinguished these two things, the authors of the *Logic* then ignored "internal" factors and focussed on the external ones. Hume's contribution to the topic was to stress that this is a big mistake. The intrinsic improbability of miracles, which we tend to underestimate, ought to affect the way we judge testimony about them.

According to the Catholic theologians who wrote the *Logic*, there is no need to believe every last miracle recounted in *The Lives of the Saints*, a famous thirteenth-century compilation. Such old collections of tattle, they wrote, "are full of so many fables that there is no reason to be sure of anything based merely on their testimony." But miracles attested by St Augustine are another matter. One should recognise as authentic anything in his *Confessions* or *City of God* that Augustine claims to have "taken place before his eyes, or about which he testifies to having been particularly informed by the persons . . . to whom these things happened." The superior credibility of Augustine is established by the usual sorts of extrapolations found in experimental reasoning. For instance, unlike some other authors, Augustine did not have a history of inventing things; he was an educated man, and such people tend to be less gullible than others; he was a public figure and had written about the evils of lying, which made it unlikely that he would risk being exposed as a liar himself. These are all reasonable points, which draw on our experience of the reliability and behaviour of people in various situations. But there is another sort of experience which the authors of the *Logic* neglected to draw on, namely the experience that is the foundation for our

* See p. 26, above.

belief in laws of nature. By definition, a miracle involves "a violation of the laws of nature," and such laws are, as Hume put it, established by "a firm and unalterable experience." So any report of a miracle goes against all the evidence on the basis of which the relevant law of nature was established in the first place. Newton's law of gravitation, for instance, would not be recognised as a genuine law of nature unless the planets had been found to behave in accordance with it. Thus any claim that some wandering planet has broken this law must be weighed against what we know about planets.

Since miracles are said to be transgressions of the laws of nature, they must be treated as so inherently improbable that our everyday standards of evidence are too lax to deal with them. As one recent commentator has noted, Hume's point about improbability may be illustrated by the example of a medical test. Suppose a particular disease affects only one person in a million, and that there is a test for the disease which produces positive results with 99 percent accuracy. That is, out of every 100 people who test positive for the disease, 99 actually have it and one does not. Now suppose that you yourself take the test and get a positive result. Ought you to con-clude from this evidence that you probably have the disease? Many people give the wrong answer to this question, because they fail to take proper account of the extreme rarity of the disease. If you get a positive result on the test, you are still very much more likely to be the one person in a hundred whose test result is wrong than you are to be the one in a million who actually has the disease.

Reports of miracles are like positive test results for very unusual dis-eases. They must be treated with extreme caution, because however remote the possibility of error or deceit may seem, it may still be less remote than the possibility that a miracle has occurred. We should therefore adopt it as a maxim, Hume wrote, that "no testimony is sufficient to establish a mira-cle unless the testimony be of such a kind that its falsehood would be more miraculous than the fact which it endeavours to establish."

Hume allowed that reports of miracles could in theory meet this high standard. But had they in fact ever done so? According to Hume, history suggests that they have not. He listed several factors that make testimony for miracles especially suspicious. Miracles seem mainly to happen to the uneducated: "they are observed chiefly to abound among ignorant and barbarous nations; or if a civilized people has ever given admission to any of them, that people will be found to have received them from ignorant and barbarous ancestors." One must also consider the fact that people love talking about marvellous or shocking things, so news of miracles spreads like romantic gossip in a village. It is well known that such tales often get embellished in the telling. The "passion of *surprise* and *wonder*, arising from miracles, being an agreeable emotion, gives a . . . tendency towards the belief of those events." Francis Bacon once noted that stories are particularly questionable if they "depend in any way on religion." Hume agreed. For one thing, religious motives may easily prompt people to be less careful than usual; a pious person may even know an account is false "and yet persevere in it, with the best intentions in the world, for the sake of promoting so holy a cause." All in all, the appalling record of reports of religious miracles counts heavily against them:

> The many instances of forged miracles, and prophecies, and super-
> natural events, which, in all ages, have either been detected by con-
> trary evidence, or which detect themselves by their absurdity, prove
> sufficiently the strong propensity of mankind to the extraordinary and
> the marvellous, and ought reasonably to beget a suspicion against all
> relations of this kind.

This seems to have been the only thing Hume ever said or wrote with which Dr Johnson agreed. Hume was right that "it is more probable . . . witnesses should lie, or be mistaken, than that [miracles] . . . should happen," the doctor told Boswell. However, this did not matter, according to Johnson, because "the Christian revelation is not proved by the miracles alone, but as connected with prophecies." (Actually, Hume claimed that his argument applied to stories about prophecies as well.)

AT THE END of his *Enquiry*, Hume discussed some extreme forms of scepticism in order to scare readers into accepting his own relatively moderate doubts as a reasonable compromise. There is, for instance, Descartes's type of "universal doubt," which enjoins us to suspend confidence in all our faculties until we can give some infallible proof of their veracity. This exercise, Hume argued, involves digging a hole so deep that nobody could ever emerge from it. Universal doubt would be "entirely incurable," because remedies for it always suffer the same fate as Descartes's invocation of God's presumed unwillingness to deceive us. They are themselves vulnerable to various doubts. Other varieties of radical scepticism focus on particular scientific findings and draw unsettling conclusions from them. The nature of perception, for example, may prompt one to wonder if there is any physical world at all. Have we not found that "nothing can ever be present to the mind but an image or perception"? And if there is thus no "immediate intercourse" between our minds and the external objects which we suppose to cause our perceptions, how can we be sure that there actually are any such external objects?

The distinguishing mark of such sceptical trains of thought is that they "admit of no answer and produce no conviction," according to Hume. They may be impossible to refute in the classroom, but they are also impossible to pursue once we venture outside it. "The great subverter of . . . the excessive principles of scepticism," Hume wrote, "is action, and employment, and the occupations of common life." As soon as these principles "are put in opposition to the more powerful principles of our nature, they vanish like smoke, and leave the most determined sceptic in the same condition as other mortals." This is rather fortunate, Hume pointed out, because any attempt to suspend judgement about everything would be suicidal. "All discourse, all action would immediately cease, and men remain in a total lethargy, till the necessities of nature, unsatisfied, put an end to their miserable existence."

NEVERTHELESS, Hume argued, much good can come from pondering sceptical arguments, provided one keeps them in perspective. A "small tincture of Pyrrhonism" helps to encourage intellectual modesty by drawing attention to the fragility and limitations of our reasoning. For example, although Descartes went too far when he pointlessly urged us not to rely on any belief until all possible doubts about it had been answered, it is indeed wise to question our principles now and then with a view to eliminating bias and rash thinking. Hume's analysis of the way our everyday reasoning depends on fallible expectations about the future was intended to serve the cause of caution. It reminds us how easily we can go wrong. Nothing, he had argued, leads us to the inference that the future will resemble the past "but custom or a certain instinct of our nature . . . which, like other instincts, may be fallacious and deceitful."

Some topics are well suited to "the narrow capacity of human understanding," but others tempt us to forget our limits. They should be left "to the embellishment of poets and orators, or to the arts of priests and politicians." It was to drive this point home that Hume brandished his Fork. If some priest or orator tries to persuade us of a questionable theory, we should demand to know whether it is supported by cautious inferences about ascertainable matters of fact, or by rigorous deductions concerning "relations of ideas"—or merely by some hybrid style of reasoning that meets the standards of neither. In Hume's opinion, theological reasoning was often this sort of misbegotten hybrid.

And what of reasoning about moral goodness or beauty? Are ethics and aesthetics as dubious as theology? They need not be, provided it is recognised what values really are and what reasoning about them amounts to. According to Hume, ethical and artistic values are "not so properly objects of the understanding as of taste and sentiment. Beauty, whether moral or natural, is felt, more properly than perceived." Still, the faculty of understanding is in one sense involved in moral thinking. He elaborated on this idea in *An Enquiry Concerning the Principles of Morals*, which was published just after he turned forty, and which he once described as "incomparably the best" of his works.

Ethics, like any other legitimate enquiry aside from pure mathematics, needs to be "founded on fact and observation." The first aim of the book was to find out, by means of the usual experimental method, what virtue, or "personal merit," amounted to. By noting the qualities of actions and of character that people tend to praise, and then analysing what it is that these qualities have in common, we can discover the "foundation of ethics." This foundation turned out to be "public utility," in a very broad sense of the term. The result of Hume's investigation was that "there never was any quality recommended by any one, as a virtue or moral excellence, but on account of its being *useful*, or *agreeable* to a man *himself*, or to *others*."

When Jeremy Bentham (1748–1832), an English jurist and philosopher, came across Hume's discussion of morality, he "felt as if scales had fallen from my eyes." Hume's treatment led Bentham to advocate "the greatest happiness of the greatest number" as the "measure of right and wrong." This "utilitarianism," as it came to be called, tends to go beyond Hume in two respects. Hume's analysis did not imply that right and wrong were capable of precise quantification. And it was not his primary aim to advocate anything. Hume purported to be describing what it is that people in fact value, not telling them what they ought to value.

The reason why people value "public utility," Hume explained, is that they have "a feeling for the happiness of mankind, and a resentment of their misery." As we have seen, Hume made incisive criticisms of the Hobbesian idea that people seek only their own gratification.* According to Hume, they feel a sympathy for others that is as natural as their desire to advance their own well-being. And it is because of the role such feelings and desires play in morality that values are, as Hume put it, more properly felt than perceived. We approve of benevolence, and so call it a virtue, because of the pleasure we get from the flourishing of humanity. It would seem to follow that if the human race had had an entirely different set of natural feelings, then our morality would have been somewhat different. Suppose, for instance, it was generally felt that there is nothing quite so delightful as a brief life devoted to the torture of infants, especially one's own. Given such feelings, our species would presumably judge any behaviour that tended to bring lives to an early close, or multiplied the opportunities for tormenting children, to be useful and praiseworthy. Hume did not address such outlandish thoughts; he would probably have regarded this sort of speculation as pointless and irrelevant to real life, just like extreme scepticism. He believed that humanity had in fact a fairly uniform set of sentiments, at least in the case of those feelings which are fundamental to morality, and that they depend on the "particular fabric and constitution" that has always been shared by humanity in general. These are the only sentiments that matter.

Working in tandem with the feelings that are natural to our species, reason has a significant part to play in our moral thinking, according to Hume. This is because only reason "can instruct us in the tendency of

* See pp. 65–66, above.

qualities and actions, and point out their beneficial consequences to society and to their possessors." In other words, although it is our feelings that make us prefer those actions which we believe to be useful to humanity, it is reason that tells us which actions actually are useful.

Philosophers and theologians, though, have tended to overstate the role of reason in ethics. Locke, as we have seen, believed that morality could be reduced to something like geometry. And Samuel Clarke, the friend of Newton's who debated with Leibniz, sought to "deduce the *original obligations of morality,* from the *necessary and eternal reason* and *proportions of things.*" A famous passage in Hume's *Treatise* took aim at such deductions, by drawing attention to the fact that they somehow jump from facts to values:

> In every system of morality which I have hitherto met with, I have always remark'd that the author proceeds for some time in the ordinary way of reasoning, and establishes the being of a God, or makes observations concerning human affairs, when of a sudden I am surpriz'd to find that instead of the usual copulations of propositions, *is,* and *is not,* I meet with no proposition that is not connected with an *ought,* or an *ought not.* This change is imperceptible, but is, however, of the last consequence. For as this *ought,* or *ought not,* expresses some new relation or affirmation, it is necessary that it should be observed and explained; and at the same time that a reason should be given, for what seems altogether inconceivable, how this new relation can be a deduction from others, which are entirely different from it.

If we press the question of how an *ought* can be conjured from an *is,* Hume continued, we shall see where the "the distinction of vice and virtue" really lies, and he then proceeded to argue that it lay in our feelings about things rather than in things themselves. Its context thus suggests that the point of this much-discussed passage is to stress, once more, the essential role played in morality by such things as sentiments and desires. Any system of ethics needs to focus on them, rather than on such abstractions as Clarke's "*necessary and eternal reason* and *proportions of things.*"

\*   \*   \*

ONE THING that did not play an essential role in morality was religion. In fact, as far as Hume was concerned, it played no useful role in morality at all. God made just one substantial appearance in Hume's *Enquiry Concerning the Principles of Morals*, in the closing words of an appendix. The tastes and sentiments of all creatures, Hume wrote, are "ultimately derived from that Supreme Will, which bestowed on each being its peculiar nature." So God is in one sense the source of morality, because He gave us the feelings on which it depends. This polite parting nod in God's direction was typical of Hume's diplomatic approach to religion.

Whenever he attacked religious views, Hume purported to be criticising only the superstitious, fanatical or dogmatic excesses of "false religion." For the sake of decorum, he presented himself as a loyal defender of the "true" variety, without going into much detail about what that might be. He also took care never to undermine all the foundations of religion at once. For example, in his *Natural History of Religion*, which gave an account of the causes and effects of faith, Hume assailed the idea that there are solid moral reasons to be religious, but made it sound as if there were still good intellectual ones, such as the argument from design. In his posthumous *Dialogues Concerning Natural Religion*, he demolished those intellectual reasons, but made it sound as if it were still acceptable to believe in God on the basis of revelation—i.e., scripture and miracles. And in his first *Enquiry*, his sceptical treatment of miracle stories pretended that faith would somehow compensate for their incredibility.

Hume told a friend that he was not at all surprised when the Parisian authorities issued a warrant for the arrest of Rousseau in 1762. The rash fellow had "not had the precaution to throw any veil over his sentiments" in *Émile*, a treatise on education, which the authorities deemed to contradict the doctrine of original sin. *Émile* was regarded as especially offensive because Rousseau had ignored propriety and issued an unorthodox book under his own name. Hume's *Treatise* and other early works had been published anonymously; it was generally known who wrote them, but anonymity was a laudable sign of modesty that helped to mitigate controversial writings.

Hume's own veils were not thrown merely to avoid punishment or professional setbacks, though such practical considerations could not be ignored. The last British execution for blasphemy had taken place in Edinburgh just fourteen years before Hume's birth, when a student, Thomas Aikenhead, was alleged to have railed against the scriptures. Another doubting Thomas—Thomas Woolston, an English theologian—was convicted of blasphemy for casting doubt on miracles, and died in prison a year or two before the young Hume's talk on the subject with a Jesuit in La Flèche. But the likelihood of severe punishment for freethinkers was rapidly receding in Britain during Hume's lifetime. When a faction in the Church of Scotland tried to excommunicate the middle-aged and then eminent Hume, one likely reason why the attempt failed is that enough churchmen realised that an excommunication would do more harm to the Church's reputation than to Hume's.

If he had merely been trying to escape persecution, Hume could have abandoned his diplomacy in the writings that he held back until he was safely in his grave. But he did not do so. The works he reserved for posthumous publication were just as reassuringly worded, even if in places they went too far for Hume to be sure that the world was quite ready for them. In a posthumous essay about immortality, he donned his usual veil of piety and told readers that "it is the gospel, and the gospel alone, that has brought *life and immortality to light.*" He then proceeded to confiscate any intellectual credentials that the afterlife may have been thought to possess. In another posthumous essay, on suicide, Hume soothingly noted that "The providence of the Deity . . . governs every thing," before undermining the conventional idea that killing oneself was a crime against God. Hume wanted to sway as many readers as possible, and he realised that the most effective way to do so was by gentle seduction. His writings were crafted so that the enlightened few would get his drift and the half-enlightened might feel comfortable enough for his arguments to have a chance of eating away at their beliefs eventually. To throw off all veils, flimsy though they often were, risked making some readers turn away in shock at his effrontery before he had had a chance to lure them. This consideration applied just as much to Hume's posthumous works as to others.

Hume's circumstances and personality must also be taken into account when interpreting his writings about religion. Quite a few of his close friends were moderate clergymen. His sister, to whom he was devoted, and who long outlived him, was, like their mother, devout. It was not in Hume's nature to offend such people.

Hume showed the manuscript of his *Dialogues Concerning Natural Religion* to some friends, several of whom thought the book was too subversive even for a posthumous work. Adam Smith was one of those who worried that its veils were so diaphanous that it had best not be published at all. Hume had been hoping that Smith would be the one to shepherd it through the press once he himself was in the underworld with Charon, so he sought to reassure him that it would be safe to do so, noting that "nothing can be more cautiously and more artfully written." Hume was proved right about this. The book is so artfully constructed that some readers still do not see through his veils. Thus one influential account of Darwinism reports, on the basis of the *Dialogues*, that Hume "caved in" to the argument from design. Such misreadings arise in part from a failure to see why a gentle eighteenth-century author would not take advantage of the protection of the tomb to write in the same brash and confrontational manner as a twenty-first-century pundit.

Hume's *Dialogues* were modelled on Cicero's *The Nature of the Gods*, which reported a debate between an Epicurean, a Stoic and a Sceptic. The three main characters in Hume's version are Demea, who is introduced by the narrator as defending a "rigid inflexible orthodoxy," Philo ("careless scepticism"), and Cleanthes, who advances a conventional form of the argument from design, thus displaying an "accurate philosophical turn." Cleanthes is presented as the winner of the debate: the narrator's closing words declare that Philo beat Demea but that Cleanthes's principles "approach still nearer to the truth." Hume gave Philo the most powerful arguments, though, and it is Philo's ideas that are closest to those in Hume's other works. However, Philo cannot be regarded as a Hume who is free at last to say exactly what he thinks. Philo implies that he is "a sound, believing Christian" and says that "no one has a deeper sense of religion impressed on his mind." This, clearly, is not the unvarnished Hume speaking. Philo is more Hume's tool than his true self. It is mainly via Philo that Hume sprinkled his gunpowder through the pages of the *Dialogues*, leaving the book primed so that its arguments would, with luck, ignite in his readers' own minds.

Philo elaborated on the points made by Hume's Epicurean spokesman in the first *Enquiry*, and subtly drained all significance from the conclusions that can be drawn about God from the evidence of nature. The God who is left after Philo has had his ingenious way is not much of a God at all. Philo's summary at the end of the debate appears to concede the idea that the natural world was designed by some sort of intelligence:

> If the whole of Natural Theology . . . resolves itself into one simple, though somewhat ambiguous, at least undefined proposition, *that the cause or causes of order in the universe probably bear some remote analogy to human intelligence*; if this proposition be not capable of extension, variation, or more particular explication; if it affords no inference that affects human life, or can be the source of any action or forbearance: and if the analogy, imperfect as it is, can be carried no further . . . what can the most inquisitive, contemplative, and religious man do more than give a plain, philosophical assent to the proposition. . . ?

It was rather an understatement to call this proposition "somewhat ambiguous." It is so ambiguous that it is compatible with atheism. A few pages earlier, Philo had argued that "all the operations of Nature . . . whether the rotting of a turnip, the generation of an animal, [or] . . . the structure of human thought . . . *probably bear some remote analogy to each other*." That is to say, all natural processes—which, for Philo, notably include thought or intelligence—are probably somewhat similar. It follows that Philo's apparent concession to the idea that the wonders of nature are caused by something like intelligence is consistent with the idea that they are caused by a natural process, because all natural processes are somewhat like intelligence, according to him. From Philo's perspective, then, to say that *the cause of order in the universe is somewhat like a mind* is to say no more than that *the cause of order in the universe is somewhat like a rotting turnip*. Religious believers can reassure themselves with the first way of putting it, if they like. But one day they might realise how little it rules out.

Philo suggested that reasonable theists and unbelievers ought to admit that neither of them has any very clear idea of what divides them on this matter:

Where then, cry I to both these antagonists, is the subject of your dispute? The theist allows that the original intelligence is very different from human reason. The atheist allows that the original principle of order bears some remote analogy to it. Will you quarrel, Gentlemen, about the degrees, and enter into a controversy, which admits not of any precise meaning, nor consequently of any determination?

Here Philo seems to have been expressing Hume's own sentiments. Hume was more inclined to combat the dogmatism of believers than to assail them with dogmas of his own. He became good friends with some outspoken atheists when he moved to France as a diplomat in his early fifties, but seems to have found their doctrinaire approach rather crude and uncouth.

∞

BY THE TIME Hume arrived at the British embassy in Paris in 1763, he was an eminent man of letters, and keenly awaited in some of the salons. A year earlier, Boswell had referred to him in his journals as "the greatest writer in Brittain." Hume's fame at this point was due above all to his *History of England*, and also to the essays in his *Political Discourses*, most of which were about economics. These essays dealt with many of the themes that were given a fuller exposition by Adam Smith a quarter-century later. Smith generously wrote that Hume was, as far as he knew, the first writer to draw attention to the fact that the development of commerce and manufacturing tended to promote liberty and good government.

Two of Hume's closest friends in Paris were the editors of the *Encyclopédie*, Diderot and d'Alembert, both of whom had at various times been regulars at the long-established salons of Baron d'Holbach. In the 1770s, d'Holbach became one of the first thinkers to advocate atheism in a book published in its author's lifetime, albeit in d'Holbach's case under a pseudonym and outside France. He liked to exaggerate the number of atheists in his coterie, as Rousseau called the d'Holbach circle, but there were certainly at least a handful of others. D'Holbach's dinners and soirees attracted several distinguished foreign visitors, including Hume,

Smith, Benjamin Franklin and Edward Gibbon, a young admirer of Hume's, whose *Decline and Fall of the Roman Empire* was published in the year of Hume's death. Gibbon wrote in his autobiography of the "intolerant zeal" of d'Holbach's coterie and of some other Parisian intellectuals: "They laughed at the scepticism of Hume, preached the tenets of atheism, and damned all believers with ridicule and contempt." By "scepticism," Gibbon meant what would now be called "agnosticism." Hume was—or ought to have been, according to his philosophy—sceptical of the idea that the question of God's existence could be settled conclusively either way. However, since he does not seem to have had any belief in God, he should probably also be reckoned an atheist in a weak sense of the term.

If d'Holbach's zealous unbelievers laughed at Hume's caution, Hume laughed back. It all seems to have been a genial affair. "The Men of Letters here are really very agreeable," Hume wrote to an old friend after a few months in the salons. The only unpleasantness to arise out of *le bon David's* high time in Paris came from Rousseau.

Hume much admired Rousseau's independence of mind, though he found some of his opinions rather eccentric. He did not, for example, share Rousseau's gloomy view of modern society. He regarded Rousseau's novel, *Julie, or the New Heloise* (1761), as his masterpiece and did not think much of the *Social Contract* (1762). When Rousseau first got into trouble over *Émile*, Hume had written to him at the suggestion of a mutual friend, the Comtesse de Boufflers, offering to help him find refuge in England. He told Rousseau that he revered him "both for the Force of your Genius and the Greatness of your Mind." Hume renewed this offer towards the end of his stay in Paris, and Rousseau accepted. They set off for England together in January 1766, which d'Holbach warned Hume was a big mistake. Rousseau had a history of biting the hand that fed him and of seeing conspiracies everywhere. "You don't know your man," d'Holbach told the departing Hume. "I tell you plainly, you're warming a viper in your bosom."

At first, this seemed to be an exaggeration. In March, Hume wrote to a friend, praising Rousseau's fine manners and modesty, though he noted that this "most singular of all human Beings" was extraordinarily emotional. Rousseau had studied very little, "and has indeed not much Knowledge: He has only felt, during the whole course of his Life; and in this Respect, his Sensibility rises to a Pitch beyond what I have seen any Example of. . . ." There had been one brief outburst of paranoia, when Rousseau accused Hume of some trivial imagined offence; but it blew over in an hour, and the unlikely couple tearfully embraced. "I think no Scene of my Life was ever more affecting," Hume reported. A few months later, however, Rousseau had come to believe that Hume lured him to England in order to destroy his reputation, and publicly accused Hume of conspiring in a plot against him. In his *Confessions*, Rousseau asserted that the plot had been hatched by the Comtesse de Boufflers and another French lady, who were trying to control him. Hume later wrote that Rousseau "is plainly mad, after having been long maddish." The quarrel got into the press, and Hume felt obliged to publish his side of the story. Rousseau returned to France the next year.

Hume lived another nine years, mostly in Edinburgh, though he spent eleven months working as an under-secretary of state in a London ministry. He wrote little after the last volume of his *History*, which had been published just before his time in Paris. His publisher asked him for more volumes of history. According to entirely plausible reports in the press, Hume replied that he was "too old, too fat, too lazy and too rich." Among his last literary efforts were revisions to his *Dialogues Concerning Natural Religion*, made in the final months of his illness. He was very careful about what he said to his posthumous audience and plainly cared what they would say about him. As we shall see next, if Rousseau had known what some people would say about him after his own death, he might reasonably have concluded that his paranoia had been justified, and that the world was madder than he was.

# 8

# WHAT HAS THE ENLIGHTENMENT EVER DONE FOR US?
## *Voltaire, Rousseau and the* Philosophes

THE REMAINS OF TWO UNLIKELY BEDFELLOWS LIE OPPOSITE ONE ANOTHER in the crypt of the Panthéon in Paris. In 1791, two years after the storming of the Bastille, Voltaire became one of the first national heroes to be buried there by the leaders of the French Revolution. In 1794, when the revolution's bloodiest phase had just ended with the execution of Robespierre, Voltaire was joined in the crypt by the ashes of Rousseau. In life, the two men had mostly been enemies. "I hate you," Rousseau wrote frankly to Voltaire in 1760. Two years later, Rousseau published a treatise on education, and Voltaire took it upon himself to spread the news that this putative educator had discarded all five of his own children in their infancy. Voltaire also mischievously alleged that Rousseau contributed to the death of these children's maternal grandmother, though she was in fact alive at the time. Voltaire once joked that the famous author of the *Social Contract* was "not very sociable." This was certainly true, and not disputed by Rousseau: "I have never really been suited to civil society, where there is nothing but irritation, obligation, and duty, and . . . my independent nature always made me incapable of the constraints required of anyone who wants to live with men."

Both men had died a decade before the revolution and were rather implausible heroes of it. Rousseau wrote that he had "the greatest aversion to revolutions" and "always insisted on the preservation of existing institutions." Although he argued that direct democracy—i.e., voting by the assembled populace—was best for small city-states, he thought that monarchy was the most suitable form of government for large countries such as France. Voltaire, too, was sympathetic to monarchism, and would have disapproved of the execution of King Louis XVI, who was guillotined by the revolutionaries in 1793. Voltaire was in many respects a champion of the liberties of the common man, but he had no desire to be counted as a commoner himself. He became very rich and joined the lower ranks of the nobility by buying grand estates. His fortune was amassed first from the sale of his writings and performances of his plays and then much enlarged by his activities as an international banker. He also profitably exploited a loophole in French lotteries that had been pointed out to him by a mathematician. Voltaire was by all accounts a particularly generous benefactor to his thousand or so villagers, and sometimes laboured alongside them— cultivating his garden, like his best-known literary creation, Candide. But his attitudes were not particularly egalitarian: "Enlightened times will enlighten only a small number of honest people," he wrote to a friend. "The vulgar masses will always be fanatics."

On the other hand, Voltaire was a supremely sarcastic and unrelenting scourge of the establishment, especially the Catholic Church. His attacks on the abuse of power by clerics, his defences of toleration, and his intervention in several infamous miscarriages of justice were much admired by later radicals, particularly those who aimed to "dechristianise" France. Like many eighteenth-century critics of the Church, Voltaire believed in some sort of God but was not much interested in Jesus. According to one plausible anecdote, he once climbed a hill at dawn with a guest and prostrated himself before the rising sun, proclaiming, "Powerful God, I believe!"— and then drily remarked to his companion, "As for *monsieur*, the Son, and *madame*, His mother, that's a different story!" Orthodox religion, Voltaire pronounced in his *Philosophical Dictionary*, "is the source of all the follies and turmoils imaginable; it is the mother of fanaticism and civil discord; it is the enemy of mankind."

Rousseau admired the "religion of the Gospel pure and simple," the gist
of which was, according to him, that all men are brothers. But he had so little respect for most theological dogmas that clerical conservatives saw him as
a dangerous enemy, and the dechristianisers regarded him as an inspiration.
His conviction that "man is naturally good and . . . it is from . . . [our] institutions alone that men become wicked" was generally taken to clash with
the dogma of original sin. Like Voltaire, Rousseau maintained that belief
in God was necessary to prevent anarchy, and he endorsed Hobbes's idea
that the state should dictate the details of an official religion. But the tenets
of Rousseau's proposed civic religion were minimal. They consisted only of
"the existence of a mighty, intelligent, and beneficent divinity, possessed of
foresight and providence, the life to come, the happiness of the just, the
punishment of the wicked, the sanctity of the social contract and the laws."

Such a diluted form of Christianity was not nearly enough to satisfy
conservatives such as Joseph de Maistre (1753–1821), a French polymath
who has been described as more Catholic than the pope and more royalist
than the king. To Maistre and his ilk, people who undermined the authority of the Church were to blame for the bloody excesses of the revolution.
It was the principles of Voltaire and Rousseau that killed those who were
guillotined:

> it is just to consider Voltaire and Rousseau as the leaders [of the
> revolution]. . . . Voltaire's corrosive writings gnawed for sixty years
> at the very Christian cement of this superb structure whose fall has
> startled Europe. It is Rousseau whose stirring eloquence seduced the
> crowd over which imagination has more purchase than reason. He
> breathed everywhere scorn for authority and the spirit of insurrec-
> tion. He is the one who . . . posed the disastrous principles of which
> the horrors we have seen are only the immediate consequences.

Napoleon agreed that Rousseau had somehow "prepared the way for
the French Revolution." It is true enough that some of its leaders, including Robespierre, took themselves to be followers of Rousseau. There were
plenty of ideas in the *Social Contract* that seemed congenial to enemies
of the old regime. The book argued that agreement is the only basis for

"legitimate authority," and it seemed plain that the average Frenchman had reached no satisfactory agreement with his rulers. The *Social Contract* discussed the common interest that unites all citizens, and it described the evils of inequality. Its rousing first words—"Man is born free, and everywhere he is in chains"— sound like an invitation to an uprising, even though that is not what Rousseau had in mind.

Rousseau's intentions can be hard to divine from his writings, not only because what he asserted in one place would fairly often be denied in another, but also because he was so idiosyncratic. "I am made unlike any one I have ever met," he wrote in his *Confessions*. "I will even venture to say that I am like no one in the whole world." His words, therefore, could not always be taken at face value, as he himself warned one correspondent: "my terms rarely have the common meaning; it is always my heart that converses with you, and perhaps you will learn some day that it speaks not as others do." There was nothing in Rousseau's heart that inclined him towards tyrannical dictatorships, yet the *Social Contract*, and especially its ill-defined concept of "the general will," could be read as providing intellectual support for them.

The true interests and desires of a society are embodied in what Rousseau called its "general will," but it is no straightforward matter to determine the contents of this will. The "multitude . . . often does not know what it wills, because it rarely knows what is good for it." So citizens have to be guided—and, when necessary, compelled—by those who have a better understanding of what they really want. The multitude must sometimes, as Rousseau put it, "be forced to be free." According to Bertrand Russell, writing in 1946, such sentiments made Rousseau "the inventor of the political philosophy of pseudo-democratic dictatorships." It followed, in Russell's view, that "Hitler is an outcome of Rousseau." Russell claimed that Rousseau's doctrine of the general will

> made possible the mystic identification of a leader with his people, which has no need of confirmation by so mundane an apparatus as the ballot-box. . . . Its first-fruits in practice were the reign of Robespierre; the dictatorships of Russia and Germany (especially the latter) are in part an outcome of Rousseau's teaching.

This goes too far, since many tyrants had held sway long before Rousseau was born, and no doubt some of them thought they were supplying the sort of leadership that the multitude really wanted. Even if Rousseau is guilty of inventing a political philosophy for dictators, he was not guilty of inventing dictators.

THERE WAS a time when Rousseau would have been honoured to be entombed alongside Voltaire. When he was in Paris in his early thirties, and Voltaire was in his early fifties, Rousseau admired the famous older man's work and sent him a letter of effusive praise. At first, Rousseau seems to have felt at home among the intellectuals who contributed to the *Encyclopédie* of Diderot and d'Alembert. He was invited to write its articles about music, and became friends with Diderot. But one day in 1749 when he was on his way to visit Diderot, who had been imprisoned for some supposedly subversive writings, Rousseau sat down dizzily under a tree and had a revelation that changed everything. He had seen an advertisement for an essay competition set by the Academy of Dijon, and he suddenly realised that he knew the answer to the question posed by the academy. The question was: "Has the restoration of the arts and sciences had a purifying effect upon morals?" The gist of Rousseau's revelation was that society ruins everything. Current intellectual developments were an example of this, and were doing more harm than good. This thought became the cornerstone of Rousseau's philosophy and it put him at odds with the intellectuals in Voltaire's and Diderot's circles—indeed, it seems to have been aimed directly at them. As Rousseau noted in the preface to his essay, he was attacking "all that is nowadays most admired. . . . But I have taken my stand, and I shall be at no pains to please . . . those who follow fashion."

Rousseau's essay won the competition and earned him his first fame. It began by conceding that mankind had recently made large strides in the understanding of itself and of nature. A few centuries earlier, Europe had lived "in a state still worse than ignorance," because it was mired in the jargon and confusion of scholastic philosophy. Now it was "highly enlightened." But unfortunately "our minds have been corrupted in proportion as the arts and sciences have improved." This had happened before, Rousseau explained, in ancient Greece and Egypt, where "the progress of the sciences soon produced a dissoluteness of manners." Rome, too, had degenerated after the rise of various obscene authors, whereas nations that had fortunately been "preserved from the contagion of useless knowledge" were virtuous and happy. The Romans managed to practice virtue only until they started to study it. They were undone by their philosophers, with the result that "military discipline was neglected, agriculture was held in contempt, men formed sects, and forgot their country."

According to Rousseau's essay, the arts and sciences not only give rise to bad behaviour but are themselves the offspring of our vices. The arts are "nourished by luxury." Astronomy was "born of superstition" (i.e., it developed from astrology), physics was the result of "idle curiosity" and geometry is the offspring of "avarice" (because it was first used to measure plots of land). Science in general leads us into error, because it is much easier to be wrong than to be right. The sciences are "futile in the objects they propose." Physics, for example, pointlessly tries to account for "the inexplicable mysteries of electricity." And they are "dangerous in the effects they produce." Since the sciences are the products of idleness, they themselves cause idleness, according to Rousseau. They do not make us better governed, more happy or less perverse. Instead they weaken religion and patriotism, and lead to the collapse of empires. In a later work, Rousseau declared that "the reasoning and philosophic spirit . . . quietly saps the true foundations of every society." He also noted that intellectual work is unhealthy. Long country walks, and agricultural labour—of which Rousseau had no firsthand experience—were better pastimes.

ROUSSEAU, it may be remembered, felt that new technology was often harmful.* In his essay for the Dijon Academy, he even condemned the technology of printing. It was a "dreadful art" because it perpetuated "the errors and extravagances of the human mind." Thanks to this unfortunate invention, "the pernicious reflections" of various writers, such as Spinoza, would be around forever. Rousseau did not mention the fact that printing also let

* See pp. 55–59, above.

him spread his own contrarian ideas about "the happy state of ignorance." In a typically provocative remark, he claimed that Socrates himself had praised ignorance. In fact, what Socrates had praised was the honest admission of ignorance when one lacks knowledge. He never implied, as Rousseau did, that ignorance was in itself desirable. If our descendants are wise, Rousseau concluded, they will exclaim to heaven:

> Almighty God! Thou who holdest in Thy hand the minds of men, deliver us from the fatal arts and sciences of our forefathers; give us back ignorance, innocence, and poverty, which alone can make us happy and are precious in Thy sight.

THE CLAIM that some parts of the world were now "highly enlightened" was repeatedly made in the middle of the eighteenth century, by Voltaire and many others. In fact, one defining characteristic of the Enlightenment as an intellectual movement is that its members "thought they were living in an Age of Enlightenment," as one recent historian has put it. Unlike grumbling Rousseau, Voltaire and his fellow spirits believed that it was on the whole a good thing to live in such times. In his book on the age of Louis XIV, Voltaire wrote that this "happy age . . . saw the birth of a revolution in the human mind," which began with Bacon, Galileo and Descartes, and gave rise to "the most enlightened age the world has ever seen." Articles in the *Encyclopédie*, which began appearing in 1751, referred to "a philosophical century" that was "full of light." Some twenty years later, another writer enthused that "the empire of reason spreads farther every day."

Diderot's co-editor, d'Alembert, published a *Preliminary Discourse* to the encyclopedia that became a manifesto for the movement, and named its heroes. The "principal geniuses that the human mind ought to regard as its masters" were Bacon, Descartes, Newton and Locke, who had helped to conquer a "multitude of prejudices" and overcome "blind admiration for antiquity." All grand systems of thought were to be rejected in favour of the cautious collection of facts. Descartes was to be praised for his questioning attitude (though he went somewhat astray with his respect for "innate" ideas). Newton put natural philosophy on a solid experimental footing, and Locke did something similar for philosophy in general, by showing how the mind works and what its limits are. Leibniz, however, had been rather a mixed blessing, according to d'Alembert. Although he was superb at demonstrating "the inadequacy of all previous solutions" to various problems, "he was not contented with formulating doubts; he tried to dissipate them." As a result, he prematurely advanced a grand system of his own, which featured some rather implausible and unhelpful ideas.

The importance of intellectual caution was underlined by Diderot in an article that explained the aims of the *Encyclopédie*: "We must . . . take care to give the reasons of things, when there are some; assign the causes, when we know them; indicate the effects, when they are certain; . . . teach men to doubt and wait. . . ." Since the point of "the philosophical or doubting spirit" was to "shake off the yoke of authority," it would defeat the object of the enterprise if one form of dogmatism were merely to be replaced by another. The *Encyclopédie*'s entry for the term "*Philosophe*" (intellectual) sheds further light on the values of these doubting spirits and on how they saw themselves. It contrasted the modern *philosophe* with the ancient Stoic sages "who wished foolishly to deny the passions." The true *philosophe*, although he is guided by reason, does not seek to eliminate his emotions, because that is impossible. Instead, "he works at not being dominated by them, at benefitting from them, and at making reasonable use of them. . . ."

Because the *philosophes* emphasised the weakness of the human mind—a constant theme in the work of their hero, Locke, and that of two of their fellow-spirits, Bayle and Hume—it is in one respect misleading to attach the familiar label "the Age of Reason" to their heyday. From the perspective of religious conservatives, the *philosophes* and their ilk took reason too far by allowing it to trespass on the province of faith. They were asking difficult questions where no questions should be asked. But in their own view, the *philosophes* sought merely to press questions that seemed reasonable and necessary, and to do so with a sense of the limits of the human intellect. "The Age of Trying to Be More Reasonable" would therefore be a more accurate, though less snappy, name for their times.

What united the *philosophes* was a distaste for undue deference to tradition, intellectual orthodoxy, scripture or religious dogma, because these things had proved to be impediments to knowledge and to the well-being of mankind. One of their campaigns, in which Voltaire played a large part, was to advocate inoculation against smallpox, on the grounds that it seemed to work. There was plenty of theological opposition to this newfangled medical practice. It was argued that it interfered with God's will and that it would make people less God-fearing. In the 1720s, religious conservatives in France, Britain and the New England colonies maintained that it was a good thing for people to worry that God might punish their sins at any moment by giving them smallpox. Inoculation was adopted more readily in England than in France: when Voltaire asserted that the lives of thousands of French people could have been saved by it, he was told, "Only an atheist who has been led astray by English nonsense could propose that our nation should do certain harm in the hope of an uncertain benefit."

The scientific case for inoculation was in fact not quite as clear-cut as Voltaire supposed. Unlike vaccination, which eventually supplanted it, the technique of inoculation carried a significant risk of sickening people who would probably not otherwise have been exposed to the disease. Some of the French opposition to inoculation came from members of the scientific establishment, and they had a point. But Voltaire and the *philosophes* had a good point, too: in a civilised society, theology had no business interfering with medicine.

Although the leading figures of the French Enlightenment shared a general commitment to fresh thinking, they were divided on many particulars. A few of them, such as Baron d'Holbach and (in later life) Diderot, were atheists. But the majority, like Voltaire, believed in God. Their political ideas varied considerably. There was no generally preferred system of government or agreed political programme—indeed, Voltaire could not agree on such a programme even with himself. Some of the *philosophes* were enthusiastic about the spread of commerce; others thought it was safer to stick with plenty of farming. Some advocated the education of the masses; others could not quite see the point of that.

The diversity of opinion among Enlightenment thinkers grows considerably if the definition of the Enlightenment is expanded beyond the *philosophes* and their associates. It has become common to gather all manner of broadly progressive thinkers, from many corners of the world, into a somewhat nebulous intellectual movement. A typical anthology of "Enlightenment" texts includes some authors who were born in the late 1500s and others who were still alive in the 1830s. This bloated conception of the Enlightenment makes it all too easy to misjudge the thinkers concerned. If a few members of this extended family can be convicted of some intellectual vice or shortcoming, then the whole sprawling tribe may unfairly be found guilty by association.

"The inflated Enlightenment," as one historian has put it, "can be identified with all modernity, with nearly everything subsumed under the name of Western civilization, and so it can be made responsible for nearly everything that causes discontent. . . ." Since we regard ourselves as children of the Enlightenment, it is tempting to lay the blame for various ills on our supposed intellectual parents. Are we now sometimes inhumane? Then that is the fault of the Enlightenment's icy rationalism. The Enlightenment has at various times been found responsible for the French Revolution's reign of terror—despite the fact that this was also somehow the fault of Rousseau, who was mainly an enemy of the *philosophes*—and for fascism, communism, psychiatric malpractice, economic exploitation, sexism, the extinction of species, madcap utopian schemes, environmental degradation and much else. It is generally admitted that none of the key figures of the eighteenth-century Enlightenment advocated or condoned any such evils (except sexism); nevertheless, it is alleged that they somehow prepared the ground for them, or influenced people who did.

Thus Isaiah Berlin (1909–1997), an influential historian of ideas, suggested that the seeds of totalitarianism may be found in some of the *philosophes*. Although Berlin wrote that he could not accuse "any of the Enlightened thinkers . . . of directly leading to authoritarianism, bullying and in the end totalitarianism itself," he did make much of the fact that some of "their interpreters in later times, in particular . . . Marxists, but also [Auguste] Comte [1798–1857] . . . did lead to something of the sort." In other words, if your ideas get mangled many decades later by people who purport to be your followers, then it is partly your fault.

In addition to the accusation that the Enlightenment negligently produced ideas that can be abused, and proposed schemes that can be taken too far, it has also been charged with setting goals that are unlikely to be reached and with promoting optimism, which is always naïve, because nothing is perfect, and something may always go wrong. In a letter, Berlin acknowledged the virtues of the *philosophes*—"these thinkers . . . effectively attacked superstition and ignorance, cruelty, darkness, dogma, tradition, despotism of all kinds, and for that I truly honour them." But such achievements are not enough to satisfy everybody. One polemicist who shares the hyperbolic pessimism of Rousseau declared that "the legacy of the Enlightenment project . . . is a world ruled by calculation and wilfulness which is humanly unintelligible and destructively purposeless."

The notion that there was something ultimately discreditable or foolish about the Enlightenment, despite the worthy intentions of the *philosophes*, was so widespread in the twentieth century that it was written into the *Oxford English Dictionary*. From 1891 until 2010, the dictionary contained the following entry for "Enlightenment":

1. The action of enlightening; the state of being enlightened. . . .

2. Sometimes used . . . to designate the spirit and aims of the French philosophers of the 18th c., or of others whom it is intended to associate with them in the implied charge of shallow and pretentious intellectualism, unreasonable contempt for tradition and authority, etc.

∞

THERE IS PROBABLY nothing that could have reconciled Rousseau to the civilisation of his day, or to that of any other. He may have praised ancient Sparta, but he only ever felt nostalgia for times in which he had never lived. It would presumably not have changed his estimation of eighteenth-century France if he had learned of the modest but undoubted success that was eventually achieved in battles against "superstition and ignorance, cruelty, darkness, dogma, tradition, despotism of all kinds"—to take Berlin's list of Enlightenment targets. Nor, evidently, have these merits sufficiently impressed some later critics of the Enlightenment who have had the opportunity to observe them. Such malcontents are comparable to the fictitious leader of the People's Liberation Front of Judea, played by John Cleese in *Monty Python's Life of Brian*, who was slow to notice any benefits from the Roman occupation of his country:

> They bled us white, the bastards. They've taken everything we had. . . . And what have they ever given us in return?!
>
> The aqueduct? . . .
>
> Oh. Yeah, yeah. They did give us that . . .
>
> And the sanitation . . .
>
> Yeah. All right. I'll grant you the aqueduct and the sanitation are two things that the Romans have done.
>
> And the roads . . . Irrigation . . . Medicine . . . Education . . . And the wine . . .
>
> All right, but apart from the sanitation, the medicine, education, wine, public order, irrigation, roads, a fresh water system, and public health, what have the Romans ever done for us?

We cannot point to any aqueducts erected by intellectuals, or to any roads, or wine. Improvements in health and education are more plausibly associated with the *philosophes*, though it can be hard to trace direct connections between books and public welfare. The case for the Enlightenment is on its firmest ground when we point to the waning power of religious authorities to interfere in and even to end people's lives, to the toleration of religious dissent, to scientific progress, and to the gradual dismantling of political institutions that were too close to feudalism and too far from democracy. Even when it is difficult to know exactly how much credit to grant philosophers, it is churlish not to admit that the eighteenth-century thinkers in this book, and their heroes in the seventeenth century, did fight on the right sides in these battles and probably helped to win them.

The heirs of Rousseau will always have their quarrels with the heirs of Voltaire. Does the pursuit of scientific knowledge, and perhaps of some of the Enlightenment's other goals, not have drawbacks and dangers, just as Rousseau complained? D'Alembert had an astute rejoinder to such worries:

> We will not reproach him [Rousseau] for having confused the culti-
> vation of the mind with the abuse that can be made of it, since he
> would doubtless answer that this abuse is inseparable therefrom. But
> we would ask him to examine whether the majority of the evils which
> he attributes to the sciences and to the arts are not due to completely
> different causes, whose enumeration would be a long and delicate
> operation. . . . In sum, even assuming that we might be ready to yield
> a point to the disadvantage of human knowledge, which is far from
> our intention here, we are even farther from believing that anything
> would be gained by destroying it. Vices would remain with us, and we
> would have ignorance in addition.

In other words, even if things were as bad as Rousseau feared, might they not have been still worse without the developments he bemoaned?

Unlike the high priest Theodorus in Leibniz's fable about an infinite palace of possibilities, we cannot inspect alternative realities and see what would have transpired if certain things had not happened. What if Descartes had not asked a passerby for help with a Flemish puzzle, and had never had his vivid dreams of a "marvellous science"? What if Leibniz had accepted a professorship, instead of racing around Europe, fizzing with ideas and suggesting schemes to sovereigns? What if Hume's career in business had gone rather well, or Oxford had not refused Locke a medical doctorate, or Hobbes had not become starry-eyed about Galileo and fallen in love with Euclid? What if Spinoza had stayed in his synagogue? Ours may not be the best of all possible worlds; but these pioneers helped to make it an intellectually adventurous and, as d'Alembert suggested, a less ignorant one.

# NOTES

## Abbreviations Used in These Notes

AL    Francis Bacon, *The Advancement of Learning, and New Atlantis*, ed. Arthur Johnston, Oxford University Press, 1974.

CDP    *The Collected Dialogues of Plato*, ed. Edith Hamilton and Huntington Cairns, Princeton University Press, 1963.

CRT    Voltaire, *Candide and Related Texts*, trans. David Wootton, Hackett, 2000.

CWA    *The Complete Works of Aristotle*, ed. Jonathan Barnes, 2 vols., Princeton University Press, 1984.

CWS    *The Collected Works of Spinoza*, trans. Edwin Curley, Princeton University Press, 1985.

DCNR    David Hume, *Dialogues Concerning Natural Religion*, ed. Norman Kemp Smith, 2nd ed., Bobbs-Merrill, 1946.

E    John Locke, *An Essay Concerning Human Understanding*, ed. P. H. Nidditch, Oxford University Press, 1975.

ECTP    *The Encyclopedia of Diderot & d'Alembert Collaborative Translation Project*, Michigan Publishing, University of Michigan Library, 2002, available at http://quod.lib.umich.edu/d/did/.

EMPL    David Hume, *Essays: Moral, Political and Literary*, Oxford University Press, 1963.

ENC    *Encyclopédie ou Dictionnaire raisonné des sciences, des arts et des métiers*, 17 text vols., Paris, 1751–65, available at http://encyclopedie.uchicago.edu/.

EW    *English Works of Thomas Hobbes*, ed. W. Molesworth, 11 vols., London, 1839–45.

HCD   Pierre Bayle, *Historical and Critical Dictionary*, trans. Richard Popkin, Hackett, 1991.

HE    David Hume, *Enquiries Concerning Human Understanding and Concerning the Principles of Morals*, ed. L. A. Selby-Bigge, 3rd ed., Oxford University Press, 1975.

HHE   David Hume, *History of England*, Liberty Classics, 1983.

HLHP  *Hegel's Lectures on the History of Philosophy*, ed. and trans. E. S. Haldane and Frances H. Simson, 3 vols., Routledge, 1892–96.

HN    Thomas Hobbes, *Human Nature and De Corpore Politico*, ed. J. C. A. Gaskin, Oxford University Press, 1994.

HT    David Hume, *A Treatise of Human Nature*, ed. L. A. Selby-Bigge, 2nd ed., Oxford University Press, 1978.

HWP   Bertrand Russell, *History of Western Philosophy*, Allen & Unwin, 1946.

L     Thomas Hobbes, *Leviathan*, ed. Noel Malcolm, 3 vols., Oxford University Press, 2012.

LAT   Antoine Arnauld and Pierre Nicole, *Logic, or the Art of Thinking*, trans. J. V. Buroker, Cambridge University Press, 1996.

LDH   *The Letters of David Hume*, ed. J. Y. T. Greig, 2 vols., Oxford University Press, 1932.

LPW   John Locke, *Political Writings*, ed. David Wootton, Penguin, 1993.

NE    Gottfried Leibniz, *New Essays on Human Understanding*, trans. Peter Remnant and Jonathan Bennett, Cambridge University Press, 1996.

NO    Francis Bacon, *The New Organon*, ed. Lisa Jardine and Michael Silverthorne, Cambridge University Press, 2000.

NPW   Isaac Newton, *Philosophical Writings*, ed. Andrew Janiak, Cambridge University Press, 2004.

OTC   Thomas Hobbes, *On the Citizen*, ed. and trans. Richard Tuck and Michael Silverthorne, Cambridge University Press, 1997.

PE    Gottfried Leibniz, *Philosophical Essays*, trans. Roger Ariew and Daniel Garber, Hackett, 1989.

PPL   Gottfried Leibniz, *Philosophical Papers and Letters*, trans. and ed. Leroy E. Loemker, 2 vols., University of Chicago Press, 1956.

PWD   *The Philosophical Writings of Descartes*, trans. John Cottingham, Robert Stoothoff, Dugald Murdoch and Anthony Kenny, 3 vols., Cambridge University Press, 1985–91.

SCD   Jean-Jacques Rousseau, *The Social Contract and The Discourses*, trans. G. D. H. Cole, Everyman's Library, 1973.

SL    *Spinoza: The Letters*, trans. Samuel Shirley, Hackett, 1995.

T     Gottfried Leibniz, *Theodicy*, trans. E. M. Huggard, Open Court, 1985.

THP    *The Hellenistic Philosophers*, ed. A. A. Long and D. N. Sedley, 2 vols., Cambridge University Press, 1987.

TPT    Benedict Spinoza, *A Theologico-Political Treatise*, trans. R. H. M. Elwes, Dover, 1951.

## INTRODUCTION

x      *Those whom we call* ... Blaise Pascal, *Préface sur le traité du vide* (1647), trans. O. W. Wight, in *Blaise Pascal: Thoughts, Letters and Minor Works*, Harvard Classics, 1910, p. 442.

x      *I am convinced is most* ... Bacon, *De augmentis scientiorum* (1623), III.IV, in *Philosophical Works of Francis Bacon*, ed. J. M. Robinson, Routledge, 1905, p. 461.

x      *to ring a bell* ... See *The Letters and Life of Francis Bacon*, ed. James Spedding, vol. 3, Longmans, 1868, p. 301.

x      *degenerate learning* ... [etc.]: Bacon, *The Advancement of Learning* (1605), I.IV.5, in AL pp. 27–28.

xi     *the Kingdome of Darknesse*: Hobbes, *Leviathan* (1651), pt. 4.

## 1 DESCARTES

1      *if a man will* ... Bacon, *The Advancement of Learning*, I.V.8, in AL p. 35.

1      *since I now wished* . . . [etc.]: Descartes, *Discourse on Method* (1637), IV, in PWD vol. 1, p. 127.

2      *ego cogito, ergo sum*: Descartes, *Principia philosophiae* (1644), 1.7.

2      *so certain* . . . Descartes, letter to Regius, July 1645, in PWD vol. 3, p. 254.

2      *a system of medicine* . . . Descartes, letter to Mersenne, Jan. 1630, in PWD vol. 3, p. 17.

2      *the principal end* . . . Descartes, letter to the Marquess of Newcastle, Oct. 1645, in PWD vol. 3, p. 275.

2      *I venture to say* . . . Descartes, *Discourse*, V, in PWD vol. 1, p. 131.

3      "final theory": See Steven Weinberg, *Dreams of a Final Theory*, Pantheon, 1992.

3      Stephen Hawking: "Is the End in Sight for Theoretical Physics?" (1980), in his *Black Holes and Baby Universes*, Transworld, 1993, p. 49.

3      Michelson: Address at the dedication ceremony for the Ryerson Physical Laboratory at the University of Chicago in 1894.

3      Born: See Hawking, "Is the End in Sight."

4      *I don't think* . . . Voltaire, *Lettres philosophiques* (1733), 14, trans. L. Tancock, in *Letters on England*, Penguin, 1980, p. 72.

5    *ridiculous enough* . . . See Geneviève Rodis-Lewis, *Descartes: His Life and Thought*, trans. Jane Marie Todd, Cornell University Press, 1998, p. 29 n6.

6    *roam about in the world* . . . Descartes, *Discourse*, III, in PWD vol. 1, p. 125.

6    *foundations of a marvellous* . . . See Desmond Clarke, *Descartes: A Biography*, Cambridge University Press, 2006, p. 59.

7    Psalms: 93.1 and 104.5.

7    Genesis: 1.1 and 1.16.

7    Joshua: 10.12.

7    *so too are the entire* . . . Descartes, letter to Mersenne, Nov. 1633, in PWD vol. 3, p. 41.

7    *Compare the deductions* . . . Descartes, letter to Morin, 13 July 1638, in PWD vol. 3, p. 107.

9    *never to accept* . . . [etc]: Descartes, *Discourse*, II, in PWD vol. 1, p. 120.

10    *they never raise* . . . Ibid., IV, in PWD vol. 1, p. 129.

10    *I would not urge* . . . Descartes, *Meditations*, preface, in PWD vol. 2, p. 8.

11    *objects of the intellect* . . . Ibid., IV, in PWD vol. 2, p. 37.

11    *the easiest route* . . . Ibid., preface, in PWD vol. 2, p. 9.

12    *shit*: See Stephen Gaukroger, *Descartes: An Intellectual Biography*, Oxford University Press, 1995, p. 323.

12    *could have occurred* . . . [etc.]: Descartes, letter to Colvius, 14 Nov. 1640, in PWD vol. 3, p. 159.

12    before Augustine: Sextus Empiricus, *Adversus mathematikos*, IX.198, in *Sextus Empiricus*, Loeb Classical Library, 1936, vol. 3, p. 101.

12    *the mind* . . . Augustine, *De trinitate*, X.10.16, trans. S. McKenna, quoted in Gareth Matthews, *Thought's Ego in Augustine and Descartes*, Cornell University Press, 1992, p. 40.

13    Hegel: *Phenomenology of Spirit* (1807), 578.

13    *only that which corresponds* . . . John Paul II, *Crossing the Threshold of Hope*, Knopf, 1994, p. 51.

13    *according to the logic* . . . John Paul II, *Memory and Identity*, Rizzoli, 2005, p. 10.

13    *When I consider* . . . Descartes, *Meditations*, IV, in PWD vol. 2, p. 37.

14    *a clear and distinct* . . . Ibid., III, in PWD vol. 2, p. 24.

14    *what the intellect* . . . Ibid., IV, in PWD vol. 2, p. 43.

14    *may not all* . . . [etc.]: Ibid., VI, in PWD vol. 2, p. 55.

14    *as for all the rest* . . . Ibid., III, in PWD vol. 2, p. 30.

14    *heaviness and hardness* . . . Ibid., 6th replies, in PWD vol. 2, p. 297.

15    *shapes and sizes* . . . [etc.]: Descartes, letter to Plempius for Fromondus, 3 Oct. 1637, in PWD vol. 3, p. 64.

16    *empty theories* . . . Ibid., p. 61.

16      *At last . . .* [etc.]: Descartes, *Meditations*, II, in PWD vol. 2, p. 18.

16      *It is true . . .* Ibid., VI, in PWD vol. 2, p. 54.

17      *the same power. . .* Ibid., III, in PWD vol. 2, p. 33.

17      *cannot be a deceiver. . .* Ibid., p. 35.

18      *A God . . .* J. E. McTaggart, *Some Dogmas of Religion*, 2nd ed., Cambridge University Press, 1930, pp. 51–52.

19      Plato's Socrates: Plato, *Theaetetus*, 158c.

19      ancient Pyrrhonists: Sextus Empiricus, *Outlines of Pyrrhonism*, I.104.

19      *every sensory . . .* Descartes, *Meditations*, VI, in PWD vol. 2, p. 53.

20      *everything that is within . . .* Ibid., 2nd replies, in PWD vol. 2, p. 113.

20      *I am not merely . . .* Ibid., VI, in PWD vol. 2, p. 56.

20      *ghost . . .* Gilbert Ryle, *The Concept of Mind*, Hutchinson, 1949, p. 15.

21      *animal spirits*: Descartes, *The Passions of the Soul* (1649), I.10, in PWD vol. 1, p. 331.

21      *you may have observed . . .* Descartes, *Treatise on Man* (written 1629–33), in PWD vol. 1, p. 100.

22      recent scholar: Desmond Clarke, "Was Descartes a Cartesian?," *Times Literary Supplement*, 28 April 2006, pp. 5–6; and see Clarke, *Descartes*, pp. 210–11.

22      *abyssal . . .* Antonio Damasio, *Descartes' Error*, Penguin, 1994, p. 249.

22      *experience within ourselves . . .* Descartes, *Principles of Philosophy*, I.48, in PWD vol. 1, p. 209.

22      *profound separation . . .* [etc.]: Al Gore, *Earth in the Balance*, Rodale Books, 2006, p. 218.

22      Prince Charles: Speech at the Foreign Press Association Media Awards, Nov. 2008, available at http://www.princeofwales.gov.uk/media/speeches /speech-hrh-the-prince-of-wales-the-foreign-press-association-media -awards-sheraton.

23      *the chief use of . . .* Descartes, *The Passions of the Soul*, III.212, in PWD vol. 1, p. 404.

23      *to try always . . .* Descartes, *Discourse*, III, in PWD vol. 1, p. 123.

23      *so impertinent, so ridiculous . . .* Descartes, letter to Mersenne, 29 June 1638, in *Oeuvres de Descartes*, ed. Charles Adam and Adam Tannery, vol. 2, L. Cerf, 1898, p. 189.

23      *stupid . . .* [etc.]: See Clarke, *Descartes*, p. 227.

24      first biographer: Adrien Baillet, *La vie de monsieur Descartes*, 1691.

25      *I love his . . .* Molière, *Les femmes savantes*, III.ii.

26      *As we can have . . .* Antoine Arnauld and Pierre Nicole, *Logic, or the Art of Thinking* (1662), I, in LAT p. 25.

27      *We must constantly . . .* Nicolas Malebranche, *The Search After Truth*, pre-

face, trans. T. Lennon and P. Olscamp, in Malebranche, *Philosophical Selections*, ed. S. Nadler, Hackett, 1992, p. 7.

27    *a man who judges* . . . Ibid., p. 6.

27    *the mind's attention* . . . Ibid., p. 7.

27    *there is only one true* . . . Ibid., VI.2.iii, p. 94.

28    two clocks: The clock analogy was invented by Arnold Geulincx (1624–1669).

28    *everyone does not have* . . . *Descartes' Conversation with Burman* (1648), in PWD vol. 3, p. 347.

29    *devote so much* . . . Ibid., p. 346.

29    *modestly written* . . . Voltaire, *Lettres philosophiques*, 13, in *Letters on England*, p. 63.

30    *relish of philosophical* . . . Damaris Cudworth (Lady Masham), quoted in Maurice Cranston, *John Locke: A Biography*, Oxford University Press, 1985, p. 100.

30    *Our Descartes* . . . Voltaire, *Lettres philosophiques*, 13, in *Letters on England*, p. 63.

30    *having destroyed* . . . [etc.]: Ibid., p. 64

31    *a natural power* . . . [etc.]: Descartes, *Comments on a Certain Broadsheet* (1648), in PWD vol. 1, p. 309.

31    *we come to know* . . . Descartes, letter to Voetius, May 1643, in PWD vol. 3, p. 222.

31    *solely from* . . . Descartes, *Comments*, in PWD vol. 3, p. 303.

33    *empiricists* . . . Kant, *Critique of Pure Reason*, 2nd ed. (1787), II.iv (A854/B882), trans. P. Guyer and A. Wood, Cambridge University Press, 1998, p. 703.

33    *who rely on experience* . . . Galen, *On the Sects for Beginners*, 1, trans. M. Frede, in Galen, *Three Treatises on the Nature of Science*, Hackett, 1985, p. 3.

33    Kant's admirer: Kuno Fischer, *Geschichte der neueren Philosophie* (1852–77).

34    *Descartes made* . . . M. Dummett, *Frege: Philosophy of Language*, Duckworth, 1973, p. 666.

35    *the empirical brand* . . . Francis Bacon, *The New Organon* (1620), I.LXIV, in NO p. 52.

35    *simply accumulate* . . . Ibid., I.XCV, in NO p. 79.


## 2 Hobbes

36    *the oddest fellow* . . . "Illustrations of the State of the Church During the Great Rebellion," *Theologian and Ecclesiastic*, XII (1851), cited by Richard Tuck, *Philosophy and Government, 1572–1651*, Cambridge University Press, 1993, p. 322.

36    *Monster* . . . [Anon.], *True Effigies of the Monster of Malmesbury; or, Thomas Hobbes in His Proper Colours*, London, 1680.

36    *profond* . . . Voltaire, *Le philosophe ignorant* (1766), ch. 37, in Voltaire, *Mélanges*, Gallimard, 1961, p. 900.

36    *such books as tend* . . . *Journal of the House of Commons*, vol. 8, 1660–67, p. 636.

37    *are extremely bad* . . . Descartes to Father ***, 1643, in PWD vol. 3, pp. 230–31.

37    *the Universe . . . is* . . . Hobbes, *Leviathan* (1651), ch. 46, in L vol. 3, p. 1076.

38    *denied the possibility* . . . Graham Greene, *Lord Rochester's Monkey*, Viking Press, 1974, p. 205.

39    *has a body of flesh* . . . *Doctrine & Covenants* (1835), 130.22.

39    *common Power* . . . [etc.]: Hobbes, *Leviathan*, ch. 13, in L vol. 2, p. 192.

39    *our most wise* . . . Ibid., ch. 19, in L vol. 2, p. 304.

39    *made you a little God* . . . James I, *Basilikon Doron* (1598), in King James VI and I, *Political Writings*, ed. J. Somerville, Cambridge University Press, 1994, p. 12.

40    *to discharge honorably* . . . James I, *The Trew Law of Free Monarchies* (1598), in ibid., p. 81.

40    *to set before* . . . Hobbes, *Leviathan*, A Review and Conclusion, in L vol. 3, p. 1141.

40    *a branch of theology*: John Dewey, "The Motivation of Hobbes's Political Philosophy," in *Studies in the History of Ideas*, vol. 1, Columbia University Press, 1918, p. 89.

40    *Hobbes's great work* . . . Ibid., p. 103.

41    Diderot: Entry "Hobbisme" in the *Encyclopédie*, vol. 8 (1765). See John Hope Mason, *The Irresistible Diderot*, Quartet Books, 1982, p. 111.

41    *The axiom, fear* . . . Hugh Trevor-Roper, *Men and Events: Historical Essays*, Harper, 1957, p. 234.

41    *Did bring forth Twins* . . . Hobbes, *Verse Life* (1672), in HN p. 254.

41    *many millions* . . . [etc.]: Lipsius, *Politica* (1589), IV.3, trans. William Jones, *Six Bookes of Politicks*, London, 1594, p. 63 (spelling modernised).

42    *Since it has been shown* . . . Hobbes, *De cive* (1642), VII.14, in OTC p. 97.

42    *quite terrifying* . . . [etc.]: Kant, "On the Common Saying: 'This May Be True in Theory, But It Does Not Apply in Practice'" (1793), II, trans. H. Nisbet, in *Kant's Political Writings*, ed. H. Reiss, Cambridge University Press, 1970, p. 84.

42    *The world may sin* . . . Dryden, *Tyrannic Love, or, the Royal Martyr* (1668/9), V.i.

42    *tend to the hurt* . . . Hobbes, *The Elements of Law* (1640), II.XXVIII.1, in HN p. 172.

43    *all men are permitted* . . . Hobbes, *De cive*, I.10, in OTC p. 28.

43    *entangled in words* . . . Hobbes, *Leviathan*, ch. 4, in L vol. 2, p. 46.

43     *Mr Hobs is very dexterous* . . . John Wallis, *Hobbius Heauton-timorumenos*, Oxford, 1662, p. 154.

43     *why would he* . . . [etc.]: Hobbes, *De cive*, VI.13, in OTC p. 83.

43     *eternal death*: Hobbes, *Elements of Law*, II.XXVIII.1, in HN p. 172.

43     *there is no reason* . . . Hobbes, *De cive*, VI.13, in OTC p. 83.

44     *he who has enough* . . . [etc.]: Ibid., p. 84.

44     *It has eternally been* . . . Montesquieu, *The Spirit of the Laws* (1748), XI.4, trans. A. Cohler, B. Miller and H. Stone, Cambridge University Press, 1989, p. 155.

44     *limited to* . . . Benito Mussolini, *Doctrine of Fascism*, trans. E. Cope, 3rd ed., Vallecchi, 1938, p. 18.

44     *all-embracing*: Ibid., p. 14.

44     *all the manifestations* . . . Ibid., p. 18.

45     *the improvement* . . . [etc.]: Hobbes, *Elements of Law*, II.XXVIII.3, in HN p. 173.

45     *the superfluous consuming* . . . Ibid., II.XXVIII.4, in HN p. 174.

45     *one man's blood* . . . [etc.]: Ibid., I.XVII.1, in HN p. 93.

45     *The infinite and immutable* . . . *Remontrances du Parlement de Paris*, ed. Jules Flammermont, vol. 3, 1898, p. 279, trans. in William Doyle, *The French Revolution: A Very Short Introduction*, Oxford University Press, 2001, p. 24.

46     *extreme malignity* . . . Edward, Earl of Clarendon, *A Brief View and Survey of the Dangerous and Pernicious Errors to Church and State in Mr Hobbes's Book Entitled Leviathan*, Oxford, 1676, p. 181.

46     *whereas in all well-instituted* . . . Ibid., pp. 182–83.

46     *exercise and have* . . . Hobbes, *Elements of Law*, II.XXVIII.5, in HN p. 174.

46     *I gloried to be* . . . *The Recantation of Daniel Scargill, Publickly Made Before the University of Cambridge, in Great St Maries*, London, 1669, pp. 3–4.

47     *that absurd and foolish* . . . Samuel Mintz, *The Hunting of Leviathan: Seventeenth-Century Reactions to the Materialism and Moral Philosophy of Thomas Hobbes*, Cambridge University Press, 1962, p. 141.

47     Bayle: *Pensées diverses sur la comète* (1682), sections 176–78, in *Various Thoughts on the Occasion of a Comet*, trans. Robert Bartlett, State University of New York Press, 2000, pp. 219–22.

47     Casanova: *History of My Life* (1790s), trans. W. Trask, Johns Hopkins University Press, 1997, vol. 8, p. 107.

47     *Fill yourselves* . . . Robert Sharrock. See Mintz, *Hunting of Leviathan*, pp. 135–36.

48     *had very early* . . . Samuel Johnson, "Rochester," *The Lives of the Most Eminent English Poets*, vol. 1 (1779).

48     *did not much care* . . . *Aubrey's Brief Lives*, "Thomas Hobbes," ed. Andrew Clark, Clarendon Press, 1898, vol. 1, p. 329.

49 *the worst Teacher. . .* Ibid., p. 357.

49 *democratical in name . . .* [etc.]: Hobbes, *Of the Life and History of Thucydides* (1629), in EW vol. 8, p. xvii.

49 *says Democracy's . . .* Hobbes, *Verse Life,* in HN p. 256.

50 *[his] opinions . . .* Hobbes, *Thucydides,* in EW vol. 8, p. xv.

50 *He read the proposition . . .* Aubrey's *Brief Lives,* "Thomas Hobbes," vol. 1, p. 332.

50 *At the age of eleven . . .* The *Autobiography of Bertrand Russell: 1872–1914,* Allen & Unwin, 1967, p. 36.

50 credibility of Aubrey's anecdote: See Douglas Jesseph, "The Decline and Fall of Hobbesian Geometry," *Studies in the History and Philosophy of Science,* vol. 3, no. 3 (1999), pp. 425–26.

51 *the Mother of all . . .* [etc.]: Hobbes, *Leviathan,* ch. 46, in L vol. 3, p. 1058.

51 *written in the language . . .* Galileo, *The Assayer* (1623), trans. Stillman Drake, *Discoveries and Opinions of Galileo,* Doubleday, 1957, pp. 237–38.

51 *whatever benefit comes . . .* Hobbes, *De cive,* epistle dedicatory, in OTC p. 4.

51 *nasty, brutish and long*: Jesseph, "Decline," p. 426.

51 *was the first that opened . . .* Hobbes, *De corpore* (1655), epistle dedicatory, in EW vol. 1, p. viii.

52 *To Matter, Motion . . .* Hobbes, *Verse Life,* in HN p. 257.

52 *there is no such thing . . .* Hobbes, *Leviathan,* ch. 6, in L vol. 2, p. 96.

52 *As, in Sense . . .* Ibid., p. 82.

52 *computation:* Hobbes, *De corpore,* ch. 1, in EW vol. 1, p. 3.

53 *His most recent arguments . . .* Descartes to Mersenne, 21 April 1641, in PWD vol. 3, p. 178.

53 *his head did not lye . . .* Aubrey's *Brief Lives,* "Thomas Hobbes," vol. 1, p. 367.

53 *as in an automatic Clock . . .* Hobbes, *De cive,* preface, in OTC p. 10.

53 *each man is drawn . . .* Ibid., 1.7, in OTC p. 27.

53 *the skill of making . . .* Hobbes, *Leviathan,* ch. 20, in L vol. 2, p. 322.

54 *if the patterns . . .* Hobbes, *De cive,* epistle dedicatory, in OTC p. 5.

54 *probably a typical example . . .* Napoleon Chagnon, *Noble Savages: My Life Among Two Dangerous Tribes—the Yanomamo and the Anthropologists,* Simon & Schuster, 2013, p. 231.

55 *blissful, non-violent . . .* Ibid., p. 7.

55 recent history of violence: Steven Pinker, *The Better Angels of Our Nature: Why Violence Has Declined,* Penguin, 2011, ch 2.

55 *For centuries . . .* Steven Pinker, in *Wall Street Journal,* 24–25 Sept. 2011, p. C1.

55 *How you exaggerate . . .* [etc.]: G. R. Harvey, *Voltaire's Marginalia on the Pages of Rousseau,* Ohio State University Press, 1933, pp. 21 and 13.

55 Montesquieu: *Spirit,* I.2.

**56**   Rousseau on the *état de nature*: See A. O. Lovejoy, "The Supposed Primitivism of Rousseau's *Discourse on Inequality*," in his *Essays in the History of Ideas*, Capricorn Books, 1960, esp. p. 29 n15.

**56**   *golden race . . .* [etc.]: Hesiod, *Works and Days*, 110–20, trans. H. G. Evelyn-White, in *Hesiod: The Homeric Hymns and Homerica*, Loeb Classical Library, 1914, p. 11.

**56**   *men of their own accord . . .* [etc.]: Ovid, *Metamorphoses*, bk. 1, trans. Mary Innes, Penguin, 1955, pp. 31–32.

**56**   *"The Noble Savage"*: *Household Words*, 11 June 1853.

**56**   *savages . . . truely Noble*: Marc Lescarbot, *Nova Francia* (1609), Routledge, 1928, p. xxv.

**57**   *only in that they . . .* [etc.]: Montaigne: *Essays* (1680), bk. 1, ch. 31, "On the Cannibals," trans. M. A. Screech, Penguin, 1987, pp. 235–36.

**57**   *bloated with . . .* Ibid., p. 241.

**57**   *There arose . . .* Rousseau, *A Discourse on Inequality*, trans. Maurice Cranston, Penguin, 1984, p. 120.

**57**   *a multitude of passions . . .* Ibid., p. 98.

**58**   *an innate repugnance . . .* Ibid., p. 99.

**58**   *One acquires the desire . . .* Voltaire to Rousseau, 30 Aug. 1755, trans. in *The Collected Writings of Rousseau*, vol. 3, ed. R. Masters and C. Kelly, University Press of New England, 1993, p. 102.

**58**   orangoutans, etc.: See Rousseau's tenth note to the *Discourse on Inequality*, pp. 154–61. (This note is omitted from most editions.)

**59**   *must have been . . .* Ibid., p. 115.

**59**   *revenge became . . .* Ibid., p. 114.

**59**   *conjectures*: Ibid., p. 68.

**59**   *as nature*: Ibid., p. 67.

**59**   *experiments*: Ibid., p. 68.

**60**   *there needeth . . .* Hobbes, *Elements of Law*, I.XIV.2, in HN p. 78.

**60**   *and hope for precedency . . .* [etc.]: Ibid., I.XIV.3, in HN p. 78.

**60**   *the wicked were fewer . . .* Hobbes, *De cive*, preface, in OTC p. 12.

**60**   *On going to bed . . .* Ibid., 1.2, in OTC p. 25.

**60**   dogs: Hobbes, *Leviathan*, ch. 13, Latin version, in L vol. 2, p. 194 n37.

**60**   *a war of every man . . .* Hobbes, *De cive*, I.12, in OTC p. 29.

**60**   *consisteth not . . .* [etc.]: Hobbes, *Leviathan*, ch. 13, in L vol. 2, p. 192.

**61**   *the savage people . . .* Ibid., p. 194.

**61**   *Petty Princes, or Kings*: George Abbot, *A Briefe Description of the Whole World* (1599), 5th ed., London, 1664, p. 265.

**61**   *centralized authority . . .* *The Cambridge Encyclopedia of Hunters and Gatherers*, ed. R. B. Lee and R. Daly, Cambridge University Press, 2000, p. 1.

62    *But (someone will say)* . . . Hobbes, *Leviathan*, ch. 13, Latin version, in L vol. 2, p. 194 n38.

63    *Original Sin* . . . Edgar Gibson, *The Thirty-Nine Articles of the Church of England*, London, 1896–97, vol. 2, p. 357.

63    *he . . . that desireth* . . . Hobbes, *Elements of Law*, I.XIV.12–14, in HN pp. 80–81.

63    *imagination or fiction* . . . Ibid., I.IX.13, in HN pp. 54–55.

64    *pitty and compassion* . . . *Aubrey's Brief Lives*, "Thomas Hobbes," vol. 1, p. 352.

65    *all society* . . . Hobbes, *De cive*, 1.2, in OTC p. 24.

65    *all the heart's joy* . . . Ibid., 1.5, in OTC p. 26.

65    *nothing else but* . . . Hobbes, *Elements of Law*, IX.13, in HN pp. 54–55.

65    sentimental moralists: See Mintz, *Hunting of Leviathan*, pp. 142–46.

65    *prevail in human nature* . . . Hume, *An Enquiry Concerning the Principles of Morals* (1751), IX, in HE p. 270.

66    *Be warned that* . . . Richard Dawkins, *The Selfish Gene*, new ed., Oxford University Press, 1989, p. 3.

66    *some particle of the dove* . . . Hume, *Enquiry . . . Morals*, IX in HE p. 271.

66    *whatever affection* . . . . Ibid., appendix 2, in HE p. 296.

66    *Immutable and Eternall* . . . [etc.]: Hobbes, *Leviathan*, ch. 15, in L vol. 2, p. 240.

67    *For there really is* . . . Aristotle, *Rhetoric*, I.13, in CWA vol. 2, p. 2187.

67    *the unwritten unalterable* . . . Sophocles, *Antigone*, lines 455–57, trans. E. F. Watling, in *Sophocles: The Theban Plays*, Penguin, 1947, p. 138.

67    Roman writers on laws of nature: See Daryn Lehoux, *What Did the Romans Know?*, University of Chicago Press, 2012, ch. 3.

67    Lucretius on magnets: *De rerum natura*, VI.906f.

67    *God . . . established those rules* . . . Robert Boyle, "About the Excellency and Grounds of the Mechanical Hypothesis," in *Selected Philosophical Papers of Robert Boyle*, ed. M. A. Stewart, Hackett, 1991, p. 139.

68    *the intelligent world* . . . Montesquieu, *Spirit*, I.1, p. 4.

68    *do not invariably* . . . [etc.]: Ibid., p. 5.

68    *what conduceth to* . . . Hobbes, *Leviathan*, ch. 15, in L vol. 2, p. 242.

68    *the first, and Fundamentall* . . . Ibid., ch. 14, in L vol. 2, p. 200.

68    *Conclusions, or Theoremes*: Ibid., ch. 15, in L vol. 2, p. 242.

68    *found out by Reason*: Ibid., ch. 14, in L vol. 2, p. 198.

68    *science*: Ibid., ch. 16, in L vol. 2, p. 242.

68    *precepts*: Ibid., ch. 14, in L vol. 2, p. 198.

69    *are the same as* . . . Hobbes, *De cive*, IV.1, in OTC p. 58.

69    *Justice, Gratitude* . . . Hobbes, *Leviathan*, ch. 16, in L vol. 2, p. 242.

69    moral rules identical to those in the Bible: See Hobbes, *De cive*, ch. 4.

69 *whatsoever is the object . . .* Hobbes, *Leviathan*, ch. 6, in L vol. 2, p. 80.

69 *more inclined to care . . .* Plato, *Republic*, bk. 3, 415d, in CDP p. 660.

70 *impious doctrines . . .* [etc.]: *The Judgement and Decree of the University of Oxford Past [sic] in Their Convocation, July 21 1683*, Dublin, 1683, p. 1.

70 Burning of *Leviathan* and *De cive* in Oxford: *The Life and Times of Anthony Wood*, ed. Andrew Clark, Oxford, 1894, vol. 3, pp. 63–64.

71 *Self-preservation . . .* Ibid., p. 2.

71 *In the state of nature . . .* Ibid., p. 3.

71 *thou shalt love . . .* Leviticus, 19.18; Matthew, 22.39 (King James Version).

71 *in matter of women . . .* Sir Charles Sedley, *Bellamira* (1687), act III, in *Works of the Honourable Sir Charles Sedley*, London, 1722, vol. 2, p. 135.

71 *the notions of Right . . .* Hobbes, *Leviathan*, ch. 13, in L vol. 2, p. 196.

72 *the state of nature has . . .* Locke, *Second Treatise of Government* (1689), II.6.

72 *Possession and strength . . . Judgement and Decree*, p. 3.

72 *there is scarce . . .* Hobbes, *Leviathan*, A Review and Conclusion, L vol. 3, p. 1135.

72 *ariseth from Pact*: Ibid., ch. 31, in L vol. 2, p. 558.

73 *is to be derived . . .* Ibid.

73 *who is so stupid . . .* Ibid., ch. 5, in L vol. 2, p. 72.

73 *as though the Christian . . .* Wallis to Huyghens, 1 Jan. 1659, quoted in Alexander Bird, "Squaring the Circle," *Journal of the History of Ideas*, vol. 57, no. 2 (1996), p. 229.

74 *all the ecclesiastics . . .* Hobbes to Samuel Sorbière, 8 Jan. 1657, trans. Noel Malcolm, in *The Correspondence of Thomas Hobbes*, Oxford University Press, 1994, vol. 1, p. 429.

74 Aristophanes: *The Birds*, lines 1000–1010.

74 Anaxagoras: Plutarch, *De exilio*, 17.

74 Dante: *Paradiso*, canto 33, lines 133–35.

74 *either I alone am . . .* Hobbes, *De principiis & ratiocinatione geometrarum* (1666), trans. in Jesseph, "Decline," p. 446.

74 *as if a hen . . .* Hobbes, *Six Lessons to the Savilian Professors of the Mathematics* (1656), in EW vol. 7, p. 330.

75 Euclid's definition of "line": *Elements*, bk. 1, definition 2.

75 doubts about Pythagoras: Hobbes to Samuel Sorbière, 7 March 1664, in *Correspondence*, vol. 2, p. 609.

76 *They display new machines . . .* Hobbes, *Dialogus physicus*, 1668 ed., trans. in Steven Shapin and Simon Schaffer, *Leviathan and the Air-Pump: Hobbes, Boyle, and the Experimental Life*, Princeton University Press, 1985, pp. 347–48.

76    *his Lordship* . . . *Aubrey's Brief Lives*, "Francis Bacon," vol. 1, p. 75.

76    Bacon's death: See Lisa Jardine and Alan Stewart, *Hostage to Fortune: The Troubled Life of Francis Bacon*, Hill and Wang, 2000, pp. 502–8.

76    *to have had many* . . . Hobbes, *Elements of Law*, ch. 4, in HN p. 32.

77    *both condemnd and stole* . . . Samuel Butler (1613–1680), "Poetical Thesaurus," in *Satires and Miscellaneous Poetry and Prose*, Cambridge University Press, 1928, p. 241.

77    Hobbes mentioned in Locke's *Essay*: 1.3.5.

77    *took Hobbes's Leviathan* . . . John Edwards, *Brief Vindication of the Fundamental Articles of the Christian Faith*, London, 1697, epistle dedicatory.

77    *no peace, no security* . . . Locke, *First Tract on Government* (1660), quoted in Cranston, *John Locke*, p. 62.

77    *must necessarily have* . . . *First Tract*, preface (1661), in *Locke: Political Writings*, ed. David Wootton, Penguin, 1993, p. 151.

78    *free from being* . . . [etc.]: Hobbes, *Leviathan*, ch. 5, in L vol. 2, p. 68.

78    *it is as insignificant* . . . Locke, *Essay*, 2.21.14.

78    *without anything correspondent* . . . Hobbes, *Leviathan*, ch. 8, in L vol. 2, p. 122.

78    *there is no conception* . . . Ibid., ch. 1, in L vol. 2, p. 22.

78    *the Attributes we give* . . . Ibid., ch. 34, in L vol. 3, p. 614.

79    *much neglected* [etc.]: Hume, *History of England*, vol. 6, ch. 62 (1762), in HHE vol. 6, p. 153.

79    Johnson on Hume: See James Boswell, *The Journal of a Tour to the Hebrides*, (1784), London, 1807, p. 278.

79    anonymous pamphlet: See Paul Russell, "Hume's *Treatise* and Hobbes's *The Elements of Law*," *Journal of the History of Ideas*, vol. 46, no. 1 (1985), p. 59.

79    Hume and Hobbes: Ibid., pp. 51–63.

79    Hume's title: Hobbes sometimes referred to his *Human Nature* as his "Treatise of Human Nature." See *De corpore politico*, pt. 2, ch. 1, EW vol. 4, p. 125. And Dr Johnson referred to it as Hobbes's "Treatise on Human Nature." See James Boswell, *Life of Johnson*, Oxford University Press, 1953, p. 1383.

79    *enemy to religion*: Hume, *History of England*, in HHE vol. 6, p. 153.

79    *Hobbes felt passionately* . . . Richard Peters, *Hobbes*, Penguin, 1956, p. 241.

80    *the Ghost of the deceased* . . . Hobbes, *Leviathan*, ch. 47, in L vol. 3, p. 1118.

80    Luther and Calvin as atheists: See Alan Kors, *Atheism in France, 1650–1729*, Princeton University Press, 1990, p. 19.

80    Christians got their atheism from Jews: Julian the Apostate, *Against the Galileans* (c. 362), bk. 1, in *The Works of the Emperor Julian*, trans. W. C. Wright, Heinemann, 1923, vol. 3, p. 321.

81    *all of us are infidels* . . . Thomas Paine, letter to Samuel Adams, 1 Jan.

1803, in Paine's *The Age of Reason*, ed. Kerry Walters, Broadview Editions, 2011, p. 135.

81    atheism in Hobbes's England: See G. E. Aylmer, "Unbelief in 17th Century England," in *Puritans and Revolutionaries*, ed. D. Pennington and K. Thomas, Oxford University Press, 1978.

81    *The Anatomy of Melancholy*: 3.4.2.1.

82    *this universall Frame . . .* "Of Atheisme" (1612), in Francis Bacon, *Essays*, Oxford University Press, 1937, p. 66.

82    first confessions of atheism: Baron d'Holbach, writing as Jean-Baptiste de Mirabaud, *Système de la nature* (1770); [Anon.], *Answer to Dr Priestley's Letters to a Philosophical Unbeliever* (1782). See David Berman, *A History of Atheism in Britain: From Hobbes to Russell*, Routledge, 1990, pp. 113–16.

82    *for the support of . . .* John Bunyan, *Grace Abounding to the Chief of Sinners*, London, 1666, title page.

82    *stirred up questions . . .* Ibid., para. 96.

82    *he that from any effect . . .* Hobbes, *Leviathan*, ch. 12, in L vol. 2, p. 166.

83    *how a thing material . . .* Robert Boyle, *An Examen of Mr. T. Hobbs His Dialogus Physicus*, London, 1682, preface, sig. a3.

83    *by the name God . . .* Hobbes, *De cive*, XV.14, in OTC p. 178.

83    *durst not write:* Aubrey's Brief Lives, Thomas Hobbes, vol. 1, p. 357.

83    passage in *Tractatus theologico-politicus*: Ch. 3, para. 4.

## 3 SPINOZA

85    *By the decree . . .* Archives of the Jewish-Portuguese community, trans. in Y. Yovel, *Spinoza and Other Heretics: The Marrano of Reason*, Princeton University Press, 1989, p. 4.

86    *There are people . . .* Uriel da Costa, *Exemplar humanae vitae* (1687), trans. in Yovel, *Spinoza*, p. 43.

87    *God exists . . .* I. S. Revah, *Spinoza et Juan de Prado* (1959), p. 64, trans. in Richard Popkin, *The History of Scepticism from Erasmus to Spinoza*, University of California Press, 1979, p. 228.

88    *all things . . .* Spinoza, letter to Oldenburg, Nov. or Dec. 1675, in SL p. 332.

88    *the love of God . . .* Spinoza, *Tractatus theologico-politicus* (1670), IV, in TPT p. 60.

88    Romantic poet: Friedrich von Hardenberg (Novalis), 1772–1801.

88    *do not differentiate . . .* Spinoza, letter to Oldenburg, early 1662, in SL p. 84.

88    *a pernicious . . .* Bayle, "Spinoza," *Historical and Critical Dictionary* (1697), in HCD p. 293.

88    *the most monstrous . . .* Ibid., p. 296.

88     *the noblest* . . . Russell, *History of Western Philosophy*, ch. 10, in HWP p. 552.

88     *Those who were* . . . Bayle, "Spinoza," p. 295.

89     Spinoza's financial circumstances: W. Klever, Erasmus University of Rotterdam, and Y. Yovel, Hebrew University of Jerusalem, personal communications.

89     *exceptional* . . . [etc.]: J. L. Fabritius, letter to Spinoza, 16 Feb. 1673, in SL p. 249.

90     *Mechanics* . . . [etc.]: Spinoza, *Tractatus de intellectus emendatione* (c. 1662), 15, in CWS p. 11.

91     *The greater* . . . Spinoza, *Tractatus theologico-politicus*, IV, in TPT p. 59.

91     *God through* . . . Ibid., XIII, in TPT p. 179.

91     *a tissue* . . . Ibid., preface, in TPT p. 7.

91     *the practice* . . . Ibid., XIV, in TPT p. 186.

91     *calculated to* . . . Ibid., XI, in TPT p. 159.

91     *adapted to* . . . Spinoza, letter to Blyenbergh, 5 Jan. 1665, in SL p. 135.

92     *were endowed* . . . Spinoza, *Tractatus theologico-politicus*, II, in TPT p. 27.

92     *the Word of God* . . . Ibid., XII, in TPT p. 165.

93     *to confuse* . . . Spinoza, letter to Blyenbergh, 28 Jan. 1665, in SL p. 153.

93     *God is described* . . . Spinoza, *Tractatus theologico-politicus*, IV, in TPT p. 65.

94     *it would argue* . . . Spinoza, letter to Blyenbergh, 5 Jan. 1665, in SL p. 133.

95     *nature is not* . . . Spinoza, *Tractatus theologico-politicus*, XVI, in TPT p. 202.

95     *I do not* . . . Spinoza, letter to Oldenburg, 20 Nov. 1665, in SL p. 192.

96     *good, evil, order* . . . Spinoza, *Ethics*, I, appendix, in CWS p. 444.

96     *nothing is in itself* . . . Spinoza, *Tractatus theologico-politicus*, XII, in TPT p. 167.

96     *Do we petty* . . . Spinoza, letter to Oldenburg, Dec. 1675, in SL p. 339.

97     *the masses* . . . Spinoza, *Tractatus theologico-politicus*, VI, in TPT p. 81.

97     *fixed and immutable* . . . Ibid., p. 82.

97     *to move men* . . . Ibid., p. 91.

97     *provided an example* . . . Spinoza, letter to Oldenburg, Dec. 1675, in SL p. 338.

98     *the mouthpiece* . . . Spinoza, *Tractatus theologico-politicus*, IV, in TPT p. 64.

98     *As to the teaching* . . . Spinoza, letter to Oldenburg, Nov. or Dec. 1675, in SL p. 333.

98     *wherever justice* . . . Spinoza, *Tractatus theologico-politicus*, XIX, in TPT p. 246.

98     *the object of government* . . . Ibid., XX, in TPT p. 259.

98     *outward observances* . . . [etc.]: Spinoza, *Tractatus theologico-politicus*, XIX, in TPT p. 245.

98     *very simple* . . . Spinoza, *Political Treatise*, ch. 8, trans. S. Shirley, Hackett, 2000, p. 118.

99     *absolutely necessary* . . . [etc.]: Ibid., XX, in TPT p. 261.

99   *everywhere plotting* . . . Spinoza, letter to Oldenburg, Sept. 1675, in SL p. 321.

100   *wretched and insane* . . . Alfred Burgh, letter to Spinoza, 3 Sept. 1675, SL p. 312.

100   *the stupid* . . . Spinoza, letter to Oldenburg, Sept. 1675, in SL p. 321.

101   *the kind of knowledge* . . . Spinoza, *Tractatus de intellectus emendatione*, 79, in CWS p. 35.

101   *consider human actions* . . . Spinoza, *Ethics*, III, preface, in CWS p. 492.

101   *if men understood* . . . Spinoza, *Descartes' "Principles of Philosophy,"* appendix, II.ix, in CWS p. 332.

102   *only one* . . . Spinoza, *Short Treatise* (c. 1660), II.17, in CWS p. 69.

103   *full of gods*: Aristotle (on Thales), *On the Soul*, 411a, in CWA vol. 1, p. 655.

104   *that the Deity* . . . John Harris (1666–1719), *The Atheistical Objections Against the Being of God*, cited in R. S. Woolhouse, *Descartes, Spinoza, Leibniz: The Concept of Substance in 17th Century Metaphysics*, Routledge, 1993, p. 46.

104   *pantheist*: John Toland (1670–1722), *Socinianism Truly Stated* (1705).

104   *a kind of mass* . . . Spinoza, letter to Oldenburg, Nov. or Dec. 1675, in SL p. 332.

104   *I do not* . . . Spinoza, *Ethics*, IV, preface, in CWS p. 544.

104   *Things could have* . . . Ibid., I P33, in CWS p. 436.

105   *with the same necessity* . . . Ibid., II P49, Schol IVB, in CWS p. 490.

105   *That thing* . . . Ibid., I D7, CWS p. 409.

105   *men are deceived* . . . Ibid., II P35, Schol, CWS p. 473.

105   *which is also* . . . Ibid., II P48, CWS p. 483.

106   *a body in motion* . . . Ibid., II P13, L3 Cor, in CWS p. 459.

107   *from the point of view of eternity (sub specie aeternitatis)*: Ibid., V P36 (my translation).

107   *salvation, or blessedness* . . . Ibid., V P36, Schol, in CWS p. 612.

107   *the mind's intellectual* . . . Ibid.

107   *the philosophy of Spinoza* . . . Hegel's *Lectures on the History of Philosophy* (1832–45), III.2.I.A.2, in HLHP vol. 3, p. 256.

108   *the more puzzling* . . . Isaac Bashevis Singer, "The Spinoza of Market Street" (1961), in I. B. Singer, *Collected Stories: Gimpel the Fool to The Letter Writer*, Library of America, 2004, pp. 159–60.

108   *disturbances of the mind*: Spinoza, *Tractatus de intellectus emendatione*, 9, in CWS p. 9.

108   *After experience* . . . Ibid., 1, in CWS p. 7.

108   *Some years ago* . . . Descartes, *Meditations*, I, in PWD vol. 2, p. 12.

109   *Human power* . . . Spinoza, *Ethics*, IV, appendix XXXII, in CWS p. 593.

111   *after I had* . . . Goethe, *Dichtung und Wahrheit* (1814), III.14, trans. R. R. Heitner in *Goethe: Collected Works*, Princeton University Press, 1994, vol. 4, p. 459.

111    *he kissed Spinoza's . . .* Diary, Reminiscences and Correspondence of Henry Crabb Robinson, 2nd ed., Macmillan, 1869, vol. 1, pp. 399–400.

111    *I believe in . . .* Albert Einstein, telegram to Rabbi H. S. Goldstein, 1929, quoted in P. A. Schilpp, *Albert Einstein: Philosopher-Scientist*, Open Court, 1949, p. 102.

111    *There is in Spinoza's . . .* Heine, "On the History of Religion and Philosophy in Germany" (1835), II, trans. in R. Robertson, *Heinrich Heine: Selected Prose*, Penguin, 1993, p. 243.

## 4 LOCKE

113    *as to the general principles . . .* Thomas Jefferson, *Writings*, ed. M. D. Peterson, Library of America, 1984, p. 479.

114    *the true system . . .* Jean Le Rond d'Alembert, Éléments de philosophie (1759), 1, quoted in G. Buchdahl, *The Image of Newton and Locke in the Age of Reason*, Sheed and Ward, 1961, p. 62.

114    *no trace . . .* Hegel's Lectures on the History of Philosophy, III.2.B.1, in HLHP vol. 3, p. 310.

114    philosophy and mere science: Ibid., introduction, vol. 1, pp. 57–58.

115    *It is marked . . .* Hans Aarsleff, "Locke's Influence," in *The Cambridge Companion to Locke*, ed. V. Chappell, Cambridge University Press, 1994, p. 260.

115    *Locke made . . .* Gilbert Ryle, "John Locke," reprinted in his *Collected Papers*, Thoemmes, 1990, vol. 1, p. 147.

116    *teaches us . . .* Ryle, "Locke," p. 152.

116    *Locke's grand work . . .* C. S. Peirce, book review, Nation, 25 Sept. 1890.

116    *there cannot be . . .* John Locke, *An Essay Concerning Human Understanding*, IV.xv.6, in E p. 657.

116    *the Mind . . .* Ibid., IV.xv.5, in E p. 656.

116    *Reason must be . . .* Ibid., IV.xix.14, in E p. 704.

116    *Above Reason . . .* Ibid., IV.xvii.23, in E p. 687.

117    *the poor of this World . . .* The Reasonableness of Christianity (1695), in John Locke, *Writings on Religion*, ed. Victor Nuovo, Oxford University Press, 2002, p. 209.

117    *men cannot be forced . . .* Locke, A Letter Concerning Toleration (1689), in LPW p. 410.

117    *ought to shut a Man . . .* Locke, A Vindication of the Reasonableness of Christianity (1695), in *Writings on Religion*, p. 211.

117    *moral Principles . . .* Locke, Essay, I.iii.1, in E p. 66.

118    *the community . . .* Locke, Second Treatise of Government (1689), XIII.

118    *are sufficient . . .* Ibid., preface.

118   *Whatsoever* . . . Ibid., XXVI.

119   *a restraint* . . . Locke, *Draft of a Representation Containing a Scheme of Methods for the Employment of the Poor* (1697), quoted in Maurice Cranston, *John Locke: A Biography*, Oxford University Press, 1985, p. 424.

119   *No-one* . . . Locke, *First Tract on Government*, "Preface to the Reader" (1661), in LPW p. 148.

119   *All the freedom* . . . Ibid., p. 149.

120   *our souls are* . . . Joseph Addison, *Spectator*, no. 413, 24 June 1712.

121   *abundance of empty* . . . Locke, *Essay*, III.x.4, in E p. 492.

121   *learned Gibberish:* Ibid., III.x.9, in E p. 495.

121   *cover their Ignorance* . . . Ibid., III.x.8, in E p. 494.

122   *no wiser* . . . Ibid.

122   *the unscholastick* . . . Ibid., III.x.9, in E p. 495.

123   *deceived by idle* . . . [etc.]: Sydenham, MS quoted in Cranston, *John Locke*, p. 92.

123   *The function of a physician* . . . Sydenham, *Works*, London, 1848, vol. 2, p. 12.

124   *the riches* . . . Abraham Cowley (1618–1667), *Ode to the Royal Society* (spelling modernised).

124   principles of morality: James Tyrrell, MS note in his copy of the *Essay*, quoted in I. T. Ramsey's edition of Locke's *Reasonableness of Christianity*, Stanford University Press, 1958, p. 9.

124   *quickly at a stand* . . . Locke, *Essay*, Epistle to the Reader, in E p. 7.

126   *A name to all* . . . Dryden, *Absalom and Achitophel* (1681), lines 151–52.

128   Locke and Tyrrell: See David Wootton's introduction to LPW, pp. 57–64, 77–89.

128   *all government* . . . Locke, *Second Treatise*, I.1.

129   *the laws of men* . . . Antiphon, Fr. 44, trans. in J. M. Robinson, *An Introduction to Early Greek Philosophy*, Houghton Mifflin, 1968, p. 251.

129   *determine that it is* . . . Plato, *Republic*, 359a, in CDP p. 606.

129   *the first men to be* . . . Diodorus Siculus, *Library of History*, I.8, trans. C. H. Oldfather, Loeb Classical Library, 1933, p. 29.

129   *Catholic Encyclopedia:* Article "Conflict of Investitures," available at http://www.catholic.org/encyclopedia/view.php?id=6159.

129   *is it not clear* . . . Manegold of Lautenbach, *Ad Gebehardum liber* (c. 1085), trans. Ewart Lewis in his *Medieval Political Ideas*, Routledge, 1954, vol. 1, p. 165.

130   compact: E.g., Locke, *Second Treatise*, VIII.97.

130   *Almost all the governments* . . . David Hume, *Of the Original Contract* (1748), in EMPL p. 457.

130   *some pack of blond* . . . Nietzsche, *On the Genealogy of Morals* (1887), II.17, trans. W. Kaufmann and R. J. Hollingdale, Vintage, 1969, p. 86.

131   *there are no instances . . .* [etc.]: Locke, *Second Treatise*, VIII.100–101.

131   *being so ancient . . .* Hume, *Original Contract*, in EMPL p. 457.

132   *we need by no means . . .* Kant, "On the Common Saying, 'This May Be True in Theory, But It Does Not Apply in Practice'" (1793), II, trans. H. B. Nesbit in *Kant's Political Writings*, ed. Hans Reiss, Cambridge University Press, 1970, p. 79.

132   *veil of ignorance . . .* [etc.]: John Rawls, *A Theory of Justice*, Oxford University Press, 1972, p. 136.

132   *original position . . .* [etc.]: Ibid., p. 120.

132   Locke and travel narratives:  Barbara Arneil, *John Locke and America: The Defence of English Colonialism*, Clarendon Press, 1996, ch. 1.

133   *the state of nature has . . .* [etc.]: Locke, *Second Treatise*, II.6.

133   *enjoyment of their properties . . .* Ibid., XI.134.

134   *nobody can transfer . . .* Ibid., XI.135.

134   *mankind in common:* Ibid., V.25 (Psalms 115.16).

134   *added something . . .* Ibid., V.28.

135   *nothing was made . . .* Ibid., V.31.

135   *he who appropriates . . .* Ibid., V.37. (This passage is omitted from some editions.)

135   business interests:  See Joseph Schumpeter, *Capitalism, Socialism and Democracy* (1942), Allen & Unwin, 1976, p. 248 n18.

136   *the will of God:* Locke, *Second Treatise*, XI.135.

136   *the Comprehension of our . . .* Locke, *Essay*, I.i.5, in E p. 45.

137   *This refined way . . .* Swift, *Remarks upon Tindall's Rights of the Christian Church &c* (1708), in Jonathan Swift, *Bickerstaff Papers*, Blackwell, 1966, p. 80.

137   *serves best . . .* Locke, *Essay*, I.i.8, in E p. 47.

137   *history-book . . .* Laurence Sterne, *Tristram Shandy* (1759–67), I.2.

138   *a man who . . .* Pierre Gassendi, *Institutio logica* (1658), pt. 1, canon II, trans. H. Jones, Van Gorcum, 1981, p. 84.

138   Stoics:  See THP vol. 1, 39E, p. 328; Aquinas, *De veritatis*, II, 3; Hobbes, *Leviathan*, I.1.

139   *having . . . got the Ideas . . .* Locke, *Essay*, II.xxiii.33, in E p. 314.

139   *like Changes will . . .* Ibid., II.xxi.1, in E p. 233.

139   *presented man's make-up . . .* Roy Porter, *The Creation of the Modern World*, Norton, 2000, p. 263.

139   *Ideas that in themselves . . .* Locke, *Essay*, II.xxxiii.5–6, in E pp. 395–96.

140   *wrong and unnatural . . .* [etc.]: Ibid., II.xxxiii.18, in E p. 400.

140   *stamped upon . . .* Ibid., I.ii.1, in E p. 48.

141   *That White is not . . .* Ibid., I.ii.18, in E p. 57.

141    *One would think* . . . Ibid., I.ii.27, in E p. 64.

141    *God is to be worshipped* . . . [etc.]: Robert South (1634–1716), quoted in John W. Yolton, *John Locke and the Way of Ideas*, Oxford University Press, 1956, p. 39.

142    *there cannot any one* . . . Locke, *Essay*, I.iii.4, in E p. 68.

143    *and you shall find* . . . Ibid., I.iv.16, in E p. 94.

143    *it eased the lazy* . . . Ibid., I.iv.24, in E p. 101.

144    *inborn* . . . Descartes, letter to Mersenne, 15 April 1630, in PWD vol. 3, p. 23.

144    *has . . . the ideas* . . . Descartes, letter to Hyperaspistes, Aug. 1641, in PWD vol. 3, p. 190.

144    *The ideas of pain* . . . Descartes, *Comments on a Certain Broadsheet* (1648), in PWD vol. 1, p. 304.

145    *inborn constitution*: Locke, *Essays on the Law of Nature* (begun in 1660), ch. 2, ed. W. von Leyden, Oxford University Press, 1954, p. 199.

145    *I deny not* . . . Locke, *Essay*, I.iii.3, in E p. 67.

145    *inherent limitations*: See, e.g., ibid., I.i.5.

145    Locke on children's characters and dispositions: Locke, *Some Thoughts Concerning Education* (1693), pp. 1–2.

145    Locke presented as opponent of the view that the mind is shaped by its inborn nature: E.g., by Steven Pinker in his *The Blank Slate: The Modern Denial of Human Nature*, Allen Lane, 2002.

145    Noam Chomsky: *Cartesian Linguistics*, Harper & Row, 1966. See also Jonathan Barnes, "Mr Locke's Darling Notion," *Philosophical Quarterly*, vol. 22, no. 88 (July 1972), pp. 193–209.

145    *proved by what lies* . . . Leibniz, *New Essays on Human Understanding* (1704), I.i, in NE p. 79.

146    *The truths about numbers* . . . Ibid., in NE p. 85.

146    Leibniz on Locke: Ibid., preface, in NE pp. 51–52.

146    *perfect Science* . . . Locke, *Essay*, IV.iii.29, in E p. 560.

146    *minute Constituent parts* . . . [etc.]: Ibid., IV.iii.25, in E p. 556.

147    *scientifical*: Ibid., IV.iii.26, in E p. 556.

147    *experimental*: Ibid.

147    *Microscopical Eyes*: Ibid., II.xxiii.12, in E p. 303.

148    Locke's friend: William Molyneux, letter to Locke, 27 Aug. 1692, in Cranston, *John Locke*, p. 360.

148    *Where there is no* . . . Locke, *Essay*, IV.iii.18, in E pp. 549–50.

148    *to demonstrate morality* . . . Berkeley, *Philosophical Commentaries* (1707–8), Notebook A, p. 690.

148    *Knowledge then seems* . . . Locke, *Essay*, IV.i.2, in E p. 525.

149    *a want of a discoverable* . . . Ibid., IV.iii.28, in E p. 558.

149    *The notice we have* . . . Ibid., IV.xi.3, in E p. 631.

150    *all we see* . . . Ibid., IV.xi.8, in E p. 634.

150    *extends as far* . . . [etc.]: Ibid., IV.xi.9, in E pp. 635–36.

151    Locke's good point about materialism: Ibid., IV.iii.6.

151    *Star Trek*: See Lawrence Krauss, *The Physics of Star Trek*, HarperCollins, 1996, ch. 5.

152    *can consider* . . . [etc.]: Locke, *Essay*, II.xxvii.9–10, in E pp. 335–36.

152    *should the Soul* . . . Ibid., II.xxvii.15, in E p. 340.

152    Criticisms of Locke, modern developments of his theory, and Pope's *Memoirs of Scriblerus*: See *Personal Identity*, ed. John Perry, University of California Press, 1975; M. A. Stewart, "Reid on Locke and Personal Identity: Some Lost Sources," *Locke Newsletter*, vol. 28 (1997); Christopher Fox, "Locke and the Scriblerians," *Eighteenth-Century Studies*, vol. 16, no. 1 (Autumn 1982), pp. 1–25.

154    *governor of the seraglio* . . . Jonathan Edwards: See Roger Woolhouse, *Locke: A Biography*, Cambridge University Press, 2007, p. 399.

154    *that thinking thing* . . . Locke, *Essay*, II.xxvii.27, in E p. 347.

154    *the Commonwealth of Learning* . . . Ibid., Epistle to the Reader, in E pp. 9–10.

154    Ayer: *Language, Truth and Logic*, 2nd ed, Gollancz, 1946, p. 52.

## 5  BAYLE

156    *the greatest dialectician* . . . Voltaire, *Poem on the Lisbon Disaster* (1756), preface, in CRT p. 98.

156    *arsenal of all* . . . Ernst Cassirer, *The Philosophy of the Enlightenment* (1932), trans. Fritz Koelln and James Pettegrove, Princeton University Press, 1968, p. 167. This remark is often misattributed to Voltaire.

157    comets and superstition: See James Howard Robinson, *The Great Comet of 1680* (1916), Zubal, 1986.

157    Callixtus III: See W. F. Rigge, "An Historical Examination of the Connection of Callixtus III with Halley's Comet," *Popular Astronomy*, vol. 18 (1910), pp. 214–19.

157    seven proofs, etc.: Bayle, *Various Thoughts on the Occasion of a Comet*, trans. Robert Bartlett, State University of New York Press, 2000, p. ix.

157    *most men remain* . . . [etc.]: Ibid., p. 90.

158    Scandinavia: See Phil Zuckerman, *Society Without God: What the Least Religious Nations Can Tell Us About Contentment*, New York University Press, 2008.

158    *it ought not to appear* . . . Bernard Mandeville, *Free Thoughts on Religion*, London, 1720, p. 4.

160    *a sincere heretic* . . . Bayle, *A Philosophical Commentary* . . . , II.x, anonymous translation of 1708, ed. John Kilcullen and Chandran Kukathas, Liberty Fund, 2005, p. 273 (capitalisation modernised).

160    Bayle on Catholic persecution: Bayle, *Dictionnaire historique et critique* (1697–1702), "Milton," note O.

161    *Man is wicked* . . . [etc.]: Ibid., "Manicheans," note D, in *Historical and Critical Dictionary: Selections*, trans. Richard Popkin, Hackett, 1991, pp. 146–47.

161    *no good mother* . . . Ibid., "Paulicians," note E, in *Dictionary*, p. 177.

161    *a father who allows* . . . Ibid., p. 176.

161    *the way in which evil* . . . Ibid., pp. 168–69.

161    *may have its value* . . . Bayle, *Dictionnaire*, "Pyrrho," in *Dictionary*, p. 194.

162    *the art of disputing* . . . Ibid.

162    *I am a good Protestant* . . . See Popkin, *Dictionary*, p. xviii n5.


## 6 LEIBNIZ

163    *When one compares* . . . Denis Diderot, "Léibnitzianisme ou Philosophie de Léibnitz," *Encyclopédie*, in ENC vol. 9, p. 370 (my translation).

164    Leibniz's cipher machine: See Nicholas Rescher, "Leibniz's Machina Deciphratoria: A Seventeenth-Century Proto-Enigma," *Cryptologia*, vol. 38, no. 2 (2014), pp. 103–15.

165    *almost perpetual jumble*: Bernard le Bovier de Fontenelle, "Eloge de Mr G. G. Leibnitz," *Histoire de l'Académie royale des sciences, 1716*, Paris, 1718, p. 95.

165    *studied incessantly*: See Maria Rosa Antognazza, *Leibniz: An Intellectual Biography*, Cambridge University Press, 2009, p. 558.

165    Leibniz and the Harz mines: See Andre Wakefield, "Leibniz and the Wind Machines," *Osiris*, vol. 25, no. 1 (2010), pp. 171–88.

166    Sir Nicholas Gimcrack: Thomas Shadwell, *The Virtuoso* (1676).

166    *mind toward* . . . See Antognazza, *Leibniz*, p. 283.

166    poverty, unemployment and bad education: Leibniz, "Memoir for Enlightened Persons of Good Intention" (mid-1690s), in Leibniz, *Political Writings*, ed. Patrick Riley, 2nd ed, Cambridge University Press, 1988, pp. 103–10.

166    *one must furnish* . . . Leibniz, "Moyens" (undated), in A. Foucher de Careil, *Oeuvres de Leibniz*, vol. 4, Paris, 1862, trans. in *Political Writings*, p. 106 n2.

166    *courtly* . . . [etc.]: Bertrand Russell, *A Critical Exposition of the Philosophy of Leibniz* (1900), 2nd ed., Allen & Unwin, 1937, p. 2.

167    *The . . . most efficacious* . . . Leibniz, "Memoir for Enlightened Persons," p. 107.

167    duchess of Orléans: See Antognazza, *Leibniz*, p. 458.

167    *one of the supreme* . . . Bertrand Russell, *History of Western Philosophy*, ch. 11, in HWP p. 563.

167 Russell's charge:  According to Russell, Leibniz suppressed his doctrine that "the individual notion of each person involves once for all everything that ever happens to him" after Arnauld objected that this was inconsistent with free will (Russell, *History*, pp. 573–74). Yet Leibniz did in subsequent published work express similar ideas—e.g., that Sextus was wicked "from all eternity" (Leibniz, *Theodicy*, 416)—that were just as likely to prompt the same complaint.

167 *My principles are such* . . . Leibniz, letter to Des Bosses, 7 Nov. 1710, in PPL vol. 2, p. 975.

168 *a sort of enchanted* . . . Kant, *What Real Progress Has Metaphysics Made in Germany Since the Time of Leibniz and Wolff?* (1793), I, trans. in Kant, *Theoretical Philosophy After 1781*, ed. Henry Allinson and Peter Heath, Cambridge University Press, 2002, p. 375.

168 *like a metaphysical romance:* Hegel's *Lectures on the History of Philosophy*, III.2.I.C.1, in HLHP vol. 3, p. 330.

168 *fairy tale:* Russell, *Critical Exposition*, p. xiii.

168 *a world of its own* . . . Leibniz, letter to Des Bosses, 5 Feb. 1712, in PE p. 199.

168 *true atoms* . . . Leibniz, "Monadology" (1714), 3, in PE p. 213.

168 *no windows* . . . Ibid., 7, in PE p. 213.

168 *pre-established harmony:* Leibniz, postcript of a letter to Basnage de Beauval (1696), in PE p. 148.

168 *several different bands* . . . Leibniz, letter to Arnauld, 30 April 1687, in PE p. 84.

169 *mirror of the universe:* Leibniz, "Monadology," 56, in PE p. 220.

169 *traces of everything* . . . Leibniz, "Remarks on Arnauld's Letter," May 1686, in PE p. 76.

169 *everything that happens* . . . Leibniz, "Discourse on Metaphysics" (1686), 8, in PE p. 41.

169 *I hear the particular* . . . Leibniz, "Principles of Nature and Grace" (1714), 13, in PE p. 211.

170 *absolute reality* . . . Leibniz, letter to de Volder, 1704 or 1705, in PE p. 181.

170 *a complete being:* Leibniz, letter to Arnauld, 30 April 1687, in PE p. 90.

170 *being which subsists* . . . Leibniz, "On Transubstantiation" (1688?), in PPL vol. 1, p. 178.

170 *result from:* Leibniz, letter to de Volder, 30 June 1704, in PE p. 179.

170 *solely through* . . . Leibniz, letter to Des Bosses, 16 June 1712, in PPL vol. 2, p. 983.

170 *the one in Ireland* . . . Leibniz, letter to Des Bosses, 5 March 1715, in PE p. 306.

171 *much here . . . is correct* . . . Leibniz, *Remarks on Berkeley's "Principles,"* in PE p. 307.

171 *there is no part* Leibniz, letter to Johann Bernoulli, Aug.–Sept. 1688, in PE p. 167.

171 *soul:* Leibniz, "Monadology," 63, in PE p. 221.

171 *there is a world . . .* Ibid., 66–67, in PE p. 222.

171 *every particle . . .* Leibniz, "Primary Truths" (c. 1686), in PE p. 34

172 *there is nothing . . .* Leibniz, "Monadology," 69, in PE p. 222.

172 *little animals . . .* See Justin Smith, *Divine Machines: Leibniz and the Sciences of Life*, Princeton University Press, 2011, p. 180.

172 *a hundred thousand . . .* [etc]: Leibniz, "Meditations on the Common Concept of Justice" (c. 1702–3), in *Political Writings*, p. 53.

172 *merely passive:* Leibniz, letter to Johannn Bernoulli, 20/30 Sept. 1698, in PE p. 167.

172 *actually subdivided . . .* Leibniz, "Monadology," 64, in PE p. 221.

172 *Truth is more widespread . . .* Leibniz, letter to Nicolas Rémond, 26 Aug. 1714, trans. in Antognazza, *Leibniz*, p. 499.

172 *right in a good part . . .* Leibniz, letter to Nicolas Rémond, Jan. 1714, in PPL vol. 2, p. 1064.

172 *Plato with Democritus . . .* Leibniz, *New Essays on Human Understanding* (1703–5), I.i, in NE p. 71.

173 *reduction of everything . . .* [etc.]: Leibniz, "Clarification of Bayle's Difficulties" (1698), in PPL vol. 2, pp. 806–7.

173 *the mechanical philosophy . . .* Leibniz, "Discourse on Metaphysics," 18, in PE p. 52.

173 *In general, we must . . .* [etc.]: Leibniz, "A Specimen of Dynamics," pt. 1 (1695), in PE pp. 126–27.

173 *derived from . . . mechanical . . .* Ibid., in PE p. 126.

174 two brothers: See Benson Mates, *The Philosophy of Leibniz: Metaphysics and Language*, Oxford University Press, 1986, p. 28.

174 *the origin of things . . .* Leibniz, "Remarks on Chinese Rites and Religion" (1708), 9, trans. in Daniel Cook and Henry Rosemont Jr, *Leibniz: Writings on China*, Open Court, 1994, p. 73.

175 *the Chinese scholars . . .* Leibniz, "Discourse on the Natural Theology of the Chinese" (1716), 67, in *Writings on China*, p. 132.

175 *the substance of . . .* Leibniz, "Remarks on Chinese Rites and Religion," p. 73.

175 *alphabet of human . . .* Leibniz, "Preface to a Universal Characteristic" (1678–79), in PE p. 6.

175 *a fundamental knowledge . . .* Leibniz, "Of the Art of Combination" (1666), trans. in G. H. R. Parkinson, *Leibniz: Logical Papers*, Oxford University Press, 1966, p. 11.

176   *should still hope* . . . Leibniz, letter to Nicolas Rémond, 10 Jan. 1714, in PPL vol. 2, p. 1063.

176   *key to all sciences*: Leibniz, letter to Christian Daum, 26 March 1666. See Antognazza, *Leibniz*, p. 63.

176   *a mind weighted* . . . George Eliot, *Middlemarch* (1871–72), ch. 20.

176   *explain correctly* . . . Descartes, letter to Mersenne, 20 Nov. 1629, in PWD vol. 3, p. 13.

176   *rightly stated* . . . Leibniz, "Of the Art of Combination," p. 3.

176   Leibniz and Gödel:  See John W. Dawson Jr, *Logical Dilemmas: The Life and Work of Kurt Gödel*, J. A. K. Peters, 1997, p. 39.

177   *life's greatest good* . . . Leibniz, "The Confession of Nature Against Atheists" (1669), in PPL vol. 1, p. 169.

178   *is not self-sufficient* . . . Ibid., PPL vol. 1, p. 170.

178   *undertake that task* . . . Leibniz, letter to Hobbes, July 1670, trans. in Noel Malcolm, ed., *The Correspondence of Thomas Hobbes*, Oxford University Press, 1994, vol. 2, p. 720.

178   *whose structure makes* . . . Leibniz, "Monadology," 17, in PE p. 215.

179   *intolerably licentious*: Leibniz, letter to Jakob Thomasius, 3 Oct. 1670, in Leibniz, *Sämtliche Schriften und Briefe*, Akademie Verlag, 2006, 2nd ser., vol. 1, p. 106.

180   *but the person he* . . . Fontenelle, "Eloge de Leibnitz," p. 126. Fontenelle's story is taken from Leibniz's first biographer, J. G. Eckhart.

180   *fatal necessity*: Leibniz, letter to Henri Justel, 14 Feb. 1678, in *Sämtliche Schriften und Briefe*, p. 592.

180   *everything happens* . . . Leibniz, letter to Arnauld, 30 April 1687, in PE p. 82.

181   *incline without necessitating*: Leibniz, *New Essays on Human Understanding*, II.xxi.13, in NE p. 178.

181   Judas: Leibniz, "Discourse on Metaphysics," 30, in PE p. 61.

182   *notion . . . another Adam*: Leibniz, "Remarks on Arnauld's Letter," May 1686, in PE p. 73.

182   *nothing happens without* . . . Leibniz, "An Answer to Dr Clarke's First Reply" (1715–16), in *The Leibniz-Clarke Correspondence*, ed. H. G. Alexander, Manchester University Press, 1956, p. 16.

182   *there is no effect* . . . Leibniz, "Primary Truths," in PE p. 31.

182   *a reason can be given* . . . Leibniz, "Specimen inventorum de admirandis naturae generalis arcanis" (c. 1686), in C. I. Gerhardt, ed., *Leibniz: Die Philosophischen Schriften*, vol. 7, Weidmann, 1890, p. 309.

182   *is oft-times no other* . . . Samuel Clarke, "Dr Clarke's Second Reply" (10 Jan. 1716), in *Leibniz-Clarke Correspondence*, p. 20.

182    *rendered every event* . . . Leibniz, "An Answer to Dr Clarke's Fourth Reply" (18 Aug. 1716), in *Leibniz-Clarke Correspondence*, p. 56.

183    *supported by inadequate* . . . Albert Einstein, foreword to Max Jammer, *Concepts of Space*, 3rd ed., Dover, 1993, p. xvi.

183    *two eggs or two leaves* . . . Leibniz, "Primary Truths," in PE p. 32.

183    *If this is the best* . . . Voltaire, *Candide*, ch. 6, in CRT p. 13.

184    *for, after all* . . . Ibid., ch. 28, in CRT p. 75.

184    *the best* [optimum] . . . Leibniz, *Theodicy*, I.8, in T p. 128.

184    *l'optimisme: Mémoires de Trévoux*, Feb. 1737, p. 207.

185    *just being glad* . . . [etc.]: Eleanor Porter, *Pollyanna* (1913), ch. 5.

185    chocolate and syphilis: Voltaire, *Candide*, ch. 4, in CRT.

185    *the most beautiful* . . . Ibid., ch. 1, in CRT p. 2.

185    *Man is exposed* . . . Leibniz, *Theodicy*, I.4, in T p. 125.

186    *difficulties:* Ibid., I.5, in T p. 126.

186    *banish . . . the false* . . . Ibid., I.6, in T p. 127.

186    *carries with it* . . . [etc.]: Ibid., I.7, in T p. 127.

186    *cannot but* . . . Ibid., I.8, in T p. 128.

186    *[we] know* . . . [etc.]: Ibid., I.10, in T p. 129.

187    *gained Jesus* . . . Ibid., I.11, in T p. 130.

187    *all of one piece* . . . Ibid., I.9, in T p. 129.

187    *the fairest* . . . Plato, *Timaeus*, 30a, in CDP p. 1162.

187    *providence has omitted* . . . Philo, *De providentia*, II.74, trans. A. A. Long in *Philo of Alexandria and Post-Aristotelian Philosophy*, ed. Francesca Alesse, Brill, 2008, p. 13.

187    Chrysippus on war and beasts: See F. H. Sandbach, *The Stoics*, 2nd ed., Bristol Press, 1989, p. 107.

188    Stoic super-optimism: See THP vol. 1, p. 311.

188    *bring forth* . . . Augustine, *Enchiridion*, 11.

188    Augustine on whether God could have done better: *De libero arbitrio*, III.v.

188    Aquinas on possible worlds: See Giorgio Pini, "Scotus on the Possibility of a Better World," *Acta Philosophica*, vol. 18, no. 2 (2009), p. 286. I owe the jigsaw simile to this article.

188    *so simple* . . . Malebranche, *Treatise on Nature and Grace* (1680), I.xiv, trans. Patrick Riley, Oxford University Press, 1992, p. 117.

189    Malebranche on fruit and deformity: Malebranche, *De la recherche de la vérité* (1674), II.vii.iii.

189    *more perfect* . . . Malebranche, *Treatise on Nature and Grace*, I.xiv, p. 116.

189    *infinity of possible* . . . Ibid., I.xiii, p. 116.

189    *Well, sir, physics* . . . Voltaire, letter to Jean-Robert Tronchin, 24 Nov. 1755, in CRT p. 132.

190    *why so many . . .* Voltaire, letter to Louis Martin Kahle, March 1744, trans. in Theodore Besterman, *Voltaire*, Harcourt, Brace and World, 1969, p. 353.

190    Voltaire on Pascal: *Lettres philosophiques*, 25.

190    *deceived philosophers . . .* Voltaire, *Poème sur le désastre de Lisbonne*, line 4.

190    *most of the physical . . .* [etc.]: Rousseau, letter to Voltaire, 18 Aug. 1756, in CRT pp. 110–11.

191    *manures the earth*: Ibid., p. 116.

191    *inevitable aspects . . .* [etc.]: Ibid., p. 117.

191    *infinite number . . .* Leibniz, *Theodicy*, I.19, in T p. 135.

191    *in a way most likely . . .* Ibid., III.405, in T pp. 365–66.

192    *serves for great . . .* Ibid., III.416, in T p. 373.

192    Sextus's garden: *"Il y achète un petit jardin; en le cultivant il trouve un trésor; il devient un homme riche, aimé, considéré; il meurt dans un grande vieillesse, chéri de toute la ville . . . ."* Ibid., III.415. See https://voltairefoundation.wordpress.com/2015/02/03/candide-and-leibnizs-garden/.

194    *nothing is moved . . .* Leibniz, "Against Barbaric Physics" (c. 1710–16), in PE p. 312.

194    *forerunner*: Leibniz, letter to Thomas Burnett, 30 Oct. 1710, in C. I. Gerhardt, ed., *Leibniz: Die Philosophischen Schriften*, vol. 3, Weidmann, 1887, p. 321.

195    *did the human species . . .* Voltaire, *Philosophical Dictionary* (1764), "Bien (tout est)," in CRT p. 137.

195    *As for the future . . .* Leibniz, "Discourse on Metaphysics," 4, in PE p. 38.

195    *leads to despair*: Voltaire, letter to Elie Bertrand, 18 Feb. 1756, in CRT p. 134.

195    *never comes . . .* Leibniz, "On the Ultimate Origination of Things" (1697), in PE p. 155.

195    *incomparably happier*: Leibniz, "Memoir for Enlightened Persons of Good Intention," in *Political Writings*, p. 104.

195    *things are bound . . .* Leibniz, "La restitution universelle" (1715), in Antognazza, *Leibniz*, p. 522.

## 7 HUME

196    survey of philosophers: The PhilPapers Survey (2009), available at http://philpapers.org/surveys/demographics.pl.

196    *dogmatic slumber*: Kant, *Prolegomena to Any Future Metaphysic* (1783), preface, trans. in *Kant: Theoretical Philosophy after 1781*, ed. Henry Allison and Peter Heath, Cambridge University Press, 2002, p. 57.

196    Reid: See Thomas Reid, *An Inquiry into the Human Mind on the Principles of Common Sense* (1764), dedication.

197    *there is no fundamental* . . . Darwin, *The Descent of Man* (1871, 1st ed.), ch. 2
       (ch. 3 in later editions).

197    *monkish virtues*:   Hume, *An Enquiry Concerning the Principles of Morals*
       (1751), IX.I, in HE p. 270.

197    *Thus died* . . . Adam Smith, letter to William Strahan, 9 Nov. 1776, in LDH
       vol. 2, p. 452 (punctuation modernised).

198    *Such . . . was the end* . . . Plato, *Phaedo*, 118, in CDP p. 98.

198    *brought upon me* . . . Smith, letter to Andreas Holt, 26 Oct. 1780, in *Corre-
       spondence of Adam Smith*, ed. E. C. Mossner and I. S. Ross, 2nd ed., Oxford
       University Press, 1987, p. 208.

199    *Have a little patience* . . . Smith, letter to William Strahan, in LDH vol. 2,
       p. 451. Smith wrote that Hume had been reading Lucian's *Dialogues of the
       Dead*, but it must in fact have been Lucian's *The Downward Journey*.

199    *till I have the pleasure* . . . Smith, letter to Alexander Wedderburn, 14 Aug.
       1776, in *Correspondence of Adam Smith*, p. 204.

199    *I had a strong curiosity* . . . [etc.]: James Boswell, *An Account of My Last Inter-
       view with David Hume, Esq* (1777), in DCNR pp. 76–77.

200    Johnson claimed that Hume was lying:   Boswell, *Life of Johnson* (1791), 17
       Sept. 1777, Oxford University Press, 1953, p. 839.

200    *no more uneasy to think* . . . Ibid., 26 Oct. 1769, p. 426.

200    *the whole of life* . . . Ibid., 19 Oct. 1769, p. 416.

200    *the confidence or* . . . Rev. William Agutter, *On the Difference Between the
       Deaths of the Righteous and the Wicked*, London, 1800, p. 11 (preached in
       1786).

200    *any belief in religion*:   Boswell, *Account*, in DCNR p. 76.

200    *with young ladies* . . . Boswell, *Life of Johnson*, 21 July 1763, p. 314.

200    Boswell and Casanova:   See Ian Kelly, *Casanova*, Penguin, 2008, p. 125.

200    *I always lived* . . . Boswell, *Journal of a Tour to the Hebrides* (1786), in
       Johnson and Boswell, *Journey to the Western Islands and A Tour to the
       Hebrides*, ed. R. W. Chapman, Oxford University Press, 1930, p. 177.

201    *Every one, who* . . . Hume, letter to [Dr George Cheyne?], March or April
       1734, in LDH vol. 1, p. 13.

202    *more upon Invention* . . . Ibid., p. 16.

202    *the Disease* . . . Ibid., p. 14.

202    *some nonsensical miracle* . . . Hume, letter to Rev George Campbell, 7 June
       1762, in LDH vol. 1, p. 361.

202    *a compleat system* . . . Hume, *Treatise* (1739–40), introduction, in HT p. xvi.

203    *making experiments* . . . Newton, *Optics* (1721), bk. III, query 31, in NPW
       p. 139.

203    *are very copious* . . . Hume, *An Abstract of . . . A Treatise of Human Nature*

(1740), in HT pp. 646–47. Hume was endorsing a remark of Leibniz's, in *Theodicy*, "Preliminary Dissertation," sec. 31.

203    *Suppose I see a ball* . . . Hume, *Abstract*, in HT p. 650 (spelling modernised).

204    *Every object* . . . Ibid., pp. 649–50.

204    *all reasonings* . . . Ibid., p. 651.

205    *is nothing but a species* . . . Hume, *An Enquiry Concerning Human Understanding* (1748), IX, in HE p. 108.

205    *'Tis not, therefore* . . . Hume, *Abstract*, in HT p. 652.

205    *demonstrative reasoning* . . . Hume, *Enquiry . . . Understanding*, IV.ii, in HE p. 35.

206    *this more perfect* . . . [etc.]: Ibid., XII.iii, in HE p. 163.

206    *just*: Hume, *Treatise*, I.III.VI, in HT p. 89.

206    *Man falls* . . . Hume, "Of the Dignity or Meanness of Human Nature" (1741), in EMPL p. 84.

206    *they suppose such* . . . Hume, *Treatise*, I.III.XVI, in HT p. 177.

206    *endow'd with thought* . . . Ibid., p. 176.

207    *sagacity* . . . [etc.]: Ibid., p. 177.

207    *can never by any* . . . [etc.]: Ibid., p. 178.

207    Aristotle on animal reason: Aristotle, *De partibus animalium*, 641B, in CWA vol. 1, p. 998; *De anima*, 3.3, in ibid., p. 681.

207    Plato on animal reason: See Richard Sorabji, *Animal Minds and Human Morals: The Origin of the Western Debate*, Duckworth, 1993, p. 10.

207    Plutarch on animal reason: Plutarch, *De sollertia animalium*, trans. H. Cherniss and W. C. Helmbold, in *Plutarch: Moralia*, vol. 12, Loeb Classical Library, 1957, pp. 319–479.

207    Montaigne on guide-dogs: Montaigne, "An Apology for Raymond Sebond," in *The Complete Essays*, trans. M. A. Screech, Penguin, 1991, p. 518.

207    *is not attained* . . . Hobbes, *Leviathan*, ch. 46, in L vol. 3, p. 1052.

208    *beasts are* . . . Leibniz, *New Essays on Human Understanding*, preface, in NE p. 50.

208    *is capable* . . . Ibid., p. 51.

208    *men so much surpass* . . . [etc.]: Hume, *Enquiry . . . Understanding*, IX, in HE p. 107 n1.

208    *we ought to* . . . [etc.]: Hume, *Treatise*, I.III.VIII, in HT p. 149.

209    *but extremely difficult* . . . [etc.]: Ibid., I.III.XV, in HT p. 175.

209    *skeleton in the cupboard* . . . C. D. Broad, "The Philosophy of Francis Bacon," in *Ethics and the History of Philosophy*, Routledge, 1952, p. 142.

209    *the glory of science*: Ibid., p. 143.

209    *Induction raises perhaps* . . . Russell, *An Outline of Philosophy* (1927), George Allen & Unwin, 1970, p. 14.

209    current encyclopedia: *The Routledge Encylopedia of Philosophy*, ed. Edward
       Craig, Routledge, 1998, vol. 4, p. 746.

209    *this operation of the mind* . . . Hume, *Enquiry* . . . *Understanding*, V.II, in HE
       p. 55.

210    *a kind of attraction:* Hume, *Treatise*, I.IV, in HT p. 12.

210    *Thoughts or Ideas:* Hume, *Enquiry* . . . *Understanding*, II, in HE p. 18.

210    *association of ideas:* Hume, *Abstract*, in HT p. 661.

210    *the only ties* . . . Ibid., p. 662.

210    talking nonsense: Ibid., pp. 648–49.

211    *Newtonian philosophy* . . . Hume, *Treatise*, appendix, note to I.II.V, in HT
       p. 639.

211    *confine our speculations* . . . Ibid., p. 638.

211    *the phenomena of* . . . [etc.]: Newton, *Principia*, general scholium to bk. III, in
       NPW p. 92.

211    *go beyond experience* . . . Hume, *Treatise*, introduction, in HT p. xvii.

211    *seemed to draw off* . . . Hume, *History of England*, vol. 6, ch. 71, in HHE vol. 6,
       p. 542.

212    *take more time* . . . Newton, letter to Richard Bentley, 17 Jan. 1692/3, in
       NPW p. 100.

212    Newton's conjectures about gravity: Newton, *Opticks* (2nd ed., 1718), query
       21.

212    *more unfortunate* . . . Hume, *My Own Life* (1776), in EMPL p. 608.

212    *Heat of Youth & Invention:* Hume, letter to Gilbert Eliot, March or April
       1751, in LDH vol. 1, p. 158.

212    *juvenile:* Hume, *Advertisement* (1775), in HE p. 2.

213    *sapping the Foundations* . . . Hume, *A Letter from a Gentleman* (1745), ed.
       E. C. Mossner and J. V. Price, Edinburgh University Press, 1967, p. 18.

213    *Principles leading to* . . . Ibid., p. 17.

213    *the propositions of morality* . . . Ibid., p. 30.

213    *the Truth of the* . . . Ibid., p. x.

213    *the manner than* . . . Hume, *My Own Life*, in EMPL p. 610.

214    *When we run* . . . Hume, *Enquiry* . . . *Understanding*, XII.III, in HE p. 165
       (punctuation modernised).

214    *founded entirely* . . . [etc.]: Ibid., p. 164.

214    *foundation in reason:* Ibid., p. 165.

215    *Atheism is so senseless* . . . Newton, "A Short Schem of the True Religion"
       (post-1710), Keynes MS. 7, King's College, Cambridge, available at http://
       www.newtonproject.sussex.ac.uk/view/texts/normalized/THEM00007.

215    *a friend who loves* . . . Hume, *Enquiry* . . . *Understanding*, XI, in HE p. 132.

216    *If the cause* . . . Ibid., pp. 136–37 (punctuation modernised).

216 *there was probably* . . . [etc.]: Ibid., p. 144.

217 *Let your gods* . . . Ibid., p. 138.

217 *I flatter myself* . . . . . Ibid., X.I, in HE p. 110.

218 *external* [etc.]: Arnauld and Nicole, *Logic*, IV.13, in LAT p. 264. See Ian Hacking, *The Emergence of Probability*, Cambridge University Press, 1975, ch. 9.

218 *are full of so many* . . . [etc.]: Arnauld and Nicole, *Logic*, IV.14, in LAT p. 267.

219 *a violation* . . . [etc.]: Hume, *Enquiry . . . Understanding*, X.I, in HE p. 114.

219 one recent commentator: Peter Millican. See the introduction to Hume, *An Enquiry Concerning Human Understanding*, ed. Peter Millican, Oxford University Press, 2007, p. l n30.

219 *no testimony is sufficient* . . . Hume, *Enquiry . . . Understanding*, X.I, in HE pp. 115–16 (punctuation modernised).

219 *they are observed chiefly* . . . Ibid., X.II, in HE p. 119.

220 *passion of surprise* . . . Ibid., p. 117.

220 *depend in any way* . . . Francis Bacon, *The New Organon*, II.XXIX, in NO p. 149.

220 *and yet persevere* . . . [etc.]: Hume, *Enquiry . . . Understanding*, X.II, in HE p. 118.

220 *it is more probable* . . . Boswell, *Life of Johnson*, 22 Sept. 1777, p. 866.

220 *universal doubt*: Hume, *Enquiry . . . Understanding*, XII.I, in HE p. 149.

221 *entirely incurable*: Ibid., p. 150.

221 *nothing can ever* . . . [etc.]: Ibid., p. 152.

221 *admit of no answer* . . . Ibid., p. 155 n1.

221 *The great subverter* . . . Ibid., XII.II, in HE pp. 158–59.

221 *All discourse, all action* . . . Ibid., p. 160 (punctuation modernised).

221 *small tincture* . . . Ibid., XII.III, in HE p. 161.

222 *but custom* . . . Ibid., XII.II, in HE p. 159.

222 *the narrow capacity* . . . [etc.]: Ibid., XII.III, in HE p. 162.

222 *not so properly* . . . Ibid., p. 165.

222 *incomparably the best*: Hume, *My Own Life*, in EMPL p. 611.

222 *founded on fact* . . . Hume, *Enquiry . . . Morals*, I, in HE p. 175.

222 *personal merit*: Ibid., p. 173.

222 *foundation of ethics*: Ibid., p. 174.

222 *public utility*: Ibid., II.II, in HE p. 180.

222 *there never was* . . . Ibid., "A Dialogue," in HE p. 336.

223 *felt as if scales* . . . [etc.]: Bentham, *A Fragment on Government* (1776), I.36, ed. Wilfrid Harrison, Blackwell, 1948, p. 50 n2.

223 *the greatest happiness* . . . [etc.]: Ibid., preface, p. 3.

223 *a feeling for the happiness* . . . Hume, *Enquiry . . . Morals*, Appendix I, in HE p. 286.

223 *particular fabric* . . . Ibid., I, in HE p. 170.

224    *can instruct us* . . . Ibid., Appendix I, in HE p. 285.

224    *deduce the original* . . . Samuel Clarke, *A Discourse Concerning the Unchange-able Obligations of Natural Religion* (1706), 1, quoted in *British Moralists 1650–1800*, ed. D. D. Raphael, Clarendon Press, 1969, vol. 1, p. 216.

224    *In every system* . . . Hume, *Treatise*, III.I.I, in HT p. 469 (punctuation modernised).

224    *the distinction of vice* . . . Ibid., p. 470.

225    *ultimately derived* . . . Hume, *Enquiry* . . . *Morals*, Appendix I, in HE p. 294.

225    *false religion:* Ibid., IX.I, in HE p. 270.

225    undermine all the foundations of religion . . . [etc.]: I am indebted to Edward Craig, *Hume on Religion*, Indian Institute for Advanced Study, 1997, p. 57.

225    *not had the precaution* . . . Hume, letter to the Comtesse de Boufflers, 22 Jan. 1763, in LDH vol. 1, p. 374.

226    *it is the gospel* . . . Hume, "On the Immortality of the Soul," in EMPL p. 597.

226    *The providence* . . . Hume, "On Suicide," in EMPL p. 588.

227    *nothing can be more* . . . Hume, letter to Adam Smith, 15 Aug. 1776, in LDH vol. 2, p. 334.

227    *caved in:* Daniel Dennett, *Darwin's Dangerous Idea: Evolution and the Mean-ings of Life*, Penguin, 1995, p. 32.

227    *rigid inflexible* . . . [etc.]: Hume, *Dialogues Concerning Natural Religion*, Pam-philus to Hermippus, in DCNR p. 128.

227    *a sound, believing* . . . Ibid., XII, in DCNR p. 228.

227    *no one has a deeper* . . . Ibid., p. 214.

228    *If the whole* . . . Ibid., p. 227 (punctuation modernised).

228    *all the operations* . . . Ibid., p. 218 (emphasis added).

229    *Where then, cry I* . . . Ibid. (punctuation modernised).

229    *the greatest writer* . . . See E. C. Mossner, *The Life of David Hume*, Oxford University Press, 1980, p. 223.

229    Smith on Hume: *The Wealth of Nations* (1776), bk. 3, ch. 4.

229    number of atheists at d'Holbach's salon: See Alan Kors, *D'Holbach's Coterie: An Enlightenment in Paris*, Princeton University Press, 1976, ch. 2.

230    *They laughed at* . . . Edward Gibbon, *Memoirs of My Life* (1796), Penguin, 1984, p. 136.

230    *The Men of Letters* . . . Hume, letter to Hugh Blair, Dec. 1763, in LDH vol. 1, p. 419.

230    *both for the Force* . . . Hume, letter to Rousseau, 2 July 1762, in LDH vol. 1, p. 364.

230    *You don't know* . . . Mossner, *Life*, p. 515.

230    *most singular of all* . . . Hume, letter to Hugh Blair, 25 March 1766, in LDH vol. 2, pp. 29–30.

231    Rousseau's *Confessions*: Bk. XII, end.

231    *is plainly mad* . . . Hume, letter to Richard Davenport, 16 May 1767, in *New Letters of David Hume*, ed. R. Klibansky and E. C. Mossner, Oxford University Press, 1954, p. 164.

231    *too old, too fat* . . . Mossner, *Life*, p. 556.


## 8  VOLTAIRE, ROUSSEAU AND THE *PHILOSOPHES*

232    *I hate you*: Rousseau, letter to Voltaire, 17 June 1760, quoted in Roger Pearson, *Voltaire Almighty*, Bloomsbury, 2005, p. 293.

232    *not very sociable*: Voltaire, "Pierre le Grand et J.-J. Rousseau," *Dictionnaire philosophique*, trans. in Leo Damrosch, *Jean-Jacques Rousseau: Restless Genius*, Mariner Books, 2007, p. 390.

232    *I have never* . . . Rousseau, *Reveries of the Solitary Walker* (1778), sixth walk, trans. Russell Goulbourne, Oxford University Press, 2011, p. 67.

232    *the greatest aversion* . . . Rousseau, *Judge of Jean-Jacques: Dialogues* (1772–75), third dialogue, trans. Judith Bush, Christopher Kelly and Roger Masters, Dartmouth University Press, 1990, p. 213.

233    *Enlightened times* . . . Voltaire, letter to Nicolas Thieriot, 13 Jan. 1757, Electronic Enlightenment Correspondence, ed. Robert McNamee et al., University of Oxford, letter D7118 (my translation).

233    sunrise anecdote: René Pomeau, *La religion de Voltaire*, Librairie Nizet, 1956, pp. 410–11.

233    *is the source* . . . Voltaire, *Philosophical Dictionary*, "Religion," trans. Peter Gay, Basic Books, 1962, vol. 2, p. 448.

234    *religion of the Gospel* . . . Rousseau, *The Social Contract* (1762), IV.8, in SCD p. 299.

234    *man is naturally good* . . . Rousseau, letter to Malesherbes, 22 Jan. 1762, trans. in *Rousseau on Philosophy, Morality, and Religion*, ed. Christopher Kelly, Dartmouth College Press, 2007, p. 152.

234    *the existence of a mighty* . . . Rousseau, *Social Contract*, IV.8, in SCD p. 304.

234    *it is just to consider* . . . Joseph de Maistre, "On the Sovereignty of the People" (1794–95), II.1, trans. Richard Lebrun, in Joseph de Maistre, *Against Rousseau*, McGill-Queen's University Press, 1996, p. 106.

234    *prepared the way* . . . See Damrosch, *Jean-Jacques Rousseau*, p. 352.

234    Robespierre and Rousseau: See Robespierre's speech to the National Convention on 7 May 1794, quoted in Maurice Cranston, *The Solitary Self: Jean-Jacques Rousseau in Exile and Adversity*, University of Chicago Press, 1999, p. 189.

235    *legitimate authority*: Rousseau, *Social Contract*, I.4, in SCD p. 185.

235    *Man is born free* . . . Ibid., I.1, in SCD p. 181.

235   *I am made unlike* . . . Rousseau, *Confessions* (1770), I, trans. J. M. Cohen, Penguin, 1953, p. 17.

235   *my terms rarely* . . . Rousseau, letter to Mme d'Épinay, March 1756, quoted in Peter Gay, *The Party of Humanity*, Norton, 1964, p. 222.

235   *multitude . . . often does not* . . . Rousseau, *Social Contract*, II.6, in SCD p. 211.

235   *be forced* . . . Ibid., I.7, in SCD p. 194.

235   *the inventor of the* . . . Russell, *History of Western Philosophy*, ch. 19, in HWP p. 660.

235   *made possible* . . . Ibid., p. 674.

236   *all that is nowadays* . . . Rousseau, *A Discourse on the Moral Effects of the Arts and Sciences* (1750), preface, in SCD p. 2.

236   *in a state still worse* . . . Ibid., p. 4.

236   *highly enlightened:* Ibid.

236   *our minds have been* . . . [etc.]: Ibid., p. 8.

237   *preserved from the contagion* . . . Ibid., p. 9.

237   *military discipline* . . . Ibid., p. 12.

237   *nourished by luxury* . . . [etc.]: Ibid., II, in SCD p. 15.

237   *futile in the objects* . . . [etc.]: Ibid., p. 16.

237   *the reasoning and philosophic* . . . Rousseau, *Émile* (1762), bk. 4, trans. Allan Bloom, Penguin, 1991, p. 312 n.

237   *dreadful art* . . . [etc.]: Rousseau, *Discourse*, II, in SCD p. 26.

238   *the happy state* . . . Ibid., I, in SCD p. 14.

238   Rousseau on Socrates: Ibid., p. 12.

238   *Almighty God!* . . . Ibid., II, in SCD pp. 26–27.

238   *thought they were living* . . . Dan Edelstein, *The Enlightenment: A Genealogy*, University of Chicago Press, 2010, p. 73.

238   *happy age* . . . Voltaire, *The Age of Louis XIV* (1751), ch. 31, trans. F. C. Green, Everyman's Library, 1961, p. 352.

238   *the most enlightened* . . . Ibid., ch. 1, p. 1.

238   *a philosophical* . . . [etc.]: See Edelstein, *Enlightenment*.

238   *principal geniuses* . . . Jean Le Rond d'Alembert, *Preliminary Discourse to the Encyclopedia of Diderot* (1751), II, trans. Richard Schwab, University of Chicago Press, 1995, p. 85.

238   *multitude of prejudices* . . . [etc.]: Ibid., p. 71.

239   *the inadequacy* . . . Ibid., pp. 86–87.

239   *We must* . . . [etc.]: Diderot, "Encyclopédie," in ECTP, available at http://hdl.handle.net/2027/spo.did2222.0000.004.

239   *he works at* . . . César Chesneau Du Marsais, "Philosophe," in ECTP, available at http://hdl.handle.net/2027/spo.did2222.0000.001.

240 *Only an atheist . . .* See Voltaire, *Poem on the Lisbon Disaster* (1756), preface, footnote, in CRT p. 96.

240 smallpox inoculation and vaccination: See David Wootton, *Bad Medicine: Doctors Doing Harm Since Hippocrates*, Oxford University Press, 2006, pp. 153–58.

241 anthology of Enlightenment texts: *The Enlightenment Reader*, ed. Isaac Kramnick, Viking Penguin, 1995.

241 *The inflated Enlightenment . . .* Robert Darnton, *George Washington's False Teeth: An Unconventional Guide to the Eighteenth Century*, Norton, 2003, p. 11.

241 blaming the Enlightenment: See Graeme Garrard, *Counter-Enlightenments: From the Eighteenth Century to the Present*, Routledge, 2006.

241 *any of the Enlightened thinkers . . .* Isaiah Berlin, letter to Mark Lilla, 13 Dec. 1993, in Isaiah Berlin, *Three Critics of the Enlightenment: Vico, Hamann, Herder*, ed. Henry Hardy, 2nd ed., Princeton University Press, 2013, p. 497.

242 *these thinkers . . .* Ibid., p. 496.

242 *the legacy of the . . .* John Gray, *Enlightenment's Wake: Politics and Culture at the Close of the Modern Age*, Routledge, 1995, p. 146.

242 *Oxford English Dictionary:* See James Schmidt, "Inventing the Enlightenment," *Journal of the History of Ideas*, vol. 64, no. 3 (July 2003), p. 421.

243 *They bled us white . . . Monty Python's Life of Brian*, dir. Terry Jones, HandMade Films, 1979, available at https://www.youtube.com/watch?v=ExWfh6sGyso.

244 *We will not reproach . . .* D'Alembert, *Preliminary Discourse*, II, p. 104.

# SUGGESTIONS FOR FURTHER READING

## Philosophers

John Cottingham, *The Rationalists*, Oxford University Press, 1988.

R. S. Woolhouse, *The Empiricists*, Oxford University Press, 1988.

Anthony Kenny, *The Rise of Modern Philosophy*, A New History of Western Philosophy, vol. 3, Oxford University Press, 2006.

Frederick Copleston, *A History of Philosophy*, vol. 5, *Hobbes to Hume* (1959), Continuum, 2003.

Margaret Atherton, *Women Philosophers of the Early Modern Period*, Hackett, 1994.

## The Enlightenment and Politics

Dorinda Outram, *The Enlightenment*, 3rd ed., Cambridge University Press, 2013.

Maurice Cranston, *Philosophers and Pamphleteers: Political Theorists of the Enlightenment*, Oxford University Press, 1986.

Jonathan Israel, *A Revolution of the Mind: Radical Enlightenment and the Intellectual Origins of Modern Democracy*, Princeton University Press, 2010.

## Science

I. Bernard Cohen, *The Birth of a New Physics*, Penguin, 1992.

Michael R. Matthews, ed., *The Scientific Background to Modern Philosophy: Selected Readings*, Hackett, 1989.

David Wootton, *The Invention of Science: A New History of the Scientific Revolution*, Allen Lane, 2015.

# ACKNOWLEDGEMENTS

I received a large amount of help over the many years during which this book was sporadically written. I especially wish to thank Oliver Black and Chaim Tannenbaum for commenting on the whole manuscript. I am grateful to Michael Ayers, Simon Blackburn, Desmond Clarke, Edmund Fawcett, Don Garrett, Zoë Heller, Cecilia Heyes, Michael Hickson, Sir Noel Malcolm, Peter Millican, Steven Nadler, Donald Rutherford, Ronald Schechter, the late Timothy Sprigge, Sir Keith Thomas and Catherine Wilson for commenting on parts of the book. And I am grateful to Maria Rosa Antognazza, Marc Bobro, Jonathan Israel, the late Lisa Jardine, Douglas Jesseph, Wim Klever, Sara Lipton, Giorgio Pini, Nicholas Rescher, Craig Walmsley, the late John Watling, the late Sir Bernard Williams and Yirmiahu Yovel for helpful correspondence or discussion. I am also grateful to the Warden and Fellows of All Souls College, Oxford, and to the Dorothy and Lewis B. Cullman Center for Scholars and Writers at the New York Public Library, and its staff, for providing support and wonderful places in which to work. Lastly, I thank Bob Weil for his patience and encouragement.

\* \* \*

Chapters one and seven of this book draw on articles of mine that were published in *The New Yorker* and *The New York Review of Books*, respectively.

# INDEX

Rousseau, Jean-Jacques (*continued*)
  *Émile*, 225, 230
  and Enlightenment, 242, 244
  on the "happy state of ignorance,"
    238
  and Hume, 229–31
  influence of, 243–44
  *Julie, or the New Heloise*, 230
  and the "noble savage," 54–57, 58
  on private property, 134
  and religion, 234
  revelation of, 236–37
  and revolution, 234–35
  *Social Contract*, 130, 230, 232, 234–35
  on stages of mankind, 58–59
  and Voltaire, 55, 58, 190–91, 234,
    236, 243
Royal Society of London, x, 67, 90,
    120, 179
  *Nullius in verba* as motto of, 124
  and scientific investigations, 75–76, 125
Russell, Bertrand, 50, 88, 235
  and empiricism, 115
  *History of Western Philosophy*, 167
  on induction, 209
  and Leibniz, 166–67, 168
Ryle, Gilbert, 115

Saturn, rings of, 90
Scargill, Arthur, 47
scepticism:
  and Bayle, 162
  and Descartes, 1–2, 8, 10, 13, 19, 26,
    28, 34–35, 151, 220–21
  and Hume, 213, 220–21, 227–29, 230
  and Leibniz, 173
  and Locke, 150–51
  radical, 221
  and Spinoza, 34–35, 83, 108
  and universal doubt, 220–21

scholasticism, 236–37
  dissatisfaction with, 35, 36, 121
  and synthesis, 172, 173
Schönborn, Archbishop of Mainz, 177,
    178
Schopenhauer, Arthur, 80
science:
  experiments in, 76, 147
  and mathematics, 147
  and philosophy, 28, 35, 147–48
secularism, 111
self-knowledge, 107
self-preservation, 106, 109
Seneca, 100
Seventh-Day Adventists, 80
Sévigné, Mme de, 25
Sextus Tarquinius, 191–92
Shaftesbury, Earl of, 113, 125, 126,
    128, 134
  earlier Ashley Cooper, 122–23, 124,
    125
Shelley, Percy Bysshe, 110
Sidney, Algernon, 114
Sidney, Sir Philip, 153
Singer, Isaac Bashevis, 107
Smith, Adam, 197–99, 227, 229–30
  *The Wealth of Nations*, 198
social contract:
  elements in, 130
  Hobbes on, 41, 130
  Hume on, 130, 131
  Kant on, 132
  Locke on, 128–32, 133
  Nietzsche on, 130–31
  Rousseau on, 130, 230, 232, 234–
    35
Socinians, 160
Socrates, ix
  death of, 198
  on ignorance, 238

on "noble lies," 69–70
questioning, 19, 137, 162
solar system, 7, 8
Sophie-Charlotte, queen of Prussia, 167
Sophists, 95
Sophocles, 67
Spinoza, Baruch (Benedict de), ix, 85–112, 237, 244
 on causes and effects, 104–5
 central role of God in universe of, 88, 91, 101–2, 109, 111–12
 and Collegiants, 90
 death of, 113, 180
 determinism of, 180
 double-aspect theory of, 103, 109
 early years of, 89–90
 enemies of, 88, 89, 99–100
 Ethics, 83, 91, 100, 101, 105, 107–8, 109–10, 111, 180
 excommunication of, 85, 87, 89, 91
 and fate, 109
 on freedom, 105, 107, 110
 and geometry, 100–101, 105, 106, 107
 on God and nature, 34, 83–84, 88, 91, 97, 101–2, 104, 109, 110
 on government, 98
 influence of, 110–12
 joy sought by, 108
 and knowledge, 90–91, 109, 111
 and mathematics, 89–90, 101, 107, 109
 mechanical philosophy of, 90, 96
 noble character of, 88
 and optics, 89, 90
 as pantheist, 104
 Parts I and II of Descartes's "Principles of Philosophy," demonstrated in the geometric manner, 100

on power, 109
on psychology, 106–7
and rationalism, 33
and religion, 90–98, 99, 110, 111–12, 117, 180
reputation of, 84, 88–89, 90, 110
and scepticism, 34–35, 83, 108
scientific interests of, 90
and search for truth, 91, 93, 97, 101, 105
and self-preservation, 109–10
Tractatus theologico-politicus, 83, 91, 99, 110, 159, 179
squaring the circle, 74–75
Stalin, Joseph, 45
Stendahl, 25
Sterne, Laurence, Tristram Shandy, 137
Stoic doctrine, 23, 108, 109, 138, 172, 187–88, 239
style vs. substance, 13–14
subjectivism, 13, 95
supernatural:
 and comets, 157, 159
 Hobbes on, 38
 and Hume, 197
 miracles, 83, 96–97, 102, 117, 215, 217–20, 225, 226
 Spinoza on, 96–97, 102, 111
 witchcraft, 38, 80
superstition, xi, 110, 140, 157, 199, 237, 242
Swift, Jonathan, 136
Sydenham, Thomas, 122, 123–24

telescope, optics of, 8
Tertullian, 38
Thomas, David, 122
thoughts, control of, 23
Thucydides, 49, 50, 74
Toland, John, Christianity Not Mysterious, 117

# ABOUT THE AUTHOR

Anthony Gottlieb is a former executive editor of *The Economist* and
author of *The Dream of Reason: A History of Western Philosophy from*
*Greeks to the Renaissance*. He has held visiting fellowships at Harvard Un
versity and All Souls College, Oxford. His work has appeared in *The New*
*Yorker*, *The New York Times* and many publications in his native Britain.
He lives in New York.

the
the
i-

# ABOUT THE AUTHOR

Anthony Gottlieb is a former executive editor of *The Economist* and the author of *The Dream of Reason: A History of Western Philosophy from the Greeks to the Renaissance*. He has held visiting fellowships at Harvard University and All Souls College, Oxford. His work has appeared in *The New Yorker*, *The New York Times* and many publications in his native Britain. He lives in New York.